Introducing narrative psychology

Self, trauma and the construction of meaning

MICHELE L. CROSSLEY

Open University Press
Buckingham · Philadelphia

Open University Press
Celtic Court
22 Ballmoor
Buckingham
MK18 1XW

e-mail: enquiries@openup.co.uk
world wide web: http://www.openup.co.uk

and
325 Chestnut Street
Philadelphia, PA 19106, USA

First Published 2000

A catalogue record of this book is available from the British Library

ISBN 0 335 20290 X (pbk)   0 335 20291 8 (hbk)

Library of Congress Cataloging-in-Publication Data
Crossley, Michele L., 1969–
    Introducing narrative psychology : self, trauma, and the construction of meaning / Michele L. Crossley.
        p. cm.
    Includes bibliographical references and index.
    ISBN 0-335-20291-8—ISBN 0-335-20290-X (pbk.)
    1. Psychology—Biographical methods.   2. Discourse analysis, Narrative—Psychological aspects.   I. Title.

BF39.4.C76 2000
155.2–dc21
                                                                99-039403

Typeset by Type Study, Scarborough, North Yorkshire
Printed and bound in Great Britain by Marston Book Services Limited, Oxford

Dust sheets cover my heart and dreams
Climb the attic stairs.
There,
Cradled in cobwebs,
Our sweet and easy intimacy lies,
Where it fell.
Joy's banner hangs in tatters.
Youth sighs out loud.
Time,
Tissue-wrapped,
Satin-bound,
Forever pressed,
Between pages of an old photograph album.

(*Not needed on Voyage,* by Dorothy Ann Crossley, 1998)

Contents

Preface

The aim of this book is to present a coherent overview of the theory, methodology and potential application of what are known as 'narrative' approaches within psychology. To this end, this book is divided into three main sections:

1 Theories of self and identity (Chapters 1–3)
2 Narrative methods for exploring the self (Chapters 4 and 5)
3 Practical applications of the study of self in traumatic situations (Chapters 6–8).

The book has a logical structure where theoretical approaches are first introduced, followed by an overview of methods encouraging you to apply those theories to your own autobiography. The third section of the book further illustrates such theories using case-study material taken from the empirical study of various kinds of psychological and emotional trauma such as childhood sexual abuse and HIV infection. Each of these issues is examined in a way which demonstrates how traumatizing events often lead to a breakdown of temporal coherence and order, creating the need to reconstruct meaning and a sense of identity through the use of contemporary narratives and discourses.

Acknowledgements

I would like to thank my many colleagues who have commented on draft chapters of this book. In particular, thanks to Phil Lee and Edge-Hill University College for granting me the sabbatical time and supportive research environment in which this book could be completed, and Justin Vaughan at Open University Press for his professional and efficient management of the initial proposal and completed manuscript of this book. Thanks to all of the people who have taken part in my research over the past five years or so, and shared their stories with me. Special thanks to CD who granted permission for his full transcript to be used in Chapter 4.

Thanks again to my mum and dad, who, as always, remain the unacknowledged background to everything I do.

I would also like to take this opportunity to pay a very special note of respect to my mum-in-law, Dorothy Ann Crossley. Narrative psychology as envisaged in this book is about how we come to terms with the losses and joys of life . . . and death. Over the past year, with our tragic loss, we have lost our backbone, the central support and meaning holding us all together. It feels like we can only stand by and watch, as we see you slowly, bravely, rebuilding and writing yourself into a new world.

My final thanks of course, as always, are reserved for a very special person – my soulmate, Nick Crossley.

February 1999

Explanatory note on 'further reading'

Each chapter of this book ends with a list of key further reading. It is intended that students studying narrative psychology should read most of the book chapters and articles related to their particular area of interest. Some of the readings, however, are marked with an asterisk (*). This means they are particularly suitable for use in seminars when the ideas covered in the chapter have already been addressed in a lecture. Many of them comprise useful extensions and interesting applications of the ideas in question.

SECTION I

Theories and methods

Theories of self and identity

Traditional psychological studies of self

We might as well begin with the age-old, perennial question. What is a self? Who am I? C.S. Lewis once commented: 'There is one thing, and only one in the whole universe which we know more about than that we could learn from external observation. That one thing is ourselves. We have, so to speak, inside information, we are in the know' (Lewis 1952: 25). But how true is this? Are we 'in the know' about ourselves? Many of us spend large portions of our life in a state of mixed confusion, subsumed by contradictory thoughts, feelings and emotions. Even on those occasions when we know exactly how we feel, we're not always sure why we feel the way we do. So perhaps the idea that we 'know' ourselves is a bit inaccurate. Wouldn't it be more accurate to say that we are 'strangers' to ourselves, our whole lives lived much as a mystery? We bumble along like second-rate detectives, fitting the pieces together as we go, but invariably failing to pull it all together, this elusive 'I' which, 'like the shadow of one's own head, will not wait to be jumped upon' (Ryle 1973: 178).

It may seem obvious to turn towards psychology in order to throw light on these complex questions regarding self and identity. After all, most people are drawn towards the study of psychology because they are interested in the 'human condition' – what makes us human, our loves, desires, passions, hates. We want insight into other people and, perhaps even more, into ourselves. But, as Freeman (1993) so accurately notes, a few months into a psychology degree you find you are dealing with very little of this. Instead, you are enmeshed in statistics, principles of learning, cognition, abstract theories and theoretical models bearing little resemblance to anything you were originally interested in studying. Somewhat ironically, a great deal of contemporary psychology, supposedly an area devoted to the study of human beings, has become a totally 'lifeless' discipline.

Where do we look, then, in the discipline of psychology, if we want to examine these questions of self and identity? There are basically four major approaches that may be of relevance: (i) experimentally based social psychology; (ii) humanistic psychology; (iii) psychoanalytic/psychodynamic psychology; and (iv) social constructivist approaches. All of these approaches are of potential importance to the study of self and identity, but, as will become increasingly clear, the 'social constructivist' approach is particularly relevant to a narrative psychology perspective. This is because it entails certain assumptions about the relationship between self, identity and social structures (especially language) which are distinct from the other three, more 'traditional' perspectives. More on this later. For the time being it is necessary to outline the kind of studies on self and identity that have been conducted from these four different approaches.

Experimental social psychology

First, experimental social psychology. In this approach it is assumed that your development of a sense of self requires the realization that you are a 'knower', an 'I', a unique processor of the information around you. This task is not at all simple, as has been shown with animal research (Povinelli 1993). One way of finding out if animals have this rudimentary sense of self is to place them in front of a mirror or a glass door and watch how they respond to their own reflection. I did this with my neighbour's cat, Bodmin, and, in confirmation of an interesting series of studies conducted by Gallup (1977), found that he stalked himself, thus displaying an inability to distinguish 'himself' as a self, separate from other members of his species. Gallup (1977) found that this was a characteristic feature of a whole range of animals except for chimpanzees, who, over time, began to use the mirror to help them groom themselves and for entertainment (e.g. making faces, blowing bubbles with their saliva). This suggested that the chimpanzees, unlike other mammals, had a sense of self and could recognize the mirror image as themselves.

Gallup tested this proposition by anaesthetizing the chimpanzees and painting an odourless red dye on one eyebrow and one ear. After coming round from the anaesthetic, when the chimps looked in the mirror they immediately reached for their red eyebrow and ear. This confirmed that they realized the image was themselves and not another chimp; it also demonstrated that they knew they looked differently than before the red dye had been painted on their faces. Research with human infants is also interesting in terms of what it tells us about the emergence of a sense of self. Babies are not born with the ability to recognize themselves in the mirror and thus to differentiate 'self' from 'others'. Experiments similar to the red dye test used by Gallup have been conducted with human infants. A dot of rouge is placed on the baby's nose and the baby is then placed before a mirror and his/her response noted. About 75 per cent of 21–25-month-old infants touched their rouged noses, compared with only 25 per cent of the 9–12-month-old infants. In general, it has been shown that the child's sense of itself emerges at about 2 years of age (Bertenthal and Fisher 1978; Crossley 1996a, Chapter 3).

Other research has looked at how the concept of self changes from childhood to adulthood by asking people of different ages to answer the simple question: 'Who am I?' (Montemayor and Eisen 1977). Findings suggest that our self-concepts start by being very concrete: for example, a typical response from a 9-year-old would be: 'I have blonde hair, I have blue eyes, I am a girl, I have an aunty called Aunty Dot . . . .' As we get older, however, we tend to place less emphasis on physical characteristics and more on our thoughts, feelings and concepts of morality and judgement: for example, 'I like to think of myself as a decent person; I think it is important to be loyal; I think it is important to work hard' and so on.

In experimental social psychological approaches, another strand of research connects to the question of how we actually achieve knowledge of ourselves. Two major 'methods' are proposed: (i) introspection; and (ii) observation of our own behaviour. Generally, researchers working in this perspective argue that we rarely use the first method, introspection (looking 'inwards' to examine thoughts, feelings and motives, see Aronson *et al.* 1994). An example of the kind of study on which such claims are made is one conducted by Csikszentmihalyi and Figurski (1982), who tried to examine how often people actually 'thought about themselves'. They asked 107 employees who worked for five different companies (aged between 19 and 63 years) to wear beepers for one week. The beepers went off at random intervals between 7.30am and 10.30pm from seven to nine times every day. At the sound of the beeper the participants answered a series of questions about their thoughts, activity and mood at that specific time. The responses were divided into categories and the results allegedly showed that people think about themselves quite infrequently because only 8 per cent of the total thoughts recorded were 'about the self'. People were more likely to think about work, chores and time. Indeed, there was a higher percentage of 'no thoughts' than thoughts about the self. These results were used to show that we do not engage in introspection very often.

The second main way in which we achieve knowledge of ourselves, according to the experimental social psychology paradigm, is by observing our own behaviour. One of the most influential proponents of this view is Daryl Bem, who developed 'self-perception theory' (Bem 1972). According to this theory, we discover the kind of person we are and our attitudes in exactly the same way as another person would – that is, by observing our own behaviour. Bem's basic argument is that we come to know our own attitudes, emotions and other internal states *partially* by inferring them from observations of our own behaviour. When our internal cues are weak, ambiguous or uninterpretable, we are in the same position as an outside observer of our behaviour; we ourselves are observers of our own emotional states and must rely on external cues (emerging from our behaviour and the environment) in order to infer the nature of our internal state of mind.

The kind of experiment used in support of self-perception theory can be seen in a study by Strack *et al.* (1988). People were asked to hold a pen in their mouths using either their teeth or their lips; the muscles in the face, particularly around the mouth, feel differently depending on how the pen is held. Then, the researchers showed participants a series of funny cartoons and asked them to rate how funny they were. Those people who held a pen with their teeth found the cartoons funnier than those who held the pen with their lips. Why? According to self-perception theory we infer how we feel from our actions, in this case our facial expressions. People who held the pen with their teeth made more use of 'smiling' muscles whereas those who held the pen with their lips were not using these muscles. Hence, so the argument goes, putting on a happy face can actually make you experience yourself as happy.

Now, although some of these findings may be reasonably interesting, you are not alone if you are beginning to feel that something is missing from these accounts of selfhood and identity. In the first place, it is a very big step from the rudimentary kind of self manifest in chimps and very young infants, to the far more complex and sophisticated understanding and experience of self chararacteristic of the human adult. But what would this complexity and sophistication consist of? This is what we want to explore in this book. One thing is for sure; we have a nagging doubt that something very essential is missing in the characteristically shallow portrayal of self and identity put forward in the experimental social psychological paradigm. In fact, this perspective's inability to capture the way in which human beings experience self and identity is not surprising when we consider its behaviouristic roots (see Pancer 1997).

Experimental social psychology, which is largely dominant in the discipline of social psychology as a whole (especially in the USA although increasingly less so in Europe), is premised on the quaint, curiously time-warped dream of behaviourism; the attempt to produce a 'hard', rigidly defined 'scientific' discipline with theories and hypotheses that can be tested under rigorous laboratory controlled conditions. This behaviouristic paradigm (with its origins in J.B. Watson's work in the 1920s) was directly pitted against any attempt to study psychology using 'introspectionist' methods (reflecting 'inwards' on one's own state of mind or consciousness), which were castigated as 'subjective' and unscientific. Watson, instead, proposed that psychologists should confine themselves to studying only aspects of human behaviour that can be measured and observed by more than one person – that is, they should confine themselves to the study of behaviour; private, mental processes should have no place in the study of psychology. The portrait of the 'self' put forward by contemporary experimental social psychological approaches is a logical correlate of this behaviourist legacy; empty, lifeless selves, devoid of any sense of privacy, feeling or humanity. It is the premise of this book that in order to develop a more adequate understanding of what human selves and identities consist of, we need a different theoretical and methodological framework.

Humanistic and psychodynamic approaches

What about the second major approach, the humanistic approach? Does that help us more accurately reflect the complexities of human self and identity? The answer is yes, undoubtedly, although as will soon become apparent, from the perspective of narrative psychology the humanistic approach has its problems. Having said that, the general tenor of the humanistic approach is consistent with that of narrative psychology, in that, unlike the experimental social psychology approach, the focus is far more on the individual as an individual; on the unique and specific meanings experienced and attributed to perceptions, events and lives by each person. The main aim of this kind of approach is to capture in all its full complexity the subjective nature of self and world experienced by each idiosyncratic individual. This is reflected in the methods used by humanistic psychologists, which are predominantly qualitative, such as auto/biographical and individual case-study methods (and in their application, counselling and psychotherapy), in contrast to the quantitative methods used in experimental social psychological approaches.

The main representatives of such a humanistic approach are people such as Abraham Maslow (1970; 1972), Carl Rogers (1961) and George Kelly (1955). For example, Maslow's classic theory of the 'hierarchy of needs' set human beings, and thus the 'essential' nature of humanity, apart from all other living things, in terms of our need for 'self-actualization', for 'becoming everything that one is capable of becoming'. In Maslow's terms: 'We share the need for food with all living things, the need for love with (perhaps) the higher apes and the need for Self Actualisation with no other species' (Maslow 1970). Both Rogers and Maslow were psychotherapists who believed that each individual has a potential for personal growth which is unique to them; their theories and therapies were designed to encourage and facilitate such self-actualization.

The main allegiance between humanistic and narrative approaches in psychology lies in their shared roots in the philosophical branches of phenomenology and existentialism (this will be explored further in Chapter 3). These two branches of philosophy are concerned with the characteristics that are distinctively and uniquely human. In particular, this includes the emphasis on human 'experience and experiencing', 'uniqueness', 'meaning', 'freedom' and 'choice' (see Cooper 1990; Hammond *et al.* 1991). Later in the book we shall see how these characteristic 'humanistic' themes become important in times of crisis, such as when a person is suffering from terminal illness or other traumatizing events. For the time being it is important to emphasize the way in which the humanistic approach, in highlighting the uniqueness of each individual, also strongly affirms a belief in our personal agency – our ability to take effective action in the world around us. This focus on choice and agency is seen by many as a positive aspect of humanistic theories but it also introduces a number of problems which some would argue place limits on the humanist portrayal of self and identity.

For example, theorists of the psychodynamic/psychoanalytic perspective, the third major approach towards self and identity previously outlined, would argue that the humanists' emphasis on conscious choice and agency is misplaced. This is because theorists from within this paradigm, sometimes alternatively known as 'depth psychology', work with a model of the human psyche that places a great deal of store in the idea that our actions and behaviours are unconsciously motivated. The very concept 'psychodynamic' implies that active forces are at work in the personality – 'inner' causes of behaviour – which include feelings, conflicts and drives, that we are largely unaware of. There is a mass of literature on the different psychoanalytic and psychodynamic approaches that have developed in contemporary psychology. We have neither the time nor space to go into these here. It is sufficient simply to point out some of the ways in which psychoanalytic/psychodynamic approaches connect with narrative psychology. Like humanistic approaches, psychoanalytic/psychodynamic approaches share with narrative psychology a focus on individual 'depth', meaning and uniqueness. Not surprisingly, the methods used by proponents of psychoanalytic/psychodynamic theories are similarly qualitative, incorporating largely case-studies based on interviews, clinical material and textual data (including works of fiction and auto/biography).

Narrative psychology and social constructivist studies of self: the fundamental role of language and meaning

Narrative approaches to the study of self and identity, however, differ substantially from both humanistic and psychodynamic/psychoanalytic approaches, in relation to the greater emphasis narrative approaches pay to the inextricable interconnection between 'self' and 'social structures', particularly the interrelationship between 'self' and 'language'. This brings me to the fourth approach towards self and identity, the 'social constructivist' paradigm of which narrative approaches form a part (other approaches falling under this title include 'discourse analysis' (see Potter and Wetherell 1987; Parker 1991; Edwards and Potter 1992), 'post-structuralist' and 'postmodernist' approaches (see Kvale 1992) and 'rhetorical' approaches (see Billig 1991)). Social constructivist approaches, sometimes called 'language-based' approaches, have arisen over the past decade or so as a major challenge to some of the implicit assumptions embedded in the three approaches previously outlined: experimental social psychology (behaviouristically based), humanistic and psychoanalytic/psychodynamic approaches.

In particular, Potter and Wetherell (1987) have argued that all of these approaches operate on the basis of 'realist' assumptions which are problematic in terms of the study of self. What this means is that all of the 'traditional' approaches just outlined are based on the assumption that the self exists as an entity that can be discovered and described in much the same way as can any object in the natural or physical world. Now, of course, as we have just seen, the actual nature of the entity 'self' as theorized in each of these paradigms is very different. For example, we have criticized the experimental social psychology paradigm for its shallow and inadequate characterization of the concept 'self'. And likewise, the humanist paradigm has been criticized for imputing too great a conception of human agency on to its concept of 'self'. Nevertheless, despite these differences, there still exists, according to some versions of the 'social constructivist' argument, a residual assumption that the 'self' exists 'somewhere', either 'externally' in terms of certain forms of behaviour (as in experimental social psychology), or 'internally' as an 'inner' self (as in the humanistic, psychoanalytic/psychodynamic paradigms). This 'realist' assumption is considered problematic by Potter and Wetherell (1987), two of the most influential proponents of the social constructivist paradigm in psychology. It is considered problematic because the alternative conceptualization of the self promoted by social constructivism is one which sees it as inextricably dependent on the language and linguistic practices that we use in our everyday lives to make sense of ourselves and other people. The main objective and, indeed, the main effect, of this new, allegedly 'critical' social constructivist movement has been to: '. . . displace attention from the self-as-entity and focus it on the methods of constructing the self. That is, the question becomes not what is the true nature of the self, but how is the self talked about, how is it theorised in discourse?' (Potter and Wetherell 1987: 102). These issues regarding the relationship between self, language and reality will be discussed in more detail in Chapter 2.

The human 'order of meaning'

For the time being it is sufficient to note that narrative psychology shares the social constructivist commitment to recognizing the central and constructive role played by language in the formation and structuring of self and identity. Narrative psychology is premised on the assumption that human experience and behaviour are meaningful and that, in order to understand ourselves and others, we need to explore the 'meaning systems' and the 'structures' of meaning that make up our minds and worlds (Polkinghorne 1988: 1). Unlike the objects of inquiry of the natural sciences on which behaviouristic psychologists model their theoretical and methodological attempts to make sense of us, as human beings, we are essentially interpretive creatures. This means that we constantly reflect on what is happening in and around us. This 'reflective' capacity characteristic of human consciousness means that the 'objects' of inquiry facing the psychological investigator are of a very different order from those addressed by the natural science investigator.

Central to grasping the unique 'order of meaning' characteristic of human consciousness is an understanding of language – one of the vehicles which makes experience meaningful. The basic principle of narrative psychology is that individuals understand themselves through the medium of language, through talking and writing, and it is through these processes that individuals are constantly engaged in the process of creating themselves. The focus on meaning and interpretation is of extreme importance. It is a focus which distinguishes narrative psychology from more traditional psychological approaches and also highlights the inadequacy of quantitative, 'scientific' methods for the study of self and identity.

Time and identity

Such inadequacy is apparent when we consider a number of the main charactertistics of the 'order of meaning' constitutive of human consciousness. One of these is the experience of 'time' (this will be explored further in Chapters 3 and 7). The human realm of meaning is different from that encountered in the natural sciences because it is not related to a 'thing' or a 'substance' but to an 'activity' (Polkinghorne 1988: 4). Everything experienced by human beings is made meaningful, understood and interpreted in relation to the primary dimension of 'activity': this incorporates both 'time' and 'sequence'. In order to define and interpret 'what' exactly has happened on any particular occasion, the sequence of events is of extreme importance. Hence, a valid portrayal of human selves and behaviour necessitates an understanding of the inextricable connection between time and identity. Quantitative approaches to the study of human psychology fail radically in the incorporation of such a temporal dimension. The attempt to numerically categorize experience through quantification and statistical procedures results in a loss of attention to this crucial dimension of human temporality – and thus to the very nature of human reality and identity.

'Connections' and relationships

Another feature of the 'order of meaning' characterstic of human consciousness is that of 'relationships' and 'connections' (Polkinghorne 1988: 4). Along with other organisms such as cats and dogs we share what can be characterized as a 'perceptual openness' to the world in which our sensory apparatus and brain structures operate to present us with a basic experience of the objects and activities going on around us. But a characteristic feature of our human realm of meaning is that we go way beyond this rudimentary perceptual level of experience as we interpret events around us in terms of connections and relationships. When we ask ourselves the question 'what does this mean?' we are asking ourselves (or others) *how* something is related or connected to something or someone else. It is the connections or relationships among events that constitute their meaning. Moreover, such meanings are not produced subjectively by isolated individuals; rather, they are formulated through cultural meaning systems such as language (and narratives) which reverberate with knowledge of connections and relationships across generations. For example, cultures transmit to children knowledge of typical patterns of relationships and meanings in their myths, fairy tales, histories and stories (see Bettelheim 1976; Polkinghorne 1988; Howard 1991). And as we will explore further in Chapters 4 and 5, we are inculcated from a very early age to seeing connections between events, people and the world in a certain way through the stories and narratives told in our families (Langellier and Peterson 1993; McAdams 1993).

To grasp the complexity of this 'order of meaning', we need methods and tools appreciative of the context-sensitivity and interrelatedness of various dimensions of human experience (as manifest in the use of language and narrative). The quantitative attempt to extrapolate and isolate discrete 'variables' as representative of various chunks of human experience is obviously inappropriate to this task. A study of narrative psychology seeks methods sensitive to the qualitative nuances of meaning; that is why history, literary criticism and philosophy, and the methods developed in those disciplines, sometimes referred to as hermeneutic techniques, are deemed more appropriate than statistical techniques.

Self as interactional process

We can turn to contemporary interpretations of the work of the social psychologist, George Herbert Mead, to help us further understand the interrelated role played by language, time and relationships in the human 'order of meaning', particularly with regard to our sense of self and identity

(Crossley 1996a). For Mead, our sense of ourselves is an activity, a process, which comes about through our engagements, relationships and connections with other people. Mead, drawing on Cooley's (1902) work, used the term 'the looking glass self' to highlight the extent to which our definition of ourselves relies on the feedback and evaluations we receive from others.

Mead presents two concepts which enable us to separate certain aspects of the self-process: the 'I' and the 'me' (see Crossley 1996a: 55). The 'I' is the part of myself which perceives, acts, speaks and feels, but as an 'I' I am not reflectively aware of myself or my world: 'It is because of the I that we say we are never fully aware of what we are, that we surprise ourselves by our own action. It is as we act that we are aware of ourselves' (Mead, cited in Crossley 1996a: 55). In order to become aware of myself, to become reflectively conscious of myself and thus to enter the 'order of meaning' characteristic of human consciousness, I have to see and experience myself in the past tense, that is, as a 'me': 'As given, it is a "me", but it is a me which was the "I" at an earlier time. If you ask then, where directly in your own experience the "I" comes in, the answer is that it comes in as a historical figure (i.e. as a "me")' (Crossley 1996a: 55).

As Crossley (1996a) argues, the 'me' is the 'I's' objectification, recollection or image of itself. This arises from the 'I' adopting an 'outside' view upon itself, that is, conceiving itself as another person would. This is what Mead calls 'taking the attitude of the other'. Thus, through Mead's account, it becomes clear how the process of self-awareness, the self-consciousness unique to the realm of human meaning, is intrinsically mediated through relationships with other people.

A great deal of emphasis is placed in Mead's account on the temporal nature of the 'me'. Whereas my 'I' actively and unthinkingly throws itself forward into situations, those actions become 'me' only in the retrospective process of accounting for my past thoughts and behaviour. But the role of the 'me' part of myself is not just relegated to the past because it also plays a crucial role in planning, anticipating, imagining and reflecting on the future. My 'me', or perhaps it is more accurate to speak in the plural, my 'me's', are the images through which I imaginatively project myself into future events; through them, I invest in hopes, fears, dreams and ambitions (Crossley 1996a: 56).

It is with regard to the interactive process between the 'I' and 'me' that we can further highlight the connection between self and social relationships. At any particular point in time it is in relation to my consideration of the continuity or discontinuity between my 'I' and my 'me' that I can engage in dialogue about the kinds of actions I will perform and, relatedly, the kind of person I have been in the past and want to become in the future. So if, for example, my 'I' feels the desire to engage in an affair, my 'me', my image of myself as a married woman, as being connected to someone else, will interpose and (perhaps) prevent my performing such an action. But this depends on how heavily invested, emotionally and/or morally, I am in the concept of 'me' relevant on any particular occasion. I may, for instance, feel that my 'me', my image of myself as a person who loves and is loyal to my husband and family, is more important than any immediate gratification I would get from an affair. On the other hand, I may feel that I have the right to assert my own freedom and that my own gratification is more important than any ties I owe to others; or I may feel so flattered by the image another person is projecting on to me, so exuberated by the prospect of a new, exciting 'me', that I feel unable to resist the lure. In all of this, I will have dialogue with the various images of myself; in my mind, I will imagine and run through the anticipated responses and consequences of my action for specific (and normally significant) others – my husband, my mother, my father, my father-in-law, my mother-in-law, my brother, my future lover. . . . Those imagined responses, good or bad, will help me to decide whether this action would commit me to the kind of self I want to be.

In addition, Mead also emphasizes that such responses may tend to be based less in the imagined attitude of specific others and more in the attitude of what he calls the 'generalized other'. This is the view not of any particular person but of the 'community as a whole'. For instance, from my community, I may have inculcated the moral value that adultery is immoral and wrong; on the other hand, I may have internalized the view that 'it's no big deal' and marriage is an outdated bourgeois patriarchal institution anyway. Whichever viewpoint my community holds, it provides a forum in which my image of myself, my 'me', can be seen from the standpoint of the community as a whole.

The development of a sense of self

What comes across from all of this is the idea that the construction of self is always a temporal process through which we have dialogue with different images of the self taken from the past and future, and mediated by the anticipated responses of significant and generalized others. Further light is thrown on the intrinsic temporality and sociality of this self-process when we look at evidence from contemporary developmental psychology (Case 1991; Fein 1991). This suggests that the dialogical and reflective self-consciousness between 'I' and 'me' just described is not innate and develops only at later stages of human development. Indeed, one of the most crucial processes for the achievement of such reflective self-consciousness is the infant's entrance into the world of language and social symbols (Crossley 1996a: 58). Both Jean Piaget and George Herbert Mead emphasized the importance of language in helping the child to develop a sense of itself and other people. This is because language, especially pronouns, provides labels which enable the child to distinguish between itself (for example, 'I', 'me') and other people and things (for example, 'you', 'it') (see also Harré and Gillet 1994). It is interesting to note that both autistic and blind children tend to use these pronouns incorrectly; for example, they use 'I' to refer to other people and 'you' to refer to themselves. This is probably related to the different forms of interactions and relationships with other people that these children experience.

Theorists such as Cooley (1902) proposed that the development of self-consciousness and self-reflective awareness among children remains dependent on the relationships they share with others, especially relationships with immediate family members or others to whom we attach significance, such as the children's play group. He called these 'primary groups'. Through this kind of relationship the growing child begins to feel part of a group, experiencing a feeling of 'we-ness' or 'togetherness', which means that s/he begins to identify him/herself as part of a social unit. Contacts with group members are particularly important for the child's growing sense of morality; it is only after continuous involvement with other people that the child learns that his/her own needs, wants and interests cannot always be paramount. Involvement in a primary group helps the child to develop a sense of moral principles such as the importance of group loyalty and the importance of adhering to rules and laws. As we are incapable of thinking about ourselves and others except with reference to some social group, Cooley argued that 'self and society are twin born' (see Berger and Luckman 1967).

Gender differences and self

One of the most significant ways in which the child develops a sense of self-reflective awareness, according to Mead and Piaget, is through play and games. Games constitute a crucial forum for mental and social development because they facilitate the child in the process of learning to take on the role of the other and coming to see themselves through another's eyes; in this way the child learns respect for rules and an understanding of how rules can be made and changed. Some studies have found sex differences between the types of games played by boys and girls, which are extremely interesting in terms of their implications for the variable development of self and identity among men and women (see Gilligan 1982). For example, Gilligan (1982) cites a study which found sex differences in the games played by 10- and 11-year-old children. Boys played outside more than girls, in larger, age-heterogeneous groups, and they played competitive games which lasted longer. The boys' games tended to last longer because when disputes arose during the course of a game, boys were more able to effectively resolve disputes than girls. Rather than elaborating a system of rules for resolving disputes, girls subordinated the continuation of the game to the continuation of relationships with their friends. Lever drew a connection between these findings and Piaget's, arguing that through childhood boys become increasingly fascinated with the legal elaboration of rules and the development of fair procedures. This, allegedly, is not case with girls who have a more 'pragmatic' attitude towards rules; they are more willing to make exceptions and to innovate. As a result, the 'legal sense', which Piaget regarded as essential to moral development, was said to be far less developed in girls than in boys.

Lever also found that girls tended to play in smaller, more intimate groups such as best friend dyads and in private places. This kind of play was thought to replicate the social pattern of primary human relationships (between infant and caretaker) in that its organization is more cooperative and less competitive. Gilligan (1982) argues that, in Mead's terms, such play could be construed as more conducive to taking on the role of the 'particular' other, and less that of the 'generalized other' (thought to be representative of the view of the community as a whole). If this is the case, we would expect men and women, in light of their differing experiences of gender socialization, to appropriate different conceptions of self, relationships to others and morality. This, indeed, is the central thrust of Gilligan's (1982) influential book. For example, in her studies of successful, professional women, Gilligan found that these women used descriptions and projections of themselves (their 'me's') primarily in terms of their relationships with other people. So they would depict their identity in terms of their intimate connections, their role as 'wife', 'mother' and so on. By contrast, the tone of identity description for men, despite them occupying similar levels of professional standing, was entirely different. Men tended to define themselves less in terms of connection with others and far more in terms of separation. Although the selves men described sometimes contained 'people' and deep attachments, no particular relationship was portrayed in the process of self-description. Hence, Gilligan concluded, whereas the female 'I' is defined largely in terms of connection and relationships, the male 'I' is alternatively construed in terms of separation and autonomy (see also Gergen and Gergen 1993: 87). These issues will be discussed further in Chapter 8 when we discuss the different forms of sense-making available to us in contemporary culture.

Self, society and morality

The intrinsic connection between the concept of self, language and society can be further illustrated if we look at differing notions of self manifest in different historical and cross-cultural societies (see Geertz 1973; Lienhardt 1985; Cousins 1989; Kondo 1990; Markus and Kitayama 1991; Triandis *et al.* 1993). Here, we will focus on differing historical conceptions of the self by drawing largely on Charles Taylor's work entitled *Sources of the Self: The Making of Modern Identity* (Taylor 1989). It is Taylor's contention that concepts of self and morality, what he sometimes calls 'the good', are inextricably intertwined. He argues that we are selves only in that certain issues matter for us. What I am as a self, my identity, is essentially defined by the way things have significance for me. To ask what I am in abstraction from self-interpretation makes no sense (Taylor 1989: 34). Moreover, my self-interpretation can be defined only in relation to other people, an 'interchange of speakers'. I cannot be a self on my own but only in relation to certain 'interlocutors' who are crucial to my language of self-understanding. In this sense, the self is constituted through 'webs of interlocution' in a 'defining community' (Taylor 1989: 39). This connection between our sense of morality and sense of self, according to Taylor, means that one of our basic aspirations is the need to feel connected with what we see as 'good' or of crucial importance to us and our community. We have certain fundamental values which lead us to basic questions such as 'what kind of life is worth living?' and 'what consitutes a rich, meaningful life, as against an empty, meaningless one?' (p. 42).

A vision of 'the good' becomes available for people in any given culture by being given expression or articulation in some form or another. This articulation most often occurs through language and symbolic systems such as custom and ritual (Taylor 1989: 91). Such articulation brings us closer to the good as a moral source and gives it further power and potency. Stories have a tremendous force in this process insofar as they have the capacity to confer meaning and substance on people's lives, to subtly influence their progression and orientation towards a particular 'good' (p. 97). The family photograph albums proudly displayed: you when you were 2 in the sea at Bridlington – holding dad's hand; you with your brother in the house where you lived as a child; all of 'us' together Christmas '76 – 'do you remember?'; 'our' wedding; 'us' with 'our' first baby. . . . This is all about articulating and reaffirming commitment to a moral good, in this case the importance of being part of a 'we', of family, love, loyalty and connection.

The central premise of Taylor's argument, then, is the essential and fundamental link between identity and moral orientation. We have a sense of who we are through a sense of where we stand in relation to 'the good'. This has the implication that radically different senses of what 'the good' is go along with different conceptions of what constitutes a 'self'. Connections between notions of 'the good', understandings of the self, the kinds of stories and narratives through which we make sense of our lives, and conceptions of society, evolve together in 'loose packages' (Taylor 1989: 105). On the basis of this thesis we would obviously predict that different societies, both cross-culturally and historically, will incorporate very different conceptions of self and morality. Indeed, arguing from a historical perspective, Taylor's main objective is to describe the way in which the modern concept of self is radically different from that of previous civilizations, a process facilitated by the interconnected development of new notions of 'the good', new forms of narration, and new understandings of social bonds and relations.

Contemporary concepts of self: the 'inward turn'

Taylor's central thesis is that for people living in contemporary Western societies, some of the basic questions about value and meaning arise in the following kind of form: 'Is my life amounting to anything?'; 'Does it have weight and substance?'; 'Is it just fading away into nothing?' Now, although these questions do suggest a continuity with previous historical eras, insofar as they display a need to aspire towards a 'higher' sense of being and morality and to be 'rightly placed in relation to the good', at the same time they also highlight a very different sense of self experienced by people in contemporary society. For instance, Taylor argues that the kind of questions troubling people today centre around concerns with 'the meaning of life', 'the meaning of self', 'where we are going' and 'what we are doing'. These 'existential predicaments' of modern life, our fears of a 'terrifying emptiness', of 'loss', 'vertigo' and 'meaninglessness', dominate our age – and yet they are very different from the kinds of predicaments experienced in previous civilizations.

Taylor suggests that in earlier times this type of question was not on the agenda because people lived in 'unchallengeable frameworks' of meaning which made 'imperious demands' on them. Although people did experience conflicts in relation to their orientation to 'the good', that 'good' was pretty much set in stone; it was relatively unproblematic and taken for granted. So, if I was a woman living in 17th-century New England who committed adultery, I would, like Hester Prynne, central protagonist in Nigel Hawthorne's novel *The Scarlet Letter*, face my Puritan judges with a red scarlet letter 'A' emblazoned across my chest. I would be in little doubt about the nature of my wrongdoing; my main fear would be of irretrievable damnation in the eternal fires of God's wrath. This is what Taylor characterizes as a 'substantive' definition of rationality and morality; one in which our sense of the 'good' is seen in terms of alliance with a pre-existent order created by God. And yet today, living in a predominantly secular society, I have no such fears. I may even question whether my action would be morally wrong, given my conflicting desires between morality and self-fulfilment. And this is Taylor's point. In modern society our 'frameworks of meaning' have themselves become problematic. We have a sense that no one framework is shared by everyone, that 'the' framework of meaning no longer exists. In a sense, it is all up for grabs.

This is partly related to the decline in religion and traditional institutions and the rise of the modern capitalist economy (see also Holifield 1983; Lasch 1984; Bellah *et al.* 1985; Cushman 1990, 1995; Giddens 1991; McLeod 1997: 1–27). Although such a dissolution of traditional strictures may be experienced as liberating, it also holds within it a terrifying and awesome responsibility. This is because our lives take on the 'object of a quest' (see MacIntyre 1981) insofar as we continuously try to negotiate and *make* its meaning while traversing our various roads. In contrast to the 'substantive' order of rationality and morality characteristic of pre-modern times, this can be defined as a more 'procedural' model in which our action is judged in terms of the standards by which we and the community to which we belong, construct, rather than discover, order (Taylor 1989: 156).

Charting the historical evolution of the modern concept of self right back to Plato, Taylor argues that our modern notion of self is constituted by a certain sense of inwardness (Taylor 1989: 111). In our contemporary language of self-understanding, the opposition between 'inside' and 'outside' plays an important role. We tend to think of our 'ideas', 'thoughts' and 'feelings' as existing 'internally', 'within' us, and objects in the world as existing 'externally', on the 'outside'. We imagine ourselves as creatures with dark, unexplored interiors (p. 111). This conception of the self comes so naturally to us that it is difficult to imagine that things could be otherwise. But in fact this concept of the self is very specific to the modern Western world. As Geertz writes:

> The Western conception of a person as a bounded, unique, more or less integrated motivational and cognitive universe, a dynamic centre of awareness, emotion, judgement and action, organised into a distinctive whole and set contrastively against other such wholes and against a social and natural background, is . . . a rather peculiar idea within the context of the world's cultures.
>
> (Geertz 1979: 229)

Of course, as Taylor recognizes, there is a sense in which people in all cultures always have some sense of themselves and distinguish between 'inside' and 'outside', 'internal' and 'external'. But having said that, there is nevertheless something unique about the modern Western concept of self (Taylor 1989: 113). This is highlighted by the fact that in our culture we tend to assume that a person's self has a certain objective status; 'it' manifests a certain degree of constancy and unity over time. Although a person will go through a whole range of differing events over the course of their life, events which may outwardly change them, essentially and fundamentally we assume that they remain the same core self. When we refer to the self we frequently do so by preceding it with the definite article 'the' or indefinite article 'a'. According to Taylor, such linguistic precision reflects something peculiar and important to the modern sense of identity (1989: 113). This characteristic sense of self has important implications for our sense of 'the good' and morality insofar as this has been internalized. The move towards a procedural definition of morality means that moral action is determined not in accordance with pre-existent rules of God, but through an internal process of interpretation and reflection.

Hence, it is this sense of the 'inner' that characterizes our modern sense of self. But how did this transformation from 'external' to 'internal' come about? One of the most important figures in this 'turn inwards' as it is sometimes called, is the philosopher St Augustine, author of *Confessions*, one of the most famous autobiographies ever written. Augustine believed that in order to achieve a higher sense of being and morality, to be 'rightly placed in relation to the good', you have to go 'inwards'. In his famous dictum, he wrote: 'Do not go outward; return within yourself. In the inward man dwells truth' (cited in Taylor 1989: 129). What Augustine does in this move, according to Taylor, is shift the focus from an 'external' field of objects to the 'activity of knowing'. If we want to know where the 'higher sense of being' is we have to look towards this 'inner turn', towards the 'self'; we have to take up what Taylor calls a 'radically reflexive' stance, to adopt a 'first-person' standpoint (p. 130). This move towards focusing on 'myself' as an agent of experience is of immense importance to the 'inward' tradition of modern Western culture. It is in this sense that Augustine introduced the 'inwardness of radical reflexivity' and 'bequeathed' it to modern culture (Taylor 1989: 131). With Augustine, we see a new orientation towards the meaning of human existence, a new method for charting the world of the self, a new fascination with the 'secret springs of personal life'.

But it is important to realize that the self Augustine concerned himself with was not strictly equivalent to our own 'modern' conception of the self. There is a fundamental difference. This is because in Augustine's case, it is none other than God who is ultimately responsible both for bringing individuality into being and also for determining the specific shape of each being. In effect, what this means is that Augustine was still working within a 'substantive' conception of reality in which he assumed a pre-existent rational order created by God. This is also sometimes referred to as a theory of 'ontic logos' which basically means a cosmic order in which notions of 'the good' pre-exist (in this case created by God). We have to wait for another famous philosopher, René Descartes, before this theory of 'ontic logos', this assumption of a pre-existent moral order, is abandoned, and ideas of the self more commensurate with our own begin to emerge.

The modern self and 'reflexivity'

According to Taylor, the internalization characteristic of the modern self holds within it two different kinds of 'reflexivity' (turning inwards) which can similarly be charted back to our philosophical heritage. These two forms of reflexivity include 'self-control' on the one hand, and 'self-exploration' on the other. Today, we take for granted the idea that we can exercise control over ourselves, that is, over our bodies, thoughts and feelings. If need be, we can 'disengage' from our desires and abstain from our passions in pursuit of a 'higher good'. This concept of 'disengagement' became very influential during the Enlightenment period with the work of philosophers such as Locke; theories promoting the ideal of the human as a being capable of making and remaking him/herself through methodical and disciplined action, by taking a logical and instrumental stance towards desires, inclinations, tendencies and so on, became very popular (Taylor 1979: 171). Philosopher/historians such as Michel Foucault in his seminal work *Discipline and Punish* (1979) have charted how these new images of self-discipline began to infiltrate into public institutions such as armies, schools, hospitals and workhouses during the Enlightenment period. Taylor refers to this stance of disengagement as an image of the 'punctual self' in which the individual is deemed capable of exercising radical self-control over his/her thoughts and behaviours. Our notion that we can achieve control over ourselves in this way embodies an ideal of responsible agency in which we are always held accountable for our own thoughts and behaviours. This ideal lies at the heart of modern popular and legal images of the self and concepts of the person.

The second form of reflexivity characteristic of contemporary 'inwardness' is that of 'self-exploration' (Taylor 1979: 177). This form of reflexivity is of particular interest to us because it is the aim of this book to critically engage us in this characteristically 'modern' enterprise. In some senses, the reflexivity involved in 'self-exploration' constitutes a total contrast to that involved in 'disengagement'. Rather than standing back from our bodies, thoughts, feelings and desires, 'objectifying' them in the pursuit of self-control, the stance of 'self-exploration' encourages us to explore these dimensions in order to establish our identity; we have to 'search for ourselves'. This search for self, as Taylor argues, has become one of the fundamental themes of modern culture, as is manifest in the widespread and increasing popularity of various forms of therapy and counselling (we will discuss this further in Chapters 6–8). It also embodies another important theme with regard to modern understandings of self and identity: the primacy of memory (see Freeman 1993). Our need to enhance self-understanding in the contemporary era turns us almost inevitably towards our pasts and our memories within which those pasts reside. The seeming inevitability of this move highlights further the assumptions characteristic of our contemporary internalized concept of self: of unity, coherence and consistency across time.

Historically, such forms of self-exploration became very popular during the Romantic period, partly as a reaction against the overly one-dimensional and exaggerated image of the self-controlled, rational and disciplined individual promoted by Enlightenment thinkers. Like children rebelling against their parents, Romantic thinkers inspired by Rousseau's philosophy affirmed the central importance of imagination, feelings, the 'inner voice', of finding the truth 'within us'. In Rousseau's terms 'The heart is the key to world and life' (cited in Taylor 1979: 371). This turn towards the 'inner voice' was immensely important in terms of concepts of 'the good' experienced by people living within the Romantic period. As Taylor argues, from this point onwards, people began to define the virtuous, 'the good', in terms of how they 'felt' about the world and their lives in general. Feelings and sentiments began to supplant the role of action and behaviour in terms of determining the 'good life'. So whether or not an event or behaviour is seen as in line with 'the good' depends not so much on objective or external consequences, but on how you feel internally about the episode. In this way, the turn towards the 'inner' reaches its full height. The moral imperative actually begins to call forth from the individual herself. 'We are called to live up to our originality' (p. 374). It is this individualistic stance, originating in the Romantic period, which remains fundamental to the reflexive self-exploratory stance characteristic of the contemporary era.

Researchers such as Cushman (1990) have drawn out the implications of Taylor's argument in terms of the visions of self most prevalent in contemporary Western societies. Cushman characterizes the kind of self that most of us live with today as an 'empty' self. This self is related, like Taylor argues, to changing economic, political and moral circumstances, which have served to accelerate the emptiness of the self experienced after the Second World War. The loss of community, tradition and shared meaning characteristic of today's society means that we experience a sense of absence that we cannot quite put our finger on. This emptiness is experienced interiorly as a lack of personal conviction and worth. Our chronic need to be 'filled up', to get rid of the vague feeling of emptiness and loss, is manifest in the characteristic contemporary obsession with food, consumer products and celebrities.

Cushman argues that two of the most lucrative professions that have emerged in the wake of this empty self are advertising and psychotherapy. Both of these professions attempt to heal and soothe this empty self but do so in such a way that the problem is exacerbated. This is because they simply substitute one form of 'filling up' for another, and thus fail to address the historical causes of the psychological symptomatology characteristic of contemporary culture. As will become apparent over the course of this book, other researchers interpret the changes associated with the contemporary self in more optimistic terms than Cushman (see Baumeister 1991; Gergen 1991; Giddens 1991).

Conclusion

So far, then, we have discussed how the concept of self is inextricably linked to language, narratives, others, time and morality. Taylor demonstrates how the modern concept of self assumes a certain 'inwardness' which incorporates assumptions about the objective and unitary status of selfhood. We have now got more idea of what narrative psychology is all about; it is an attempt to study the language, stories and narratives which constitute selves and the implications and permutations of those narratives for individuals and societies. The experience of self takes on meaning only through specific linguistic, historical and social structures.

It is also important at this point to emphasize that issues of power and control are intrinsic to this process of the narrative construction of self. The choice of one narrative over another often has serious implications for the construction of images of self, responsibility, blame and morality. At the heart of this book is the attempt to demonstrate and discuss how the selection of particular narratives presents certain visions of self at the expense of others, and the implications, both psychologically and socially, of such formulations. Although we are unable to step out of dominant narrative structures of power and control in experiencing and developing an understanding of self, nevertheless, the essential message of this book is intended as one of liberation and transformational possibility. Recognition and acknowledgement of the role played by particular narratives in our understanding of ourselves should, hopefully, enable us to stand back and become more critical and reflective about the kind of person we are, and the kind of person we would like to be.

Chapter summary

By the end of this chapter you should understand the following issues and concepts:

- The various different approaches to the study of self in psychology:
  (1) Experimental social psychology
  (2) Humanistic
  (3) Psychodynamic/psychoanalytic
  (4) Social constructivist.
- The connection between narrative psychology and social constructivist approaches.
- The uniquely human 'order' of meaning which includes an emphasis on the interrelationship between the following factors and identity: language; time; relationships with others and morality.
- How the sense of self develops during childhood through interactions with others.
- Gender differences in the experience of self and identity.
- Contemporary experiences of self, for example the 'inward' turn, 'reflexivity' and the associated moral implications.

Discussion points

- How do social constructivist approaches to the study of self and identity differ from more traditional social psychological approaches?
- How might the self that girls and women experience be influenced by the interactions they experience with significant others? Discuss some of the practical and moral implications of this.
- Outline some of the ways in which our experience of self in contemporary Western society may be different from that of previous historical eras. Think about some of the consequences of this.

Key further reading

*Cushman, P. (1990) Why the self is empty: toward a historically situated psychology, *American Psychologist*, 45(5): 599–611.

Freeman, M. (1993) *Rewriting the Self: Memory, History, Narrative* (Chapters 1 and 2). London: Routledge.

Gilligan, C. (1982) *In a Different Voice: Psychological Theory and Women's Development* (Chapters 1 and 6). Harvard: Harvard University Press.

McLeod, J. (1997) *Narrative and Psychotherapy* (Chapter 1). London: Sage.

Polkinghorne, D.P. (1988) *Narrative Knowing and the Human Sciences* (Chapter 1). Albany, NY: SUNY Press.

Taylor, C. (1989) *Sources of the Self: The Making of Modern Identity* (Chapters 1–4 and Chapter 25). Cambridge: Cambridge University Press.

Note on further reading

The Freeman, Polkinghorne and McLeod readings are all essential for understanding developments in contemporary narrative psychology. Chapters in Taylor's book are excellent in terms of their exposition of the historical development of concepts of self. Gilligan's book is a classic in its exploration of the differing concepts of self and identity held by men and women.

The *Cushman reading constitutes a highly engaging and readable account of the major problems faced by most of us in contemporary Western societies, particularly in relation to our 'empty' selves and our endless search for a sense of meaning and connection.

Introduction

In the last chapter we used the term 'social constructivist' to characterize the distinction between newer approaches towards the study of self and identity, which recognize and prioritize the inextricable relationship between self and language, and more traditional approaches, which allegedly adopt more realist conceptions in which the self is assumed to exist independently of language in some mysterious 'inner' domain (as in the case of humanist/ psychodynamic approaches) or in 'external' behaviour (as in the case of experimental, sometimes also referred to as behaviouristic, approaches). In this chapter our aim is to examine in more detail the various research approaches that are frequently brought together under the umbrella of 'social constructivism', sometimes also referred to as 'discursive' or 'language-based' approaches. In particular, we shall address the relationship between narrative and other discursive approaches towards the study of self and identity. These include postmodernism, discourse analysis, rhetorical analysis, interpretive phenomenological analysis and critical feminist psychological analysis. As will become clear, there are many confusions and contradictions in this debate and it will be suggested that the distinctions between the old and new paradigms are not nearly as clear-cut as they are often made out to be. It will be argued that, on a philosophical level, the narrative psychological approach developed in this book shares the 'realist' assumptions associated with more traditional social psychological approaches. On the other hand, these approaches are commonly limited in their study of self and identity by their over-reliance on quantitative, experimental methods. In order to achieve greater depth, it is argued that qualitative methods and analysis are required. These are associated more with the newer 'social constructivist' paradigm.

Postmodernist approaches

Before describing how postmodernist theory relates to the study of self and identity, we need first to clarify what the word 'postmodern' means. To do this, we need to distinguish between the modern and the postmodern (see Featherstone 1988; Best and Kellner 1991). The term 'modernity' is often used to describe the modern age which, from a Marxist perspective, is the historical period referring to the epoch following the Middle Ages. Some other social theorists use the term modernity in opposition to 'traditional' or less developed societies (Best and Kellner 1991: 2). Modernity refers to a variety of economic, political, social and cultural transformations. It can be characterized by the changes in society which came about through the process of industrialization and advancing capitalism, sometimes referred to as 'modernization' – a term denoting processes of individualization, secularization (the decline in religion), commodification, urbanization, bureaucratization and rationalization (the celebration of 'reason' as the source of progress in knowledge and society). All of these processes have together constituted the modern world.

Postmodernity, as its name suggests, describes the period which follows modernity (sometimes also referred to as the period of 'high modernity'). We are allegedly living in the postmodern era now. The postmodern era is characterized by the increasing proliferation of high technology such as computers and the media, the Internet, virtual reality and hyperspace, all of which create the capacity for new forms of communication and knowledge, and consequent changes in social and economic formations. Not surprisingly, the social and cultural context of postmodernity produces changes in psychological experience because it creates a new sense of space and time, and new modes of experience and culture (see also Giddens 1991).

In academia in recent years, post-structuralist theory (which underlies most postmodern approaches in psychology) has become very popular across a whole range of social science disciplines (it is sometimes also called 'deconstructionism'). This approach is represented by figures such as Michel Foucault (a philosopher/historian), Jacques Derrida, Jean François Lyotard (critical philosophers), and Jacques Lacan (a psychoanalyst). These authors see individuals and selves as being enfolded in language and thus constituted through social and historical relations of power and modes of discipline. The task of postmodernism is to 'deconstruct' linguistic structures and socio-historical narratives in order to find out what our knowledge is actually based on.

A central theme of postmodernism is the idea that knowledge is determined not by logic or rationality (as the 'modernist' theorist would argue) but by the twists and turns of language. Although we may believe ourselves to be the masters of language, it is more apt to say that language masters us (Lovlie 1992: 119). Language can be described as a 'structure of signs' which is itself the repository of meaning, independent of the 'reality' of the self or the world. Instead of meaning residing in a correspondence between 'sign' and 'referent', meaning is to be found in the relation between signs. That is, signs do not have meaning in themselves but get their meaning by the place they occupy in relation to other signs in the language network.

The idea that meaning consists of a system of signs has particular implications for our concepts of self and identity, and this is manifest in the famous postmodern declaration of the 'death of the subject' (Lovlie 1992: 120). This phrase reflects the postmodernists' critical stance towards the 'inwardness' characteristic of contemporary individuals' understanding of themselves. As we have already seen, this sense of 'inwardness' incorporates certain assumptions about the self. One of these is the idea that we 'have' a self and despite undergoing a whole range of conflicting, challenging experiences over the course of our lives, we nevertheless maintain a certain constancy, a unity, within our core self. We assume a linear progression and continuity through life, as in the 'romantic image of the child unfolding its innate abilities and talents towards a final ripening' (Lovlie 1992: 120). The postmodernist views such images as nothing more than the fond delusions of our culture and attempts to displace them with images of fragmentation and discontinuity. The postmodernist vision of the individual is one which defies any sense of development, order or progression. It is in this sense that the 'subject' is pronounced dead. I am no longer viewed as the 'centre' or 'essence' of my personality, a unique individual with the ability to 'authentically' or independently reflect on how to act or how to understand my life and its meaning. Instead, the locus of meaning shifts to the play of linguistic signs, narratives and power.

One of the most influential proponents of postmodernism in psychology is Kenneth Gergen (1991) who characterizes postmodernity as the era of the 'saturated self'. This vision of the contemporary self, unlike Cushman's 'empty' self discussed in the last chapter, is full of optimism and potentiality. Gergen argues that the increasing complexity of society and new technologies for communication and travel results in a self saturated with the 'voices of humankind'. 'Newspapers, television and video recorders, radio, easy long-distance travel, computer communications, junk mail and even answerphones engulf us with a plethora of images and information' (Stevens and Wetherell 1996: 346). Gergen believes that this information explosion, which has emerged only over the past 20 years or so, is having a profound impact on modern-day consciousness.

Social saturation has the capacity to change our consciousness, according to Gergen, because it results in the fragmentation of our self-conceptions and relationships. Gergen argues that:

> . . . social saturation brings with it a general loss in our assumption of true and knowable selves. As we absorb multiple voices, we find each 'truth' relativised in our simultaneous consciousness of compelling alternatives. We come to be aware that each truth about ourselves is a construction of the moment, true only for a given time and within certain relationships.
>
> (Gergen 1991: 16)

It is clear here how Gergen's position fits in with the general postmodern claim of 'death of the author' or 'death of the subject'. Instead of a consistent, coherently defined 'inner' self, a more 'open slate emerges on which a person may inscribe, erase and rewrite their identities as the ever-shifting, ever expanding and incoherent network of relationship invites or permits' (Gergen 1991: 228). For Gergen, the kind of self that this postmodern world promotes is one full of adventure and what he calls a 'free play of being'. It is a world that encourages 'experimentation . . . risk and absurdity', our opening up to a 'multiplicity of possibilities', a world 'free from the limiting constraints of the past' (pp. 248–9; see also Turkle 1996).

Discourse analysis: Parker's approach

In psychology, the influence of postmodernism has also been represented by Ian Parker's (1990; 1991) version of 'discourse analysis', which is informed by French post-structural writers such as Foucault and Derrida. Parker's aim is to locate and describe the variety of 'discourses' proliferating within societies which implicitly shape the way we see ourselves and the world. For example, in contemporary Western societies there are a number of dominant discourses which inform and shape various aspects of our lives. As we shall explore in more detail in this book, for example, in recent years 'therapeutic' or 'healing' discourses have become very popular in informing the way in which we experience ourselves in the aftermath of various traumatic events and experiences. In addition, various 'feminist' discourses have had a radical and profound effect on the way in which both women and men experience themselves in contemporary societies.

Parker defines discourses as 'coherent systems of meaning'. Alternative discourses compete with one another so that their specific vision of self, world and morality will be accepted and incorporated into dominant institutional and political structures through and by which power and influence are reproduced. It is in this sense that Parker argues that discourses have a material and almost 'physical' presence because once created they proliferate within society. It may be useful to recall historian Michel Foucault's work *Discipline and Punish* (1979), briefly discussed in Chapter 1, to illustrate this point. Foucault showed how the discourse of 'self-discipline' emerging during the Enlightenment period began to infiltrate into public institutions such as armies, schools, hospitals and workhouses. In addition, the ideal of responsible agency incorporated within the discourse of self-discipline now lies at the heart of modern popular and legal images of the self and concepts of the person. Parker's approach has a political edge insofar as some discourses function to legitimate and buttress existing institutions, reproduce power relations and inequities in societies and have certain ideological effects (Parker 1990). Hence, 'discourse analysis should become a variety of action research in which the internal system of a discourse and its relation to others is challenged. It alters and so permits different spaces for manoeuvre and resistance' (Parker 1990: 201).

Discourse analysis: Potter and Wetherell's approach

Perhaps the most popular form of discourse analysis in social psychology is represented by Potter and Wetherell and was put forward in their influential book, *Discourse and Social Psychology: Beyond Attitudes and Behaviour* (1987). Like postmodernist approaches, this discursive approach was conceived as a radical alternative to more traditional approaches in social psychology insofar as it allegedly challenged the 'epistemological' status of many traditionally accepted concepts such as 'self', 'attitudes', 'emotions' and so on. Basically, this means that Potter and Wetherell had a different theory about both what and how the knowledge of concepts such as 'self' could be built up. For instance, one of their central arguments with regard to traditional concepts of self is that they incorporate 'cognitivist' or 'mentalistic' assumptions – that is, they assume that something like a 'self' can be identified and located 'within' an internal, mental world (see also Coulter 1979, 1983). Like the postmodernists, Potter and Wetherell argue that such 'cognitivist' assumptions are problematic. They propose the suspension of such assumptions and the turning of attention towards what people have to say about the self and the functional actions inherent in such discourses.

Potter and Wetherell's central idea is that people use language to 'do things' and to achieve certain ends. Words are not just abstract tools used to describe things. Rather, they are used to construct the self and the world and thus to make things happen. Thus, people use language to excuse, blame, justify, persuade and present themselves in certain ways. In other words, language is functional. Potter and Wetherell's interest is therefore in how people use language to understand and make sense of everyday life. Hence, in terms of the study of self and identity, Potter and Wetherell argue that we need to '. . . displace attention from the self-as-entity and focus it on the methods of constructing the self. That is, the question becomes not what is the true nature of the self, but how is the self talked about, how is it theorised in discourse?' (Potter and Wetherell 1987: 102).

A pervasive theme in Potter and Wetherell's work is the variability of people's talk and thus the importance of interactional and social context. What people say about 'self', for instance, depends on the particular context in which it is spoken and the function it serves. This is in contrast to more traditional approaches in social psychology which look for stability, consistency and order in people's accounts and concepts of self. This is all part of the move from a traditional 'realist' view which treats language as descriptive and reflective of a relatively stable pre-existent 'self' and 'world', towards a 'constructivist' concern with how such a sense of coherence and order is 'manufactured' through the use of linguistic practices.

Although Potter and Wetherell's version of discourse analysis is in some senses similar to Parker's, Potter and Wetherell have criticized Parker's notion of discourse because they claim it is too abstract (Potter *et al.* 1990). Parker claims that discourses, existing as 'real' material entities, exist independently of the people who use them. By contrast, Potter and Wetherell use the concept discourse only when it can be located in the speech practices of individuals. In this sense, their conception of discourse analysis is one which is much more narrowly focused on the specific practices of individuals. They claim that this provides a more social psychological focus to discourse analysis.

Shotter's 'rhetorical-responsive' approach

Another influential social constructivist approach in psychology is John Shotter's 'rhetorical-responsive' approach (see Shotter 1993, 1997). Drawing on the work of the philosopher Wittgenstein (1953, 1980), the literary theorist Bakhtin (1984) and the social psychologist Billig (1987), Shotter argues that this approach throws light on what we call our 'inner' lives and selves (Shotter 1997). Shotter argues that 'everything of importance to our studies should be seen as happening' in the 'momentary relational encounters occurring between people in their dialogic exchanges' (p. 9). It is in the 'brief interactive moments between people, in which speakers and listeners must continually react to each other spontaneously and practically, with an active, responsive understanding, that we must focus our studies'. Our conversational activities are not just one of our activities in the world. Rather, they are foundational in that they provide the living basis for everything we do (Shotter 1997: 9).

According to Shotter, this focus on conversational, relational activities occurring between people is of great importance to the way in which we understand the 'inner, psychic lives of individuals – their feelings or experience, their thoughts and thinking, or those inner moments when, all alone, we try and make sense of our own lives' (p. 11). This is because the 'things supposedly in our "inner" lives are to be found not within us as individuals, but in the momentary relational spaces occurring between ourselves and an other or otherness in our surroundings' (p. 12). In practice, the 'psyche' is 'less an entity and more a strategy or set of strategies, a set of characteristic ways of responding to the others around us. Its nature appears only in our practical activities, at that point of contact with others, in our relational encounters with them' (p. 20). It is clear here that Shotter's perspective is very similar to postmodernist and discourse analytic approaches insofar as his emphasis is not on meaning which in some way 'pre-exists' within the individual (or within language – 'the sign'), but which emerges in the context of interaction and is thus to be found 'in relation' to that context.

Thus 'a person's psyche (if such an entity can be said to exist at all)' exists 'according to social conditions' and is thus 'an entity with constantly contested and shifting boundaries, something that can be recollected one way one day and in another the next' (Shotter 1997: 20). Here again, we see a by now familiar attempt to challenge the traditional notion that our selves and identities maintain a certain constancy and unity. The rhetorical approach, like the postmodernist and discourse analytic approaches, is concerned to highlight the contextually and pragmatically constructed nature of self and thus its unstable, variable and fragmentary nature as it is brought into being in 'certain fleeting and momentary (dialogical) occurrences' (see Katz and Shotter 1996).

Shotter argues that the task of developing a conversational, rhetorical-responsive account of our selves and identities is not merely a theoretical task. It also has practical implications. He argues that 'we must develop new practices, new stances, new ways of talking and being' in order that we can sustain new forms of 'relating ourselves to each other' (Shotter 1997: 22). The study of how this might be achieved is characterized by Shotter as 'social poetics'. An example of social poetics in practice is provided by Katz and Shotter (1996) in a study of doctor–patient interaction where a third person occupies the position of a 'cultural go-between' who mediates between doctors and patients in diagnostic interviews. The task of the cultural go-between is to be open to being arrested or 'moved by certain fleeting, momentary occurrences in what patients do or say' (Katz and Shotter 1996: 919). The aim of this process is to 'begin to sense the unique nature of (the patient's) inner world of pain and suffering' (p. 919).

Problems with social constructivist approaches – 'losing the subject'

As has been pointed out by other researchers such as Parker, the problem with both postmodernist and discourse analytic approaches is that they repeatedly beg the question: 'what is going on inside human beings when they use discourse?' (Parker 1991: 83). Parker argues that the capacity to be reflexive (to think about oneself, to reflect inwardly) is at the core of human agency and understanding and it is this capacity to be reflexive which is 'the point of connection between the individual and the social' (Parker 1991: 105). Unfortunately, it is this ability to be reflexive that both postmodernist and discourse analytic approaches tend to omit from their accounts of human subjectivity.

As we have just seen, the postmodernist, discourse and rhetorical analytic commitment to 'deconstructing' the self stems from an appreciation of the inextricable connection between linguistic structures and concepts of self. This leads to an understanding of the 'self' as a phenomenon characterized by interpretation, variability, relativity, flux and difference. From this perspective, it is impossible to make universal claims about the nature of human selves because such selves differ in relation from different historical, cultural and practical contexts. It is from this theoretical recognition of a lack of unity and constancy that postmodernists declare the 'death of the subject'. If there is no 'one' essential nature of self to describe, then the concept of 'a' self, of 'having' or 'possessing' a self, must be abandoned. Discourse and rhetorical analysts, in recognition of the variable and functional nature of talk about selves, similarly reject the traditional assumption of 'a' central and unitary concept of self. I want us now to look at the type of self or 'subject' that emerges from both postmodernism and discourse analysis when the claims regarding variability and lack of unity are taken seriously.

Consider the following short prose narrative written by the novelist Jean-François Bory. This piece is intended to illustrate the postmodern conception of self as a 'play of linguistic signs':

> And after the subject, the verb, followed by an adjective agreeing in gender and number with the subject. The same subject, an adverbial pronoun, an auxiliary verb, an article, a noun, an object of the predicate, an indefinite pronoun and an infinitive verb.
>
> (cited in Nash 1990: 199)

And now consider the example used by Potter and Wetherell in their book to illustrate how discourse analysis might be used to study the self. They draw, somewhat obscurely, on interviews 'conducted with New Zealanders concerning the question of sporting links with South Africa and more specifically the 1981 Springbok rugby tour of New Zealand' (Potter and Wetherell 1987: 111). Because this tour was highly controversial in New Zealand and not supported by most of the population, a great deal of inter-group conflict was apparent. In interviews, people were asked to give an account of or explain the conflict and violence surrounding the tour and to articulate their own position. When people did so, it became apparent that 'varying constructions of the self were brought into play in the process'. Potter and Wetherell admit that these were generally '. . . third person models in the sense that other people rather than one's own self were being described. But from our discourse perspective, the same analytic principles apply, and discourse about others' selves is just as interesting as discourse about one's own self' (Potter and Wetherell 1987: 111).

It is important to draw out from these two characteristic examples the image of 'self' or 'subject' that the postmodern and discourse analytic approaches promote. In the quote from the postmodern novelist Jean-François Bory, it is clear that although the author repeatedly refers to a 'subject', this is literally the grammatical 'subject' of each sentence. In this example the 'subject' is reduced to a mere grammatical shell, empty of meaning, intention and information, simply interplaying between different linguistic signs. We have no way of knowing what kind of 'person' this 'subject' is. A similar reductionism and depersonalization of the subject is evident in Potter and Wetherell's justification of their decision to use third person descriptions of 'other' people rather than first person descriptions of 'self'. Of course, it may be the case that in terms of the analytic principles of discourse analysis, talk about oneself and talk about other selves is very similar. Having said that, however, one cannot help thinking that the selection of this kind of 'social' example, taken from an episode of intergroup conflict, enables Potter and Wetherell to avoid some of the nitty-gritty questions and issues that come up when we focus on how people talk about and try to understand their own more 'personal' selves.

This links into a more general critique of the discursive approach to the understanding of human psychological and social life highlighted by Augustinous and Walker (1995: 276). This is the argument that the 'individual purposive-agent' seems absent in such accounts which deliberately avoid the suggestion that human beings have any fundamental or internal 'sense' of themselves as a self. Self is studied only in terms of individual, discursive acts which perform various social activities such as presenting a certain image of the self, excusing, blaming and so on. This results in a conception of self in which 'subjective experience . . . is made so context-dependent, so fluid and flexible, that there seems to be little beyond a personal psychology which is a moment-to-moment situated experience' (Augustinous and Walker 1995: 276). Language and context are emphasized to such an extent that the self is 'engulfed, if not annihilated' (Dunne 1995: 140). Similarly, critics such as Smith (1994) have questioned the extent to which the ruminations of postmodernist theorists actually connect with the empirical realities of most people's selves and lives. For example, Smith asks how relevant the conceptions of saturated, empty or fragmented selves are to the concerns of 'children growing up in central city poverty and in fractured families' or of 'HIV infected people around the world facing the prospect of AIDS' (p. 406)?

It is in this sense that both postmodern and discourse analytic approaches have been characterized as a 'retreat from the investigation of core questions' (Abraham and Hampson 1996: 226). This is what I mean in the subtitle to this section when I refer to the postmodernist and discourse analytic tendency to 'lose' the subject. We need to find some way in which we can appreciate the linguistic and discursive structuring of human psychology without losing sight of the essentially personal, coherent and 'real' nature of individual experience and subjectivity.

Retrieving the subject – interpretive phenomenological analysis?

One of the social constructivist approaches currently achieving recognition within psychology which enables us to explore the experiential reality of the self is that of Interpretive Phenomenological Analysis (IPA), mainly represented by Jonathan Smith (see Smith 1996; Smith *et al.* 1997). Smith uses this style of analysis mainly in areas relating to the study of health and illness, which, as we shall see later in this book, often radically changes a person's conception of themselves, others and the world.

According to Smith *et al.* (1997) it is important to distinguish between IPA and discourse analysis as represented by Potter and Wetherell's approach. This is because although IPA shares with discourse analysis a commitment to the importance of language and qualitative analysis, the two approaches differ in terms of the status they afford to 'cognition' and experience of the self and body. As we have already seen, discourse analysis is generally sceptical of mapping what people say on to underlying subjective experiences. It prefers to treat people's verbal accounts as behaviours in their own right which should be analysed in accordance with the functions and activities they are performing in particular situations. By contrast, IPA is concerned with cognitions and experiences, that is, with getting to grips with how a person thinks or feels about what is happening to them. It does this by assuming a 'chain of connection' between what a person says (verbal response) and how they think and feel about themselves, their bodies, other people and the world more generally (cognition and experience). Hence, IPA is based on 'realist' assumptions drawn from traditional approaches in social psychology such as social cognition (Smith *et al.* 1997). In other words, it operates with a 'realist epistemology': that there is a knowable domain of facts about human experience and consciousness that can be discovered through the application of certain methods (Augustinous and Walker 1995: 262). As we have already seen, this epistemological position, this assumption of a chain of connection between language and the experiencing 'self', is questioned in discourse analysis which brackets assumptions about the 'reality' of the self and can therefore tell us very little about how the person subjectively thinks or feels about the phenomena being talked about (see also Abraham and Hampson 1996; Smith 1996).

Smith *et al.* argue, by contrast, that IPA is a 'method which attempts to tap into a natural propensity for self reflection on the part of participants' (Smith *et al.* 1997: 68). A central premise of the method consists of 'allowing participants to tell their story, in their own words, about the topic under investigation' (p. 68). The aim of IPA is to 'explore the participant's view of the world and to adopt, as far as is possible, an "insider's perspective" (Conrad 1987)' (p. 69). The approach is phenomenological, according to Smith *et al.*, insofar as it is 'concerned with an individual's personal perception or account of an object or event as opposed to the attempt to produce an objective statement of the object or event itself' (p. 69).

Smith acknowledges that whereas his IPA and related qualitative methods have only recently begun to establish a higher profile in psychology, they have a long history in the social sciences more generally. This is especially the case within medical sociology where phenomenological and qualitative methods have been extremely important in studying a whole variety of issues related to health and illness (Smith *et al.* 1997: 72). For example, a number of medical sociologists have attempted to get closer to the individual's own sense of what chronic illness means by conducting qualitative studies (for collections see Anderson and Bury 1988; Social Science and Medicine 1990). Smith *et al.* argue that these studies are concerned less with 'testing predetermined constructs than with examining individual themes elicited from the transcripts of intensive, semi-structured interviews with patients' (Smith *et al.* 1997: 73). As yet, however, apart from exceptions such as Shelly Taylor's qualitative work with cancer patients, and my own and Steven Schwartzberg's work with HIV/AIDS patients, there have been few qualitative studies from within psychology on people's illness experiences (see Taylor 1983; Schwartzberg 1993; Crossley 1997a, 1997b, 1998a, 1998b, 1998c, 1999a, in press, forthcoming; Davies 1997). As Smith *et al.* (1997) argue, 'it seems somewhat ironic that in order to explore this phenomenology of illness one turns to sociological rather than psychological studies' (p. 73).

Potential problems with phenomenological approaches – losing 'discourse'

There are, however, potential problems with phenomenologically inspired approaches insofar as the attempt to achieve insight into the perspective of others may lead to the 'uncritical presentation of their understanding of a phenomenon' (Yardley 1997: 30). This problem has been debated in the discipline of qualitative medical sociology in terms of the 'insider' view of illness. This 'insider' view tends to celebrate the authority of the individual in managing illness or health risks and, relatedly, challenges the authority of 'outside' professionals such as doctors or those involved in health promotion. Some of the most fundamental problems with such 'insider' views are that they often become romanticized and, in the process of celebrating the individual's experience, tend to neglect structural factors which can lead to the perpetuation of inequality and unwittingly reinforce relations of domination and subordination (see Crossley 1998b). From a social constructivist perspective this is problematic because it fails to take adequate account of the social structuring of individual, personal experience.

An example will be helpful at this point. Smith *et al.* (1997) present an illustration of how IPA can contribute to the psychology of sexual health.

More specifically, they report results from a study which aimed to enhance understanding of gay men's attitudes towards sex, sexual behaviour and sexual decision making, as a means of reducing HIV infection among the gay community. Smith *et al.* (1997) criticize many of the studies conducted from within the disciplines of health psychology, epidemiology and health promotion because they are premised on what they characterize as a limited 'medicalized' model of sex (p. 82). This model creates an oversimplified image of sex which only focuses on the body: the sexual organs and reproduction. This is problematic for a psychology of sexual health because it provides an 'incomplete account of sexual decision making' and a 'unitary understanding of sexual behaviour' (p. 82). For example, much health psychology fails to consider the fact that the sexual act of anal intercourse (considered one of the most 'risky' activities in terms of HIV transmission) takes on different meanings in relation to different interpersonal contexts. Smith *et al.* quote Richard, a gay man, describing two differing understandings of the same physical act (penetrative anal sex):

> 'If it's somebody casual, a fuck's a fuck isn't it? But when you're making love with somebody, there's like the emotional feeling. It's not just the feeling that you get your dick in and once you've, you know, once you've come, I mean that's it isn't it, but when you're making love with somebody, you can come and then still carry on from there, you know. It's just totally, totally different.'
>
> (cited in Smith *et al.* 1997: 83)

According to Smith *et al.*, the failure of many health interventions to take such differential meanings into account means that they will have a limited impact on gay men's sexual behaviour because they take inadequate account of the significance of those acts for the individual.

This is particularly important when one considers recent findings that 'relationship status' is associated with unsafe sex more than any other variable. In particular, the closer the relationship, the greater the chance of unsafe sex (de Wit 1994; Lowy and Ross 1994). Smith *et al.* argue that their qualitative study can shed light on this finding and illustrate this by drawing on a gay man, Daniel's, discussion of the 'problematic relationship between condom use and intimacy' (p. 84). Daniel's account highlights the way in which he perceives unprotected penetration as a 'natural' act and hints at its 'symbolic and historical legitimacy as the culmination of sex and the expression of a couple's togetherness' (p. 85). He feels that the condom acts as a barrier to this fulfilment. Hence, for some gay men, unprotected sex comes to represent an 'expression of love and commitment' as is evident in the following quote when 'Philip' told his partner he loved him: 'I says, "I love you enough to fuck you without a condom on". Yeah, yeah, I says, "I want to fuck you without a condom on or you fuck me, I want you to come inside me or I'll fuck you and come inside you"' (cited in Smith *et al.* 1997: 85). 'Daniel' takes such thoughts to their 'logical conclusion' in the following comment:

'I've not been in the situation but if you really loved somebody and that's what you wanted to do, even if you knew they were HIV, I think that would even come into the equation, if, you know, if you were wanting, you know, wanting to die with somebody, or even if you loved somebody that much I suppose, wanting somebody's virus inside 'em. You know, that they've got it, then you want it as well, sort of thing.'

(Smith *et al.* 1997: 85)

Smith *et al.* argue that in this way, becoming infected knowingly can be seen as 'the ultimate expression of prioritizing the relationship' and the prioritizing of the 'selves above the bodies' and the 'couple above the individuals'; this might also be described as 'the ultimate expression of love' (p. 85).

This example demonstrates how important it is to understand the meaning and significance of certain behaviours from the point of view of the individual. Having said that, however, it also clearly points to some of the potentially problematic dimensions of phenomenologically inspired approaches. For example, adopting an 'insider' view of illness it is all too easy to slip from an understanding of the individual's perspective (for example, becoming infected with HIV knowingly as an 'ultimate expression of love'), to an uncritical advocacy of that subjective viewpoint as the best way of understanding the situation.[1] To avoid such problems, the comments of individuals should not be taken at face value, rather, they need to be located in wider structures of discourse and power so that their implications and ramifications can be fully understood. For example, from my own interviews with HIV-positive individuals, I found this 'romantic' discourse in evidence, particularly among heterosexual couples where women were willing to demonstrate their love for HIV infected male partners by trying to conceive, despite risking infection of both themselves and their potential child. As other researchers such as Hollway (1984) and Ingham and Kirkland (1997) have shown, such discourses of 'romance' surrounding sexuality have served to rationalize and perpetuate inequalities in relationships, particularly among men and women (see also Joffe 1997).

In addition, especially in the HIV/AIDS arena, it has been argued that we need to go beyond the kind of individual or relationship perspective encouraged by the 'insider' view of illness. This kind of approach draws on the popular discourse of empowerment which frequently encourages people to think individualistically in terms of the 'rights' and 'needs' of themselves, their relationship or their individual family unit, without any corresponding sense of 'duty' to the wider social body (this will be discussed further in Chapter 8). As recent critics in both the USA and Britain have argued, from the very beginning of the AIDS crisis the possibility of producing an adequate response to a potential world health crisis has been hampered and plagued by the prioritization of individual civil liberties over the needs of society more generally (see Fumento 1990; Scheper-Hughes 1994; Hodgkinson 1996). For example, Scheper-Hughes asks if it is possible 'to control an epidemic such as AIDS in a purely democratic fashion . . . [and if not is the]

1998: xv). For instance, feminist approaches such as Irigiray's place a great deal of emphasis on celebrating the experiences of motherhood, the body and nature. This forms part of the attempt to challenge the dominant values of 'masculinist' culture which emphasize the importance of rationality, work (the 'public' world), objectivity and culture. By contrast, Irigiray celebrates the opposing culturally 'feminine' values of irrationality, home (the 'private' world), subjectivity and nature. As the radical feminist Daly (1979: 44) argues, 'we are rooted, as are animals and trees, winds and seas in the earth's substance. Our origins are in the elements'. And Irigiray (1985) comments that 'woman has sex organs just about everywhere. She experiences pleasure almost everywhere'.

The problem with approaches such as these which attempt to retrieve women's experiences, whether through 'voices' as in the case of Gilligan, or 'bodies' in the case of Irigiray and Kristeva, is that they can easily slide into romanticism. We have already discussed this problem in relation to phenomenological approaches towards the study of health and illness. The main point is that when experiences are reproduced in this way, there tends to be an inadequate exploration of the social and political factors undergirding such experiences (see Soper 1990; Ussher 1991; Segall 1997; Woodward 1997). In addition, critics have suggested that such approaches 'impose a false homogeneity upon the diversity of women's voices across differences of age, ethnicity, (dis)ability, class and other social divisions' in much the same way as traditional psychological approaches have done (see Davis 1994).

In sum then, feminist approaches, like IPA, are involved in a struggle to present individual (women's) experiences in a 'realistic' way which appreciates both their 'personal' idiosyncratic nature, and also their linguistic and discursive structuring. The need to maintain an element of individuality, agency and autonomy, and not simply to 'die' into the fragmentary, disordered condition characterized by postmodern theorists, is particularly important from a feminist perspective. This is because feminism is partly about enabling women to 'discover' the independence and autonomy that comes from experiencing the kind of self postmodernists are in the business of deconstructing. As many women have never experienced such a self in the first place, it is unlikely that they will be as willing to give it up as the postmodern acolytes. As Waugh (1992) argues, feminism cannot necessarily afford the luxury of a postmodern, fragmented self; it 'needs coherent subjects'.

Where does narrative psychology fit into all this?

So far we have looked at various social constructivist approaches prevalent in contemporary psychology: postmodernism, discourse analysis, rhetorical analysis, interpretative phenomenological analysis and critical feminist analysis. We have argued that although postmodernism and discourse analysis are important in terms of their ability to extrapolate and highlight the linguistic, social and practical nature of selfhood, they fail to adequately address the experiential and personal dimensions of human experience. In order to achieve this, it has been suggested that the 'realist' epistemology associated with traditional social psychology and Smith's IPA approach may be more appropriate. Having said that, however, we have also expressed a concern with the potential for phenomenologically inspired approaches (and some radical feminist approaches) to perpetuate a 'romanticist' image of self and experience which potentiates the uncritical acceptance and perpetuation of relations of power and domination. Our next question is: where does a narrative psychological approach fit into all this?

As we discovered in Chapter 1, a narrative psychological approach clearly shares the postmodernist, discourse and rhetorical analytic concern with language as a tool for the construction of reality, especially the reality of the experiencing self and the way in which the concept of self is inextricably linked to language, narratives, others, time and morality. Indeed, as was argued in that chapter, the experience of self takes on meaning only through specific linguistic, historical and social structures. The aim of narrative psychology is therefore to study the language, stories and narratives which constitute selves and the implications and permutations of those narratives for individuals and societies. In this sense, the narrative psychology approach is entirely consistent with social constructivist approaches such as postmodernism, discourse, rhetorical and critical feminist analysis.

Having said that, however, a narrative psychological approach has developed in relation to issues such as the psychology of trauma and in the attempt to understand the way in which people adapt and respond to traumatizing events such as the experience of terminal illness (and as we shall see in Chapter 3, the experience of mental illness). This points to one of the major ways in which it differs from postmodernism, rhetorical and discourse analysis: it basically has a very 'topical' or 'substantive' orientation to it. What I mean by this is that narrative psychological approaches tend to be very much grounded in the attempt to understand the specific experiences undergone by individuals. This is in contrast to the postmodern approach which tends to be pitched at a more abstract, theoretical level, and the discourse and rhetorical analytic approaches which have a more methodological focus. We have argued that these approaches tend to 'lose' the experience of the subject by operating at these levels. By contrast, narrative psychology, like IPA and some feminist psychological approaches, is concerned to retrieve that subjectivity by specifically focusing on the lived experience of the individual. It is in this regard that narrative psychology recognizes the need, again like IPA and feminist psychology, to operate with a realist epistemology which is able to accord sufficient respect to the experiences of specific individuals.

For example, 'realist' critics of postmodernism and discourse and rhetorical analysis have argued that despite the fact that discourse may be fragmentary, contradictory and changeable within different interactive and social contexts, nevertheless, it is normally possible to discern a degree of 'coherence', or a 'chain of connection', between what people say and how they experience themselves (Augustinous and Walker 1995: 274; Abraham and Hampson 1996: 229). It is the central premise of this book that when we actually turn to examine the full range of experiences, knowledge and understandings of self that people live and struggle with, therein resides a sense of unity, continuity and coherence which simply does not gel with the radical fragmentation, disunity and absence promoted in the theoretically and methodologically confined agendas of postmodernism and discourse analysis respectively. This book demonstrates that experiential struggle, the fight between a sense of self (unity) and non-self (disunity, fragmentation), remains a central feature of human existence. Nowhere is this more apparent than in cases of trauma. For instance, consider the following quote from Simon, a man who described to me the 'identity crisis' he experienced in the early days of his HIV-positive diagnosis:

> '. . . Absolutely everything, everything that you have in life just breaks down, becomes dust, powder, you know, and you become completely naked and utterly lost. You do not know what to do; Where did you come from?; Where do you go and where are you standing at this moment? This is something indescribable and nobody can help you. You have to build up by yourself; it is an extremely difficult and helpless situation. It is very traumatic.'
>
> (Davies 1997: 565)

Simon's comments illustrate the essential difference between the kind of self or 'subject' narrative psychology on the one hand, and postmodernism/discourse analysis on the other, are interested in studying. Simon depicts what might best be characterized as an 'old-fashioned' or 'realist' narrative. This is:

> . . . the kind of narrative that has a 'subject'. 'Subject' in two important senses of the word: a 'subject matter' that demands to be 'told', to be 'borne witness to'; the narrative is about something – something stable, clear, and readily identifiable. And the narrative has in it or behind it a 'subjectivity' – a person, a 'subject' who experiences the truth to which he or she must bear witness; a being, a mind that is in some vital respect stable, clear and readily identifiable.
>
> (Nash 1990: 20

This kind of 'subject' contrasts directly with the empty 'grammatical' depersonalized 'object' which is generally the focus of postmodernist and discourse analytic approaches. The postmodern vision of a fragmented, anonymous, dead self simply does not accord with the reality of how people contend with their experiences and sense of themselves. The plain fact is that the kinds of experiences many of us undergo cry out for the kind of 'old-fashioned' narrative depicted above, that is, we frequently find ourselves having to make sense of what is going on; we have to create a stable, solid version of what and why this or that happened; and in order to do this, we have to have some sense of ourselves as a unified, coherent person. To reiterate Waugh (1992) in relation to feminism, when selves are at risk or in the process of being built, 'we need coherent subjects'.

But in committing ourselves to a realist epistemology which recognizes the need to empathically portray the trials and tribulations, the joys and tragedies of human lives, we must also be aware of the converse 'romanticist' trap of accepting the rendition of such events as simply idiosyncratic (individual or personal) expressions of experience. Consider, for instance, the following quote from another HIV-positive man, Sean, who describes a similar 'personal' or 'identity' crisis to Simon:

> 'I think the most difficult thing to come to terms with in living with HIV, if you are going to be honest with yourself and acknowledge it, is that there are so many uncertainties. Suddenly, you discover things which you had been led to believe were certainties can't be taken for granted anymore, not just issues around health or relationships or your career or your economic position. Suddenly, they all become uncertainties and that is the nearest I have come to feeling that the supposed rules, like set in stone or whatever, no longer apply to you and somehow you feel that it is legitimate for the rest of the population to claim it is true for them but suddenly it isn't for you. . . .'
>
> (Davies 1997: 565)

Sean's comments illustrate that his very 'personal' crisis is inextricably related to the society in which he lives and the predominant narratives, inscribed goals and moralities intrinsic to that culture. For, as we saw in relation to Charles Taylor's work in Chapter 1, in order to answer that most personal of questions 'who am I?', I basically need to know where I stand in relation to 'the good'. To know who I am, I have to know how I am oriented in moral space, a space in which questions of good or bad, worthless or worthwhile, have meaning for me (Taylor 1989: 29). In other words, our routine sense of unity, of coherence and continuity, shaken in relation to the identity crisis, is all about our connection to others and morality. We have to take a stand in relation to 'the good'. It is only then that we know who we are.

Conclusion

In this chapter it has become evident that the various social constructivist approaches towards the study of self leave a gap that needs to be filled. There is a need to develop an approach which, while recognizing the inextricable connection between individual 'personal' experience and 'social' forms of meaning such as discourse and narrative, retains the capacity to accord a sufficient degree of 'reality' to the experiential 'domain'. Other authors have suggested various routes by which this might be achieved. For instance, Parker suggests that we turn to writers such as Lacan and Habermas, who pay particular attention to the role of language in human consciousness and reflexivity (Parker 1991: 105). Augustinous and Walker (1995: 285) draw attention to Vygotsky's work (Vygotsky 1978, 1986;

Wertsch 1991) which informs us of the essentially social and cultural nature of cognition. However, in this book we shall pursue the narrative psychological approach which shares similar concerns with these perspectives but has as yet received very little exposure in psychology. In the next chapter, our aim will be to outline in more detail some of the central themes associated with a narrative psychology approach and to argue that narrative structure is intrinsic to the structuring of human experience in contemporary Western societies.

Chapter summary

By the end of this chapter you should understand the following issues and concepts:

- How various social constructivist approaches approach the study of self. These include:
  Postmodernist approaches
  Discourse analysis – both Parker's and Potter and Wetherell's
  Shotter's 'rhetorical-responsive' approach
  Smith's IPA approach
  Critical feminist psychological approaches.
- Problems with social constructivist approaches – their tendency to 'lose the subject'.
- Problems with phenomenological and feminist psychology's 'retrieval' of the subject – tendency to romanticization and 'essentialism'.
- Narrative psychology's attempt to retain a sense of subject and discourse.

Discussion points

- How does a narrative psychological approach differ from:
  (1) traditional social psychological approaches;
  (2) other social constructivist approaches.
- What are some of the problems associated with some forms of discourse analysis?
- Discuss some of the problems associated with postmodern approaches to self (see Smith 1994).
- Why is it important not to simply naïvely accept the versions of reality put forward by respondents? Discuss in the light of some of the potential pitfalls of a phenomenologically inspired approach (see Crossley 1998b; Joffe 1997).

Key further reading

Abraham, C. and Hampson, S. (1996) A social cognition approach to health psychology: philosophical and methodological issues, *Psychology and Health*, 11: 233–41.

Augustinous, M. and Walker, I. (1995) *Social Cognition: An Integrated Introduction* (Chapter 10). London: Sage.

Crossley, M.L. (1998) Sick role or empowerment: the ambiguities of life with an HIV-positive diagnosis, *Sociology of Health and Illness*, 20(4): 507–31.

Joffe, H. (1997) Intimacy and love in late modern conditions: implications for unsafe sexual practices, in J. Ussher (ed.) *Body Talk: The Material and Discursive Regulation of Sexuality, Madness and Reproduction*, pp. 159–76. London: Routledge.

Smith, J. (1996) Beyond the divide between cognition and discourse: using interpretative phenomenological analysis in health psychology, *Psychology and Health*, 11: 261–71.

*Smith, M. (1994) Selfhood at risk: postmodern perils and the perils of postmodernism, *American Psychologist*, 49(5): 405–11.

Note on further reading

These readings all provide further background in relation to the development of narrative and discursive psychological approaches. Abraham and Hampson (1996), Augustinous and Walker (1995), and Smith (1996) all provide important expositions of the differences between social cognition, discursive and phenomenological approaches. The Crossley and Joffe readings, with particular reference to HIV, explore the importance of locating 'insider'/lay accounts within the contemporary social and economic structure. The *Smith (1994) article provides an interesting, engaging critique of postmodern approaches towards the self.

End note

1 This is not to say that Smith *et al.* (1997) fall into the trap of uncritically 'siding' with the 'insider'. The whole point of their work on the detailed examination of gay men's accounts of sex is to inform health promotion work and thus to find ways of changing unsafe sexual practices (see Flowers *et al.* 1997).

3 Narrative: living and being in time

A self without a story contracts into the thinness of its personal pronoun.

(Crites 1986)

Stories are the womb of personhood. Stories make and break us. Stories sustain us in times of trouble and encourage us towards ends we would not otherwise envision. The more we shrink and harden our ways of telling, the more starved and constipated we become.

(Mair 1989: 2)

Always in emergencies we invent narratives. We describe what is happening as if to confine the catastrophe. When people heard that I was ill, they inundated me with stories of their own illnesses, as well as the cases of friends. Storytelling seems to be a natural reaction to illness. People bleed stories and I've become a bloodbank of them.

(Broyard 1992: 21)

Introduction

A narrative theory of psychology advocates the need to focus attention on human existence as it is lived, experienced and interpreted by each human individual. As we have seen in the last two chapters, our experience of self, others and the world more generally is inextricably tied up with our use and understanding of the linguistic and moral resources made available to us in the cultures we are brought up in. Narrative theories suggest that the primary way in which such meanings are transmitted is through our embeddedness, from the moment of birth, in familial and cultural stories. In this chapter, our aim is to examine some of the predominant theories which explore the relationship between human experience and narrative, and thus to emphasize the centrality of narrative in human experience and existence. Of particular importance in this discussion is our everyday experience and orientation towards time. As will become apparent, our temporal orientations are of central importance to our understanding of self and others and are crucially related to the idea that human experience takes place in the context of narrative configurations.

What is narrative? Narrative as an 'organizing principle' for human life

As Sarbin (1986) points out, narrative is coterminous with *story* as it is used by English speakers:

> A story is a symbolised account of actions of human beings that has a temporal dimension. The story has a beginning, middle, and an ending. . . . The story is held together by recognisable patterns of events called plots. Central to the plot structure are human predicaments and attempted resolutions.
>
> (Sarbin 1986: 3)

Numerous authors such as MacIntyre (1981), Carr (1986) and Sarbin (1986) have put forward the idea that human psychology has an essentially narrative structure. For example, Sarbin proposes what he calls the 'narratory principle'; this is the idea that human beings think, perceive, imagine, interact and make moral choices according to narrative structures. In support of this theory, Sarbin argues that if you present two or three pictures or descriptive phrases to a person, they automatically connect them together to form a 'story', an account that relates the pictures or the meaning of the phrases in some patterned way. On reflection, we discover that the pictures or the meaning of the phrases are held together by an implicit use of *plot*. If the pictures or phrases presented depict people, the story will reflect human sentiments, goals, purposes, valuations and judgements. The plot will influence the flow of action of the narrative figures in the story (Sarbin 1986: 9).

A number of researchers have tried to classify the plots we use in making sense of events, into different dimensions. For example, White (1973) suggested four major plot structures: tragedy, romance, comedy and satire. And Gergen and Gergen (1983), looking at the kind of narratives people produced when they were suffering from serious illnesses, identified three main plot dimensions: stability, progression and regression. For the moment, the important point to understand is that the narrative is a way of organizing episodes, actions and accounts of actions; it is an achievement 'that brings together mundane facts and fantastic creations; time and place are incorporated. The narrative allows for the individual to include their reasons for their acts, as well as the causes of happening' (Sarbin 1986: 9).

Sarbin treats narrative as the 'organizing principle for human action'. By this, he means that the concept of narrative can be used to help account for the observation that human beings always seek to impose structure on the flow of experience. The narrative principle, however, presents a very different portrait of the human individual to those encountered in traditional psychology which routinely promote abstract images or 'dead metaphors' of individuals processing information in a machine or computer-like way. Instead, the narrative principle invokes a more humanistic image of the self as a teller of stories; of heroes and villains, plots and images of actors performing and engaging in dialogue with other actors. According to Sarbin, to seriously entertain the proposal that the narrative principle guides human thought and action, we can reflect on any slice of life. Our hopes, dreams, fears, fantasies, plannings, memories, loving, hating, the rituals of daily life (for example, sitting down to eat a meal with the family), the pageantry of rites of passage (such as marriages, christenings, funerals) – all of these are guided by narrative plots and are organized to tell the stories of the individuals involved.

Hence, storytelling is a pervasive activity and can be traced back to the ancient and still common practice of guiding moral behaviour through the reciting of parables and fables. Shortened fables such as traditional proverbs are still widely used to give counsel, urge wisdom, entertain and enlighten. MacIntyre's (1981) description of the narratory basis of experience sums this up:

> It is through hearing stories about wicked stepmothers, lost children, good but misguided kings, youngest sons who receive no inheritance but must make their own way in the world and eldest sons who waste their inheritance on riotous living and go into exile to live with the swine, that children learn, or mislearn, both what a child and what a parent is, what the cast of characters may be in the drama into which they have been born and what the ways of the world are. Deprive children of stories and you leave them unscripted, anxious stutterers in their actions as in their words. Hence, there is no way to give an understanding of any society, including our own, except through the stock of stories which constitute its initial dramatic resources. Mythology, in its original sense, is at the heart of things.
>
> (MacIntyre 1981: 54)

As Bettelheim (1976) argues along similar lines, the classic fairy tales children are exposed to during childhood are not just silly or superficial. Tales such as *Cinderella*, *Sleeping Beauty* and *Pinocchio* play out the eternal conflicts of good versus evil, life and death, love and hate. This is psychologically heavy material packaged in a medium attractive to young children and infuses them, from their earliest days, with a sense of the moral conflicts and problems important to their particular culture (see Howard 1991). And this does not stop during childhood either. As adolescents and adults we are exposed on a daily basis to TV dramas, soap operas, movie blockbusters and talk shows, all of which play out, in the same way as the fairy tale does for the child, these eternal moral conflicts (see Priest 1996; McLeod 1997).

Human experience and narrative structure

Carr (1986) argues that the reality of contemporary Western human life can be characterized as one which has a narrative or story-telling character (Carr 1986: 18). What would it be, he asks, to experience life as a 'mere' or 'pure' sequence of isolated events, one thing after another? In order to illustrate his thesis Carr draws upon phenomenological approaches such as Husserl's theory of time consciousness, which depicts the way in which humans ordinarily experience time. He basically makes a distinction between three levels of human experience: passive experience, active experience and experience of self/life. At each of these levels, human experience can be characterized by a complex temporal structure akin to the configuration of the storied form (see also Bruner 1990, 1991). In the following exploration of human time consciousness, we will look at each of these experiential levels in turn.

Passive experience

According to Husserl, even as we encounter events at the most passive level (that is, when we are not consciously aware that we are encountering them), they are charged with the significance they derive from our anticipation of the future ('protention') and our memory of things past ('retention'). His point is not that we have the capacity to project and remember but that we cannot even experience anything as happening, as present, except against the background of what it succeeds and what we anticipate will succeed it. Hence, when we experience time, we have no option but to experience it as an interrelated 'configuration' of past–present–future. Our experience automatically assumes temporally extended forms in which future, present and past mutually determine one another as parts of a whole. Husserl gives the example of a note in a melody. When we are listening to a melody we do not encounter notes in that melody as isolated elements or components. Rather, the note is encountered and 'understood' as part of a sequence as a whole. It takes on 'meaning' only in relation to the note that has preceded it and in anticipation of that which will succeed it. Hence the 'presence' of the note can be encountered only in relation to a mutually determined retentional–protentional structure. This kind of temporal experience is analogous to the Gestalt phenomena often discussed in relation to spatial perception.

Active experience

Carr proceeds to argue that if this 'configurational' dimension is true of our most passive experiences, it is true even more of our active lives in which we 'explicitly consult past experience, envisage the future and view the present as a passage between the two'. Carr argues that the 'means–end' structure of action that we experience in everyday life is akin to the beginning–middle–end plot structure of narrative and thus, 'the structure of action . . . is common to art and life' (1986: 61). This idea is also central to literary theorist Paul Ricouer's notion that 'time becomes human to the extent that it is articulated through a narrative mode' (Ricoeur 1984: 85). According to Ricoeur there are two sorts of time in every story told: on the one hand a discrete succession that is open and theoretically indefinite, for example, a series of incidents for which we can always pose the question, 'and then? and then?', much like a chronicle of events. The other sort of time is characterized by integration, culmination and closure owing to which the story receives a particular configuration. In this sense, composing a story involves drawing together a series of events in order that they make sense in relation to one another (Ricoeur 1991: 121). We tend to experience activities, both short and long term, in relation to this latter mode, sometimes referred to by Ricoeur as the process of emplotment.

For example, if I were to account for my present activity with regard to the writing of this book, theoretically, I could just present a chronicle of events that have led up to it. This would read much like a formal CV. So, I got a first-class honours degree from Manchester University in 1990 *and then* I worked for a while as an Assistant Clinical Psychologist *and then* I got my PhD from The Open University in 1993 *and then* I published *Healing Sylvia*, a book based on my PhD, *and then* I got a lectureship at Keele University *and then* I got a research fellowship at Sheffield University *and then* a senior lectureship at Edge-Hill University College . . . and so on. But this kind of description fails to depict the characteristic past–present–future configuration of my current activity. I am writing this book not just because I happen to have got to this 'point' along a whole 'sequence' of events. This 'present' activity can be understood in relation to a complex configuration of past retentions and future protentions and, to make things even more complicated, a criss-crossing array of intellectual, professional, emotional and social ambitions and associations. For example, there are emotional 'retentions', voices from the past echoing in my head which form the background or horizon to my writing this book. Mum and dad telling others that 'Michele always loved to read and write – we always knew she'd be a writer'. These voices push me forward in my 'protentional' anticipation of its successful completion. And then there are intellectual considerations.

How to fit this piece of work into what has gone before and what will succeed in the future. My previous works on childhood sexual abuse and HIV/AIDS can be brought to bear on this current project and, in their combination, they open further possibilities for the future. In writing this book, I anticipate these horizons in preparation for the next book, the next project. Even at the level of writing each chapter, I work in a complex backward–forward motion, retaining knowledge of what has been covered in the previous chapter, projecting what has to be covered in the next, and thus creating a space for what has to be covered in the present. And then there are professional and social considerations. Why do I want to write the book? Maybe I want promotion, to become a professor in the future? As I write, past images from when I first went to university swim around my head. I walked around the department at Manchester, in awe of the name plates on the doors, Dr this, Dr that, Prof. this, Prof. that. I imagine such a name plate on *my* door. Or maybe I just anticipate getting letters from people who have read this book telling me how much they enjoyed it. Such is the imagination! The point is, this present activity only makes sense, and is framed in terms of, a vast array of interrelated memories from times past and anticipations of and for the future. Hence, the temporal configuration characteristic of narrative structure is akin not only to passive but also to active human experience.

Experience of self/life

If we can talk of narrative structure in connection with individual passive and active experiences, then the notion of a 'life story' requires yet a further, more comprehensive grasp which brings separate 'stories' together, takes them all as 'mine' and establishes connections among them (Carr 1986: 75). Although we have argued that there is a past–present–future temporal configuration (a narrative structure) at the level of passive and active experience, it is not difficult to see that at this more complex level (life as a whole) something special is required in the way of a reflexive (looking back) temporal grasp, to hold together the phases of these longer-term phenomena and preserve their coherence. This, of course, is the classic process of autobiography in which there is an attempt to envisage the coherence of a life through selection, organization and presentation of its component parts. Some authors such as Kierkegaard (1987) have argued that it is through this process of autobiographical selection that we become ethical beings; in the telling of our life stories, we become responsible for our lives. Ricoeur makes such responsibility central to his concept of 'narrative identity', arguing that the self comes into being only in the process of telling a life story (Ricoeur 1986: 132). These issues of ethics, self and responsibility will be discussed in more detail in Chapters 6–8 when we explore how identities are constructed and reconstructed in the aftermath of illness and trauma.

For the moment it is important to point out here that we may be in danger of suggesting that in order to help us understand ourselves and our lives we actually need literary creations such as works of fiction, biography and autobiography. Indeed, Ricoeur has been accused of placing too much emphasis on the role of 'story' as the instance where meaning is created, at the expense of 'human life' (Widdershoven 1993). However, if we bring forth the conception of the narrative structure of human experience and action developed by Carr, we can see that the meaning created in the auto-biographical act of reflection, and that found within everyday experience and action, actually exist on a continuum rather than being radically dis-continuous. In Carr's terms, 'lives are told in being lived and lived in being told' (1986: 61). The actions and sufferings of life can be viewed as a process of telling ourselves stories, listening to those stories and acting them out or living through them. Hence:

> It is not the case that we first live and act and then afterward, seated around the fire as it were, tell about what we have done. . . . The retro-spective view of the narrator, with its capacity for seeing the whole in all its irony, is not an irreconcilable opposition to the agent's view but is an extension and refinement of a viewpoint inherent in action itself . . . narration, intertwined as it is with action, [creates meaning] in the course of life itself, not merely after the fact, at the hands of authors, in the pages of books.
>
> (Carr 1986: 61)

When Carr refers to narration here, he is not just referring to the fact that a great deal of our everyday conversations are devoted to telling stories (although this is true). His point about narrative is more to do with its role in constituting the sense of the actions we engage in and the events we live through, its role in organizing temporally and giving shape and coherence to the sequence of experiences we have as we are in the process of having them (p. 62). Hence, the notion of narrative structure or the act of narrative struc-turing does not necessarily take on the form of explicit verbalization. It refers more to the fact that, as the agent or subject of experience, I am con-stantly attempting to 'surmount time in exactly the way the storyteller does'. I constantly 'attempt to dominate the flow of events by gathering them together in the forward–backward grasp of the narrative act . . .' (p. 62).

Carr further argues that our constant attempt to achieve a sense of struc-ture and order in the course of our everyday activities and lives is firmly based on our practical orientation in the world. In order to get on in every-day life we need things to hang together, to make sense, to have some sense of connection. If, for instance, I found myself writing this book and it bore very little resemblance to anything I had ever done before, I would have great difficulty pursuing it because I would be unable to see the point – Why am I doing this? Where will it take me? Where do I go from here? And for the most part it is 'normal' for us to experience such narrative coherence in the sense that, for most of us, most of the time 'things do, after all, make sense, hang together' (Carr 1986: 90).

It is in this sense that Carr insists that everyday reality is permeated with narrative and that the human experience of time is one of configured time. 'The narrative grasp of the story-teller', he claims, 'is not a leap beyond time but a way of being in time. It is no more alien to time than the curving banks are alien to the river or the potter's hands to the clay' (p. 89). According to this perspective, literary stories such as fiction and autobiography do not in any sense 'impose' a structure and order on human action and life. Instead, they tend to reinforce and make more explicit the symbolization that is already at work in a culture at the level of practical human action. The function of narratives such as autobiographies, then, is simply to reveal structures or meanings that previously remained implicit or unrecognized, and thus to transform life and elevate it to another level.

But is human life narratively configured?

In characterizing psychological life through the concept of narrative, however, are we not overplaying the significance of the storied form in human experience? There are two interrelated levels on which to address this argument: the 'personal' and the 'socio-cultural'. At the level of 'personal' experience, some researchers have argued that although human experience may bear some resemblance to the story, the idea that it takes on a narrative structure is mistaken. The core of this argument is that the coherent temporal unity lying at the heart of stories (the connection between beginning, middle and end) is something that is not at all intrinsic to real human events, real selves and real life. As literary theorist Frank Kermode argues, such 'narrative properties cannot be ascribed to the real' (cited in Wood 1991: 160). The historian Louis Mink argues a similar point: 'Stories are not lived but told. . . . Life has no beginnings, middles and ends. . . . Narrative qualities are transferred from art to life' (cited in Wood 1991: 161).

A related point is made by literary theorist Roland Barthes with regard to the selective capacity of the author of the story and his/her ability to create and determine coherence and order in the text. The literary text has a sense of structure and order because the elements and events making up the story have been 'put there' by the author. Disruptive elements have been 'eliminated'. Life, in contrast to the careful manipulation of the story, cannot possibly have such a structure. Thus, it has been argued, whereas the story has an 'implicit contract' towards order, life has no such contract (Bell 1990: 174). In this sense, it is claimed, the story differs radically from 'life' insofar as in the latter, everything is 'scrambled messages', 'chaos rather than order' (see Carr, cited in Wood 1991: 161).

There is some truth to this argument. However, is it the case that life admits of no selection, that everything is 'left in', a vast array of 'scrambled messages'? For example, Carr argues that our most basic capacity for attention and following through various activities or projects is premised on our capacity for selection. Hence, just like the author of the literary text, we partially determine the course of our own lives by selecting and omitting certain elements and events. As Carr argues:

> Extraneous details are not left out but they are pushed into the background, saved for later, ranked in importance. And whose narrative voice is accomplishing all this? None but our own, of course. In planning our days and our lives we are composing the stories or the dramas we will act out and which will determine the focus of our attention and our endeavours, which will provide the principles for distinguishing foreground from background.
>
> (Carr, cited in Wood 1991: 165)

This may be story planning or plotting, but is it story telling? 'Most assuredly it is, quite literally, since we are constantly explaining ourselves to others. And finally each of us must count himself among his own audience since in explaining ourselves to others we are often trying to convince ourselves as well' (Carr, cited in Wood 1991: 165). Hence, through the interrelated processes of story plotting and story telling we partially determine the stories of our lives.

The word 'partial' is important here, however, because we should not take this point – the self as a teller of her own story – too far. The critical arguments of theorists who dispute the analogy between 'life' and 'narrative' are important insofar as they emphasize the fact that, unlike the author of fiction, we do not totally create the materials we are to form. To a certain degree, we are stuck with what we have in the way of characters, capacities and circumstances. For instance, if, when I was a child, my parents had not placed a great deal of emphasis on the importance of books and education, it is very unlikely that I would now be in an academic position where the writing of books is a distinct possibility, indeed, an expectation. I was born into a working-class environment in Sheffield where my father was (and still is) a steelworker and we lived in a council maisonette for the first 14 years of my life. I went to a very poor comprehensive school where out of a total of 900 pupils in my year, only nine stayed on into the sixth form. Four of those were retaking their O-levels. The remaining five studied for A-levels. I was the only girl. I think if I had been born into any other family in our block of maisonettes, an environment where we were considered 'snobs' for visiting the public library, no matter what stories I had told myself, it is very unlikely that I would be writing this book now.

In addition to our inability to control the beginnings of our stories, it is also important to note that we are not, unlike the author of fiction, describing events that are already completed. Instead, we are in the middle of our stories and we cannot be sure how they will end. Hence, although I may have a plan to write this book, I do not have any idea what may await me around the corner. As the proverb goes, 'There's many a slip 'twixt the cup and the lip' (Crites 1986: 166). All manner of things could happen to forestall this plan and render it irrelevant. For example, I may be made redundant, in which case I would probably feel there is little point in continuing to write this particular book. I may get breast cancer and become too ill to complete the project; or even if I didn't become too ill, my goals and values may change in the face of confrontation with the possibility of death. Or my husband may die or decide to leave me. In which case, thrust forth by the waves of trauma, I may have to rethink my aims and projects, change direction, and start a new story. Hence, the fact that we cannot wholly determine either the beginning or the end of our stories suggests that our activities and projects do lack the formal order and coherence of literary stories. Life, unlike the story, does not have an 'implicit contract' towards order.

The second level at which to address the adequacy of the concept of narrative configuration as a characterization of human life is that of the sociocultural. For example, numerous historical and cross-cultural studies have looked at the way in which concepts of time vary across cultures (Wax 1959, cited in Roth 1963; Zerubavel 1979, 1981; Pollner 1987; Bourdieu 1990; Elias 1992). Hence, even if the experience of people in contemporary Western societies can be adequately characterized as incorporating a narrative configuration, it should not simply be assumed that this is universally true for all societies and cultures. For example, Elias (1992) has argued that the introduction of clocks and calendars into developed industrial states served to introduce changes in patterns of self-regulation which eventually led to relatively high levels of self-regulation and the development of moral concepts such as individual responsibility and individual conscience. Rooted deep in the psyche of people living in advanced industrialized nations is a conception of time which encourages us to exercise control over its 'passing', make 'plans' for its presence, and find activities and thoughts to 'fill' it in order that it will not be 'wasted'. Time is tacitly understood as the platform from which we live our lives and the means by which control over its course can be exercised. Hence, we all experience a sense of responsibility with regard to the way in which we 'spend' our time, and subsequent degrees of 'guilt' for having 'wasted' it. In this way, we live in and for the future, believing that our actions in the present will, at the very least, have a bearing on what we will become.

This characteristic projection into the future may, however, just be an idiosyncratic feature of relatively modern, industrialized societies. Certainly, some anthropological studies of 'primitive' and pre-literature cultures have suggested the absence of future projection and the experience of time as 'mere sequence' or 'flux', a mass of undifferentiated images and sounds in which events occur relationally and rhythmically as a series of repetitions or cycles rather than having any sense of 'linear' order (Wax 1959, cited in Roth 1963). Some more recent feminist studies of time have also suggested that women experience time differently from men. The basic idea here is that 'women's time' is conceptualized as cyclical, following the biological rhythms and phases of life, in contrast to men, whose experience is more linear and progressive, approximating more closely to the 'industrial' time characterized by Elias (see Kristeva 1981; Forman and Sowtin 1989).

However, as Glucksmann (1998) argues, we should be very careful in drawing such general distinctions between men's and women's experience. If we accept the argument that our assumptions and orientations towards time have a crucial impact on our psychological and social life, affecting our sense of identity, self-concept and moral responsibility, such studies could be used to suggest that women and people in less developed societies have a retarded sense of individual conscience and moral development.

A final point to consider here is the temporal experience of those of us living in high or postmodernism. Is the notion that we still live with a sense of unity and temporal coherence hopelessly outdated, an old-fashioned modernist dream? Think back to Chapter 2, where we discussed the impact of technological and information changes on our contemporary experiences of time, space, and the ultimate implications this has for selves, relationships and morality. Gergen, for instance, in his concept of the 'saturated self', suggests that it is no longer possible to characterize the modern experience of self as one of unity, wholeness and coherent integrity. Rather, we exist in a state of 'multiphrenia' in which we are constantly bombarded with multiple relationships and truths. The kind of self this produces is one characterized by fragmentation, variability and context-specificity. We are not the same person across different times and spaces; we change in accordance with each social and interactional encounter. Two cultural examples of this postmodern shift are manifest in literature and music.

For instance, Gergen notes that, traditionally, a good novel is one which proceeds according to plot; as we have already noted in this chapter, such a story has a recognizable beginning, middle and end, a central protagonist and some kind of point or action orientation. Postmodern genres of the novel, however, are deliberately attempting to subvert such conventions. Gergen uses Milan Kundera's novel, *The Unbearable Lightness of Being*, as one such example. Very few of the events related in this novel proceed in accordance with 'linear' time. Rather, 'one moves through the novel as if in a dream' (Gergen 1991: 130). Brown (1996) similarly provides an interesting analysis of the TV programme *Twin Peaks*, highlighting ways in which it challenges narrative conventions in typical postmodern style.

Gergen also argues that music television – MTV – has 'carried the postmodern breakdown of narrative rationality to its furthest extreme' (Gergen 1991: 132). Drawing on Kaplan's (1987) book, Gergen argues that MTV is a 'quintessentially postmodern medium' which relies heavily on the 'breakdown of objective reality' (p. 133). When viewing MTV:

> The shape or identity of an object or person may change several times within a given video clip. . . . Rock videos represent a full breakdown in the sense of a rationally coherent world. Few of the videos offer a linear narrative; most will jolt the viewer with a rapid succession of images – often less than two seconds long – that have little obvious relation to each other. . . .
>
> (Gergen 1991: 133)

Hence, Gergen argues, 'to enter the world of MTV is to abandon the concept of a coherent world' (p. 133).

It is important to bear in mind these differing conceptions of time and the implications they have for the idea that our experience of self and identity is narratively configured. We cannot assume that such narrative configuration is universal. Indeed, Gergen's concept of the saturated self casts some doubt on whether such a characterization is even adequate for understanding people's experiences in contemporary society. However, returning to some of the points first introduced in Chapter 2, it is my argument that postmodern approaches such as Gergen's considerably overplay the disorderly, chaotic and variable nature of contemporary human experience. On a routine, daily basis, there is more order and coherence than such accounts suggest. This is nowhere more apparent than when we examine traumatizing experiences, which have the capacity to painfully highlight the 'normal' state of narrative coherence which is routinely taken for granted and thus remains 'unseen'.

Trauma and narrative breakdown

The existentialist philosopher Martin Heidegger (1962) developed his concept of Angst (a kind of intense anxiety or dread) to characterize the feeling and experience of disintegration that can, at times, be radicalized and generalized in a person's life to such an extent that the whole complex of projects in which an individual is involved becomes problematic. The experience of Angst is like that of vertigo, when a person is brought face to face with the presence of an abyss and the absence of a supporting ground; the experience of groundlessness and the absence of anything holding one in place and anchoring one's actions (Cooper 1990). In this kind of existential crisis, often brought about by seriously traumatizing events such as bereavement and other forms of loss such as relationship breakdown, divorce, terminal illness and depression, nothing 'makes sense' any more. In this kind of experience the loss of 'grounding', of things making sense, highlights the way in which we routinely take for granted the sense of implicit connection between events, people, plans, aims, objectives, values and beliefs. When one 'element' in the chain disappears, for example, if a loved one dies or leaves, the whole complex configuration of memories, associations, plans, hopes and fears shatters like shards of glass – and with it our sense of who we are and why we are here. Frank (1995) uses the metaphor of 'narrative wreckage' to characterize such experiences.

It is at such times of distraction and disconnection that the events, experiences and actions of real life really do assume the character of a 'mere sequence', the senseless progression of one thing after another, when our only objective is to 'get through the day'; when we sit there in the deep depression of the glass bell jar, separate yet stifled, mind blurred and fuzzy, just waiting for the hands of the clock to turn; when time drags; when time does not mean anything except for the meaningless passage of the seconds, minutes, hours. As Carr (1986: 88) argues, this incoherence of the 'mere sequence' is '. . . the dark and looming outer limit of experience, the chaos which stands opposed to order . . . this is a threat which is, admittedly, in varying degrees, permanently present at the periphery of our consciousness, the very threat and possibility of madness'.

This threat of chaos, of meaninglessness, is evident in the following quote from Paula, an HIV-positive woman I interviewed, whose husband, a haemophiliac, had recently died from HIV infection. When I asked her about her plans for the future she said:

> 'I don't think of the future as in what is going to happen in a year's time or whatever. My future seems to have stopped when Mark [her husband] died because I am on my own and I just live from day to day. . . . I am only 28 and I feel as if I have been put in a shop and left there . . . It is as if I am stuck in a sort of bubble and nothing seems to, I can't get out of it . . . it's frightening to think that I am going to be like that until I die . . . It's terrible when you have got no one to talk to . . . that's a large part of it now for me, it is the loneliness, especially of a night-time when the kids are in bed . . . I often keep the baby up just to keep me company, it is horrible, I shouldn't because he needs his rest . . . but . . . if I do send him to bed, it is so silent, it is just me. Often I go to bed early because I can't stand being on my own. . . .'

These kinds of traumatizing events and experiences and the sense of disorientation accompanying them are likely to happen to most of us at some point in our lives. Having said that, however, they can be characterized as traumas precisely because they do not conform to our more everyday, normal sense of reality. This, instead, can be characterized as having a more stable, ordered structure, or at least by the fact that we constantly struggle to create or maintain such stability in the face of 'an ever-threatening, impending chaos at all levels, from the smallest project to the overall "coherence of life"'(Carr 1986: 91).

Narrative and psychotherapy

We have just suggested that traumatic events in a person's life can lead to a radical sense of disorientation and the breakdown of a coherent life story. Similarly, the experience of mental illness has been characterized as amounting, at least in part, to suffering from 'an incoherent story', 'an inadequate narrative account of oneself' or a 'life story gone awry' (Polkinghorne 1988: 179; Howard 1991; Showalter 1997: 11). It has also been argued that Freud's case histories incorporate the underlying assumption that mental health corresponds to a coherent narrative account of one's life. Hence, some theorists and therapists characterize the practice of psychotherapy as an 'exercise in story repair' (see Spence 1982; Cox and Theilgaard 1987; Mair 1989; White and Epston 1990; Howard 1991; Schafer 1992;

McAdams 1993; Roberts 1994; Dwivedi 1997). In the following section we will address in further detail some of the issues related to this 'narrative' conception of psychotherapy.

Spence (1982) argues that the narrative tradition in psychotherapy dates back to Freud:

> Freud made us aware of the persuasive power of a coherent narrative – in particular of the ways in which an aptly chosen reconstruction can fill the gap between two apparently unrelated events, and in the process, make sense out of nonsense. There seems no doubt but that a well constructed story possesses a kind of narrative truth that is real and immediate and carries an important significance for the process of therapeutic change.
>
> (Spence, cited in Polkinghorne 1988: 178)

Psychotherapeutic work with individual clients is centred in narrative statements. Invariably, therapy begins with an invitation to the client to tell his or her story in the form of statements such as 'Can you tell me what brings you here?'; 'How can I be of help to you?' (Howard 1991: 194). Or, in the more colloquial tradition of popularized images of psychoanalysis: 'Tell me about your childhood'. From a narrative perspective of psychotherapy, the 'plot' brought by the client tends to 'lack the dynamic necessary to create a sequence, or design, that integrates and explains' (Polkinghorne 1988: 179). The general aim of therapeutic work is therefore to create a 'fuller plot' that will ideally lead to a 'more dynamic and thus more useful plot which serves as a more powerful and connective force' (Polkinghorne 1988: 179).

Although the narrative tradition of psychotherapy can be dated back to some of Freud's case studies, in another sense the psychoanalytic enterprise, as originally envisaged by Freud during the early years of this century and as manifest in much contemporary clinical psychotherapeutic theory and practice, is totally anathema to hermeneutic and narrative approaches towards knowledge (Josselson 1995: 331). This is made clear in a radical critique of the foundations of psychoanalysis in a book entitled *Narrative Truth and Historical Truth*, written by Spence in 1982. Spence criticizes the classic Freudian model of the mind, especially the idea that the secrets of the psyche can be 'found' or 'discovered' in the hidden depths of the 'unconscious'. Spence's book raises the question of whether psychoanalysts are really engaged in the 'archaeological project of unearthing the historical past', or, rather, can better be described as 'pursuing a narrative task – that of shaping bits of memory, fantasy and association into a coherent and plausible story' (Davies 1993, 1995a; Freeman 1993; Josselson 1995: 331). In Spence's view, the work of psychoanalysis and psychotherapy is on meanings, communicated and altered through language.

One illustration of this idea that therapists are in the business of 'constructing' meanings through stories rather than 'discovering' meanings 'in' the mind, can be seen when we consider dreams. The classic Freudian formulation depicts dreams as 'the royal road to the unconscious'. However, in a recent book entitled *The Rhetoric of Dreams*, States (1988) argues that there is nothing psychologically 'deep' in dreams at all, insofar as they 'do not *mean* to mean anything' (States 1988: 29, original emphasis). From this perspective, the therapeutic act of 'retrieving' meaning from the dream, as though it holds some kind of hidden secret, is a misnomer. The dream has no meaning in itself but gains its meaning only by being put into the network of a person's beliefs. We are persuaded to confer meaning on dreams in a creative and constructive act of interpretation (Lovlie 1992: 129). Hence, 'dreams are not products of (unconscious) meanings, but rather *productive* of meanings. Dreams are what we make of them' (emphasis in original).

For example, imagine you are involved in a piece of psychology research in which you are encouraged to write down your dreams in a dream diary as soon as you wake in the morning. As part and parcel of this process, at a later date, you will go back over these dreams and interpret their meaning and significance. Simply by virtue of the fact that your dreams have been written down, they will become more significant than if this had not been the case. For example, we often have to engage in a conscious act of recollection if we want to remember what we dreamt the previous evening (unless the dream was particularly vivid and upsetting, in which case it may haunt us through the morning and its impact recede gradually as the day proceeds). When we engage in this conscious act of recollection we are providing the dream with a forum in which it will take on more meaning and significance than would normally be the case. This is because the dream does not routinely intrude into waking consciousness and is not therefore 'experienced' as it is in the conscious act of reflection; it typically recedes into oblivion as we emerge from a sleeping to a waking state. In this sense, dreams are what we make of them because it is only by working with a theoretical model that considers dreams to be significant and meaningful that they become so.

It is important to note that this conception of the individual as constructing and creating the meaning of his/her own life through the use of language, narratives and stories, is one which, as we saw in Chapter 1, connects him/her inextricably to the interpersonal, social and moral context in which his/her life is lived. Meaning and stories do not just 'emerge' from 'within' the isolated individual; rather, they develop in the context of specific interactive episodes and contexts. This point is particularly important when we consider the way in which meaning is constructed in the therapeutic encounter. Typically, this kind of interactive episode takes place between two people, the client and the therapist. Recent narrative conceptions of the psychotherapeutic process have therefore emphasized the fact that therapy does not just involve the therapist listening to the story of the client. Rather, the therapist also plays a role as a collaborator in the production of the story or narrative; the therapist is like the editor of a living text (Polkinghorne 1988: 178; Parry 1991; Hoffman 1993; Wax 1995; Dwivedi and Gardner 1997). Schafer (1992) therefore describes the process of psychoanalysis as follows:

> People going through psychoanalysis – analysands – tell the analyst about themselves and others in the past and present. In making interpretations, the analyst retells these stories. In the retelling, certain features are related to others in new ways or for the first time; some features are developed further, perhaps at great length. . . . The analyst's retellings progressively influence the what and how of the stories told by analysands. . . . The end product of this interweaving of texts is a radically new, jointly authored way of working.
>
> (Schafer, cited in Polkinghorne 1988: 179)

This process is characterized by Schafer as a project of 'reauthoring' a life through 'coauthoring' it; 'a dialogue' through which the person's (problematic) life story is transformed (Polkinghorne 1988: 179; Gergen 1996a; McNamee 1996).

There are, however, problems with this conception of the psychotherapeutic process as a narrative dialogue. As Josselson (1995) points out in relation to Schafer's work, although he talks about 'coauthoring' the client's story, the therapist remains in a privileged and powerful position in the therapeutic situation and often operates with a 'master narrative' that guides understanding. What this master narrative consists of will depend on the particular theoretical orientation of the therapist. In Schafer's terms, it is a psychoanalytic perspective which serves to present a particular image of the client's problems (the implications of adopting a psychoanalytic perspective will be addressed further in Chapter 7 when we see how a woman uses this framework to interpret the child sexual abuse she suffered as a child). Josselson argues that Schafer's implicit use of the psychoanalytic framework means that the alleged 'coauthoring' of the client's life would more accurately be construed as a 'reauthoring', a process which involves the imposition of a powerful cultural narrative on the individual's life. This is an important point and raises the more tricky question of what constitutes a 'better' life story and how, if at all, life stories can and should be reauthored. This, in turn, leads us in later chapters to address the relationship between narratives, identity and power in contemporary culture (see Chapters 6–8).

The importance of this relationship (between narrative, identity and power) can be highlighted further with reference to White and Epston's (1990) book *Narrative Means to Therapeutic Ends*. These authors also see themselves as 'restorying' lives through the therapeutic process. Clients are encouraged to 'externalize' their problems and in the process of so doing, enter a 'space for reauthorship'. Clients are invited to imagine 'alternative stories for their lives' in which their problem is 'demonized'; the therapist is encouraged to help people 'perform' these revised stories. The core of the therapeutic technique they describe consists of composing written interventions that tell different stories about their clients' lives and their future course (Josselson 1995: 337). For example, White and Epston write letters to their patients narrating alternative versions of their life circumstances. This technique was originally used in family therapy whereby family members were encouraged to write letters to each other that disrupted fixed social roles and static perceptions of each other – frequently a factor contributing to the family's 'problem'. The basic idea here is that people are encouraged to exercise their imaginations, to write themselves into different stories and alternative projects, and thus to free themselves from the deadening conception of the present and future which serves only to tie them to a restrictive past (see also Watzlawick *et al.* 1974; Penn and Frankfurt 1994; Turkle 1996 (for an interesting analysis of how people create 'new' stories of themselves in virtual communities on the Internet); Dwivedi and Gardner 1997: 36; Frosh 1997; and McLeod 1997: 76–80).

It is important, however, to recognize that there are some rather basic problems here and these connect to the issue of the relationship between therapeutic narratives and historical 'facts' or 'reality'. In discussing this problem Spence (1982) makes a distinction between 'historical truth' – what has actually happened in the past – and 'narrative truth' – a story about what has happened. This issue is very similar to the one we discussed earlier in this chapter regarding the relationship between 'life'/'reality' on the one hand, and 'narrative' or 'story' on the other. We suggested that some of the basic differences between 'life' and 'story' relate to the degree of freedom we have in configuring the past and the future. For example, in life, as with 'historical truth', past events have occurred which are to some degree unchangeable. Similarly with regard to the future, although we can to a certain degree exercise free will, imagination and positive thinking in order to determine our futures, at the same time we are constrained by the limitations (social, economic, psychological, political and so on) of our current existence. For example, if I were a woman with three young children, no educational qualifications and economically dependent on my alcoholic husband who beat me up every night, then a future full of independence and freedom would seem unlikely unless I were able to radically change the circumstances in which my life was being lived. If we are committed to a 'realistic' view of life and history, we must recognize that there are certain structural limits, characterized by relations of power, which serve to constrain our visions of the past and the future.

Having said that, however, if certain psychotherapeutic techniques encourage us to imagine alternative possibilities and imaginatively rewrite our stories, to what extent are they committed to historical truth? Does narrative truth, the construction of a pleasing, coherent and persuasive story, take precedence? For instance, it may be that a woman who suffered severe emotional abuse as a child at the hands of her parents finds it more pleasing to imagine that she had a wonderful childhood in which she was totally loved and cared for. Or that the woman who is beaten up by her husband every night manages to convince herself that everything is hunky-dory, her husband totally loves her, the future will be bright and so on. Yet neither of these images conforms with the 'historical truth' of the past or the 'life' of the future. Does this matter? As Eagle asks: 'Why should the analyst not disregard those factual truths that do not fit in with or that disturb the elegance, coherence and persuasiveness of the narrative?' (Eagle, cited in Polkinghorne 1988: 180).

Both Spence and Eagle argue that the therapeutic narrative *does* need to include 'factual' events that did happen in the past and a realistic assessment of the future. A personal story that neglects or denies the events of one's life in order to make it more pleasing or coherent is 'counter to the therapeutic commitment to truth' (Polkinghorne 1988: 181). This commitment to a true historical narrative of oneself is a 'value' commitment. Although it is true that individual 'events' and 'facts' take on meaning only when they are placed in a particular 'organizing scheme' or 'narrative framework', nevertheless, there is a difference between acknowledging that a variety of frameworks can fit the same set of facts rendering them differentially significant, and denying the existence of those facts. For example, for the woman who is battered by her husband, the significance of this event can vary, depending on whether it is incorporated into a narrative of opportunity/growth (for example, it may be seen as the catalyst which led her to become involved with feminist groups which enabled her to find strengths she never knew she had), or a narrative of tragedy. However, if this woman wants to deny ever having been battered in order to retain a life story that supports a positive self-image, she would be seen as 'overstepping the value commitment of therapy to recognize and accept the "factual" happenings' (Polkinghorne 1988: 181). Thus it is argued, in the interests of both psychological growth and in recognition of the imbalanced power relations intrinsic to many human relationships, although committed to the pursuit of narrative reconfiguration, therapy also maintains a commitment to the 'historical truth'.

Conclusion

To conclude this section then, both psychotherapy and narrative have in common the 'construction of meaningful human existence' (Polkinghorne 1988: 182). When clients come into therapy they already have life narratives of which they are both the protagonist and author:

> This life narrative is open-ended: future actions and occurrences will have to be incorporated into the present plot. One's past events cannot be changed. . . . However, the interpretation and significance of those events can change if a different plot is used to configure them. Recent events may be such that a person's plot line cannot be adapted to include them. The life plot must then itself be altered or replaced.
> (Polkinghorne 1988: 182)

The idea is that therapists can assist clients in the reconstruction of life narratives that have become too restrictive. Questions can be asked about the 'quality of existence' and the 'freedom of choice' that a client's narrative allows. Therapists can draw attention to events not accounted for by the client's narrative which can 'challenge and test the story as told'. They can also offer 'alternative narratives' that 'more fully incorporate' a client's life events in a 'more coherent and more powerful narrative' (Polkinghorne 1988: 182). Hence:

> The therapist helps clients articulate and bring to language and aware-ness the narratives they have developed that give meaning to their lives. The clients are then able to examine and reflect on the themes they are using to organise their lives and to interpret their own actions and the actions of others. The reflective awareness of one's personal narrative provides the realisation that past events are not meaningful in themselves, but are given significance by the configuration of one's narrative. This realisation can release people from the control of past interpretations they have attached to events and open up the possi-bility of renewal and freedom for change.
>
> (Polkinghorne 1988: 183)

As we shall see in the next chapter, however, we do not necessarily need a therapist to help us with this autobiographical process of reflective articu-lation because we can do it for ourselves. As we have already argued in Chapter 1, at the heart of this book is an attempt to create liberating and transforming ways of experiencing ourselves. Part and parcel of this ap-proach, as with some critical approaches in sociology (see Habermas 1971; 1987), is the suggestion that we should not rely too much on the kinds of knowledge produced by powerful professional groups within society such as medics and, increasingly, therapists and psychiatrists. From this perspective, our own, lay knowledge, although of course not divorced from dominant narrative structures of power and control, should be acknowledged as having an equal and sometimes superior status to professional knowledge with regard to issues such as the experience of self and identity (see Rappo-port and Simkins 1991; Birren and Birren 1996; Pilgrim and Rogers 1997). The aim of the next chapter is thus to encourage us to pursue this potentially liberatory task.

Chapter summary

By the end of this chapter you should understand the following con-cepts and issues:

- The debate about whether or not human action and experience expresses a narrative form.
- The way in which the breakdown of meaning in experiences of trauma or mental illness allows us to understand our more routine narrative configuration.
- Psychotherapy and narrative approaches.

Discussion points

- Is lived experience structured in accordance with a 'narrative configuration'? Do we live our lives without a beginning, middle and end?
- How does the experience of trauma or mental illness help us to understand the way in which we routinely structure our everyday lives?
- If psychotherapy is committed to the 'repair' of stories, does it matter if a patient produces a story which is 'pleasing' but fails to accurately convey the circumstances of his/her life?
- What does the practice of Internet users logging into 'MUDs' (multi-user domains) and creating 'new' identities for themselves reveal about contemporary concepts of identity? What are the possible positive and negative implications of such practices? (see Turkle 1996).

Key further reading

Carr, D. (1986) *Time, Narrative and History* (Chapters 1, 2 and 3). Bloomington: Indiana University Press.

McLeod, J. (1997) *Narrative and Psychotherapy* (Chapter 2). London: Sage.

Polkinghorne, D.P. (1988) *Narrative Knowing and the Human Sciences* (Chapter 6). Albany, NY: SUNY Press.

*Turkle, S. (1996) Parallel lives: working on identity in virtual space', in D. Grodin and T. Lindlof (eds) *Constructing the Self in a Mediated World*, pp. 156–77. London: Sage.

Wood, D. (1991) *Paul Ricoeur: Narrative and Interpretation* (Chapters 2 and 10). London: Routledge.

Note on further reading

All of the above readings are important in terms of their theoretical development of ideas regarding the relationship between temporality, experience and identity.

The *Turkle reading constitutes an interesting exploration of the way in which people create 'new' and multiple stories of themselves in virtual communities on the Internet. As such, it represents a useful way of addressing the relevance of the above theoretical ideas to experiences of self in contemporary society.

SECTION II

Applying methods

Preface

This section of the book encourages you to explore and apply the principles of narrative psychology to your own self and life. Interviewing and autobiographical techniques are introduced and you are set the practical task of conducting your own autobiographical research. This section draws mainly on the methodology put forward by McAdams (1993) in his book entitled *The Stories We Live By: Personal Myths and the Making of the Self*. This autobiographical methodology leads the reader/student through their life story: the identification of 'life chapters', 'key life events', 'significant people', 'future script', 'stresses and problems in living', 'personal ideology' and the identification of an overall 'life theme'. The aim of the chapter is to provide a practical application and to form the basis for an assessed coursework project as part of the narrative psychology course. Chapter 5 demonstrates how to analyse the results of the narrative psychology investigation and how to write it up in the form of a research report.

If you want to know me then you must know my story, for my story defines who I am. And if *I* want to know *myself*, to gain insight into the meaning of my own life, then I, too, must come to know my own story.

(McAdams 1993: 11, original emphasis)

What is a personal narrative?

The personal narrative is a special kind of story that every one of us constructs to bring together different parts of our selves into a purposeful and convincing whole. Like all narratives, the personal narrative has a beginning, middle and end, and is defined according to the development of plot and character. A personal narrative represents one of the ways in which we narratively structure and configure life (discussed in Chapter 3) insofar as it is an 'act of imagination that is a patterned integration of our remembered past, perceived present and anticipated future' (McAdams 1993: 12).

It is important to emphasize that we do not 'discover' ourselves in narrative, rather, we make or create ourselves through narrative (McAdams 1993: 13). Even before we consciously know what a story is we are gathering material for the 'self-defining story we will someday compose' (p. 13). Maturity demands the 'acceptance and meaningful organisation of past events' (p. 92). Thus, as adults we impose a narrative plan on our lives where no plan existed before. We create a narrative so that 'our lives, and the lives of others will make sense' (p. 92). Through narrative we define who we are, who we were and who we may become in the future. Hence, to make meaning in life is to create 'dynamic narratives that render sensible and coherent the seeming chaos of human existence' (p. 166). McAdams argues that if we fail in this act of narrative configuration we experience the 'malaise and stagnation that come with an insufficient narration of human life' (p. 166). It is useful at this point to recall our discussion in the last chapter of traumatizing events which have the capacity to produce 'narrative wreckage' in the life story and the subsequent attempts of therapy to repair such rifts in order to create a greater sense of coherence, continuity and meaning for the individual. We will also explore in more detail the devastating effects of 'insufficient narration' in Chapter 7 when we look at how some people adapt to living with an HIV-positive diagnosis.

A method for exploring personal narratives

In contemporary life, as we already noted in the last chapter, the two most common means used to identify personal narratives and stories are psychotherapy (more on this in Chapters 6–8) and autobiography. Beyond these two approaches are other methods that can be used to enhance self-understanding and identify your personal narrative. These include 'private' explorations such as keeping a diary, recording your dreams and engaging in dialogue with your many 'selves' or 'inner voices'. Although these methods may be very useful, the autobiographical method of exploration created by McAdams (1993) is particularly interesting from our point of view because it provides a useful way of eliciting material for autobiographical research. In addition, it emphasizes the importance of interpersonal dialogue in the exploration of self and identity. This is important in terms of the concept of self and identity put forward so far in this book which, drawing on theorists such as Charles Taylor and George Herbert Mead, emphasizes that individual self-consciousness presumes 'otherness' and an 'answerability' to others (see also Josselson 1995: 332; Crossley 1996a; McLeod 1997). In the last chapter we also saw how important this concept was to therapeutic approaches which emphasize dialogue and focus on the act of 'coediting' a life story.

Choosing a listener

As in certain forms of therapy then, the telling of your life story to a sympathetic listener can be illuminating. But unlike in therapy, your listener does not have to be a trained professional (McAdams 1993: 254) and should not adopt an advisory or judgemental role. Instead, s/he should serve as an 'empathic and encouraging guide and affirming sounding board' to your life story (p. 254). Who, then, should you choose to be your listener? Your listener can be a friend, spouse, sibling, lover, parent or your adult child. Of course, one of the main points of a hermeneutic inquiry such as this involves the recognition that the story you tell about yourself will be crucially affected by the person who is serving as listener. As Sass (1988) writes, 'If meaning is social, if it exists in the dialogue, then it legitimately depends, to a significant extent, on the person who listens. All this implies that the meaning (in our case of our life stories) is essentially indeterminate, since it depends and varies with the contexts of understanding within which it is received' (cited in Messer *et al.* 1988: 252).

You should also bear in mind the implications of this fact for subsequent interactional encounters. For instance, if you choose a friend to serve as listener, you should be ready for the 'intensification of your relationship that such an exploration will [may] produce' (McAdams 1993: 254). Your exploration needs to be evaluated in the context of a particular friendship. What might happen to the friendship as a result of such an exploration? How might your feelings about each other change? As McAdams suggests, it may be enriching for your friend to explore his/her own personal narrative as well. You may wish to switch roles. You become the listener as your friend takes on the role of story teller.

If you choose a relative things become more complicated, primarily because these people are likely to have been intimately involved in the events you will be describing from your past, and also plans you have for the future. So you may be less able to be open about your desires and feelings than if you were speaking to a friend who has less stake in the events of your life. Nevertheless, the value of such encounters may exceed the potential liabilities. As McAdams points out, the process of exploring your own self not only promotes your own self-understanding, but may also enrich your ongoing relationship with a lover, spouse or family member.

So, in considering who your listener should be, there are two important criteria to consider: (1) the nature of your relationship with the prospective listener; and (2) the listener's suitability for the role (McAdams 1993: 255). In relation to the first, you and the listener must feel that 'such an exploration is appropriate and comfortable for both of you at this point in your relationship' (p. 255). And with regard to the second, the listener should be able to take on an 'enthusiastic, affirming and non-judgemental perspective'. In addition, the listener should be familiar with the concept of personal narratives; by way of preparation you and the listener should discuss some of the central concepts we have already talked about in this book, for instance, the meaning of stories in lives.

If you prefer not to share your story with another person, you may serve as your own listener. However, McAdams does argue that, from his own research in this field, this kind of approach does not lead to the kind of intimate self-disclosure that typically emerges from interpersonal dialogue. Even if you feel that you are the kind of person who finds it extremely difficult to talk about yourself with others, or if you feel that you cannot find an appropriate listener, you are urged to make every effort possible to do the exploration through interpersonal dialogue (McAdams 1993: 256).

Finally, it should also be noted that identifying your personal story or narrative is not something that is achieved simply in the context of a single interview. It should, rather, be seen as a 'life process', an 'endless quest' to use MacIntyre's (1981) words. You should make time to get to know yourself and share yourself with the listener because the whole process is enjoyable in itself (McAdams 1993: 264). This project should help you to identify your narrative and see more clearly how you are living it. Identifying your narrative is a valuable enterprise in and of itself. 'You don't need to change anything to be enriched and enlightened about yourself' (McAdams 1993: 270). But should you wish to change, then identification is the first step.

The interview protocol

McAdams puts forward an interview protocol that we can use for exploring our own personal narratives (see McAdams, Chapter 10). This protocol is summarized in the outline that follows. It is important to note that this is a 'semi-structured' interview, which basically means that the list of questions set out in the protocol serve as a guide rather than something that should be strictly adhered to (see Smith 1995). The whole point of using the semi-structured interview is to try and enter, as far as possible, the 'psychological and social world of the respondent' (Smith 1995: 12). Because of this, the interviewer has to try to achieve a substantial degree of rapport with the respondent and this sometimes means allowing the respondent to have greater influence over the direction of the interview and the order in which certain topics are covered. In addition, the interviewer is freer to probe any interesting questions that may arise which are not listed on the interview protocol.

Question 1: Life chapters

Begin by thinking of your life as if it were a book. Each part of your life composes a chapter in the book. Certainly, the book is unfinished at this point; neverthless it still contains a few interesting and well-defined chapters. Choose as many or as few as you like, but McAdams suggests dividing it up into at least two or three chapters and, at most, about seven or eight. Think of this as a general table of contents for your book. Give each chapter a name and describe the overall contents of each chapter. Discuss briefly what makes for a transition from one chapter to the next. The first part of this interview can go on for a long time but try to keep it relatively brief, say in 30–45 minutes. You don't (and can't) tell the 'whole story'; just a sense of the story's outline – the major chapters in your life.

Question 2: Key events

Ask about eight key events. A key event is a specific happening, a critical incident, a significant episode in your past. It is helpful to think of such an event as constituting a specific moment in your life that stands out for some reason. For example, a particular conversation you had with your mother when you were 12 years old or a particular decision made one afternoon last summer might qualify as key events in your life story. These are particular moments in a particular time and place, complete with particular characters, actions, thoughts and feelings. For each event describe in detail what happened, where you were, who was involved, what you did and what you were thinking and feeling in the event. Try to convey the impact that this key event had in your life story and what this event says about who you are or were as a person. Did this event change you in any way? If so, in what way? Be specific. People are most articulate and insightful when talking about particular, concrete episodes in their lives. You should, therefore, focus considerable time and energy on each recalled event, providing as much detail as possible.

The eight key events to be dealt with in this way are:

1 *Peak experience* – A high point in your life story; the most wonderful moment of your life.
2 *Nadir experience* – A low point in your life story; the worst moment in your life.
3 *Turning point* – An episode where you underwent a significant change in your understanding of yourself. You don't need to have understood it as a turning point at the time when it happened, but only now, in retrospect.
4 *Earliest memory* – One of your earliest memories complete with details of setting, scene, characters, feelings and thoughts. It doesn't have to be especially important. The main point is that it is an early memory.
5 *An important childhood memory* – Any memory from your childhood, positive or negative, that stands out.
6 *An important adolescent memory* – Any memory from your teenage years that stands out today – positive or negative.
7 *An important adult memory* – A memory, positive or negative, that stands out from age 21 onwards.
8 *Other important memory* – One particular event from either your recent or distant past that stands out – positive or negative.

Question 3: Significant people

Every person's life is populated by a few significant people who have a major impact on the narrative, for example, parents, children, siblings, spouses, lovers, friends, teachers, co-workers, mentors and so on. Describe four of the most important people in your life story. Specify the relationship you had or have with each person and the specific way in which s/he has had an impact on your life story. After this, describe whether or not you have any particular heroes or heroines in your life.

Question 4: Future script

You have talked about the past and present; what of the future? What might be your plan or script for what is to happen next in your life? Describe your overall plan, outline or dream for the future. Most of us have plans or dreams which provide our lives with goals, interests, hopes, aspirations and wishes. These plans may change over time, reflecting growth and changing experiences. Describe your present dream, plan, outline. How, if at all, does your plan enable you to (a) be creative in the future; (b) make a contribution to others?

Question 5: Stresses and problems

All life stories include significant conflicts, unresolved issues, problems to be solved and periods of great stress. Consider some of these. Describe two areas in your life in which you are experiencing at least one of the following: significant stress, a major conflict, a difficult problem, a challenge that must be addressed. For each of the two areas describe the nature of the stress, problem or conflict in some detail, outlining the source of the concern, a brief history of its development and your plan, if you have one, for dealing with it in the future.

Question 6: Personal ideology

This question is all about your fundamental beliefs and values:

1 Do you believe in the existence of some kind of god or deity, or force that reigns over or in some way organizes and influences the universe? Explain.
2 Describe in a nutshell your religious beliefs.
3 In what ways, if any, are your beliefs different from those of most people you know?
4 How have your religious beliefs changed over time? Have you experienced any rapid changes in your personal beliefs? Explain.
5 Do you have a particular political orientation? Explain.
6 What is the most important value in human living? Explain.
7 What else can you tell me that would help me to understand your most fundamental beliefs and values about life and the world?

Question 7: Life theme

Looking back over your entire life story as a book with chapters, episodes and characters, can you discern a central theme, message or idea, that runs through the 'text'? What is the major theme of your life?

Taking part in the interview

Semi-structured interviews such as this often take a considerable amount of time to complete (ususally an hour or more). It is likely that the interview may become quite intense and involved so it is sensible to make sure that it can proceed without interruption (as far as is practically possible). You need to find a room where the two of you can sit down in peace and quiet in order to conduct and tape the interview.

Tape-recording and transcription

The interview should be taped because it will provide the raw material on which your analysis and subsequent research report will be based. Tape-recording obviously allows a much fuller record than notes taken during the interview and allows the interviewer to concentrate on how the interview is proceeding rather than laboriously writing down what the interviewee is saying (see Smith 1995: 18 on the advantages and disadvantages of tape-recording). After the interview, you will need to transcribe the tape. This basically means reproducing on paper (or disk) the interview material recorded on the tape. It is a laborious procedure which involves sitting down with the tape, playing and replaying, stopping and starting, until you have an adequate copy of the material. The question of what constitutes an 'adequate' copy and how detailed the transcription should be (for instance, should it include pause-lengths, hesitations, overlaps and intonation?) is a thorny one (Potter and Wetherell 1987: 166). For example, some forms of conversation analysis (Heritage 1984; Hutchby and Wooffitt 1998) place a great deal of emphasis on the importance of timing and intonation in the interactional process. How-ever, as Potter and Wetherell point out (1987: 166), for many sorts of research questions such fine details are not crucial and may actually interfere with the readability of the transcript. For our purposes, bearing in mind the sorts of questions we are interested in, the fine details of discourse are not crucial. Basically, what we require is a full transcription of the content of the interview, including questions and answers. An example is provided below. It generally takes about 4 hours to transcribe 1 hour of an interview, so make sure you leave yourself sufficient time to do this. Leave a wide enough margin on both sides of the paper to make your analytic comments. It is essential that you number each line of the interview transcript because you will have to keep referring back to it during the process of analysis (see Chapter 5).

An example of a transcribed interview

The following example consists of a transcription from an interview where I served as 'listener' for a 21-year-old male student, CD. It is reproduced here with his consent. The names of places and people are changed in order to preserve anonymity. It is important to reproduce the interview in full because this will provide the 'raw data' for our example of how to analyse material from our autobiographical interviews in the next chapter.

1   MC: Let's begin by thinking of your life as if it were a book. Can you divide
2   your life into chapters?

3   CD: Erm, let me think . . . This is really difficult . . . I'm not sure I can do it.

4   MC: Well try thinking about an early memory, that might get you started.

5   CD: Yes. OK. There are loads and loads of things coming into my mind but
6   they're not really ordered in any way. I'm not sure how old I am. I guess I'm
7   pretty young. I can remember the first house we lived in – my mum and me.
8   It was in the middle of the town, there was never any peace and quiet. I used
9   to lay in bed at night and feel my bed shudder as the big buses went past on
10 the road outside. And I'd watch the flashing of their headlights against the
11 wall. I suppose this would be the first chapter in my life. Me with my mum
12 in this big house, well, what seemed like a big house then, because my father
13 died when I was 2, I never knew him. I don't remember him at all. Or
14 there may be something there but I'm not sure that's not just what I've
15 been told about him. And there's two parts in this as well because there is
16 school – but home and school belong in very different components of my
17 memory.

18 MC: How do you mean?

19 CD: Well they're really quite separate parts. And I think I made them like
20 that. I used to hate the idea that there would be any connection between
21 home and school. I liked to keep home separate. I think that's because I had
22 a pretty bad time at school and I didn't want it to enter home as well. At
23 home with my mum, I felt quite happy. She always made me feel safe. I
24 always got this feeling I wasn't like the other lads because they were
25 always playing football in the park and running around being rough,
26 shouting, hitting each other. I used to like sitting at home in front of the TV.
27 I would just sit there all day during the school holidays when mum was out
28 at work. I never got bored. I just used to sit there watching TV. It made me
29 feel safe. When the other kids came and knocked on the door to ask if I was
30 playing out, mum would try and persuade me. But I really hated and
31 resented her when she did that. I just wanted to be left on my own in peace.
32 I suppose I was a real loner really. At that time I didn't have any brothers or
33 sisters. It was just me and mum.

34 MC: How would you describe this chapter. What title would you give it?

35 CD: Innocence.

36 MC: Innocence?

37 CD: Yes, I was very innocent then. Everything just seemed to sort of

38   happen around me. I felt like I didn't have any control over what happened.
39   Maybe that was made worse by the fact that my dad died when I was so
40   young. But I don't think I ever felt bad about that. In some ways, the feeling
41   of lack of control was quite a nice feeling. Mum did everything for me and
42   catered for all my needs. So I certainly didn't have any responsibilities. At
43   school though, it was totally different. Whereas mum made me feel
44   important, like I was the centre of the world, school couldn't have been
45   more different. There I felt very small, not at all important. I was really
46   scared of the teachers and of adults in general. I think that might have been
47   another reason why I never liked playing out with the other kids. 'Cause when
48   you went to their houses their parents were in. The fathers in particular put
49   the fear of God into me. They were always big with booming voices, and
50   again, always roughing up the kids and brawling about on the floor. I just
51   felt totally uncomfortable with that. But I remember this as a time when I
52   didn't make things happen – they just happened. I was vulnerable and
53   powerless outside of home because nothing I ever did seemed to be taken
54   seriously. I felt like that for a long time. My memory of it is all very dark.
55   Like a dark hole where I can't remember much – I suppose this must be up
56   to the age of about 7 or 8. I remember coming home from school one day
57   when I was about 6 and my mother had burned my teddy bear on the fire
58   in the garden. She said I was a big boy now, too old for things like that. I
59   went hysterical. I used to cling on to things. I still do now. I wonder if that's
60   because my dad died when I was so young. I think that's about the end of
61   that chapter, when I'm about 7 or 8.

62   MC: What about the next chapter then?

63   CD: Oh, hang on. It's difficult to say when the first chapter ends. It's more
64   the fact that the second chapter begins when I'm about 10. That's when my
65   mother remarried. And that's when things got really bad. From then, the
66   small bit of security I had at home was lost. It was like the badness
67   infiltrated from school to home. I'd always been scared of that. Everything
68   changed then. Mum married this big bloke called Terry. I had to call
69   Terry 'dad' and I hated that, still do now. I hated it because I didn't see why
70   this stranger, who came and took away my mother, and brought
71   three other kids into the house who were now my 'brothers and sisters' and,
72   even worse, who called *my* mum 'mum', should be my dad. And, of course,
73   he never treated me very well anyway. He was always very rough with me.
74   He used to box my ears and kick me as if I was a dog. I mean, it wasn't just
75   me who he was rough with. He was with his own kids as well, but I suppose
76   they were used to it. But I used to see him and my mother standing there
77   with their arms around each other and it made me feel physically sick. It was
78   like she'd betrayed me. And whenever there was an argument or anything,
79   she never stood up for me any more. She always sided with him. I couldn't
80   even sit and watch TV in peace any more because there were loads of other
81   kids running around and Terry was in charge of what we could watch. So I
82   didn't stay in the house any more. I used to roam the streets on my own.

83 Oh, and incidentally, in fact it wasn't incidentally because it was another
84 massive change in my life at the time, we moved house to another town
85 when my mother remarried. I had to go to another school which turned out
86 to be as bad as the old one. I didn't fit in there either. Stuck out like a sore
87 thumb. And that was all made worse by the fact that I was shooting up
88 really fast. I was much taller than any of the other kids who were my age
89 and that made me feel really gawky and stupid. I was never any good at
90 sports either. I just didn't have any sense of timing or movement.

91 MC: So this school was no better than the last?

92 CD: No. And it just seemed like everything had suddenly changed for me.
93 And I had no control over any of it. Like I was a piece of unwanted baggage
94 being carted around. People thought I was weird because I was so quiet and
95 withdrawn. I wasn't accepted because I was an outsider.

96 MC: So, why do you think you had such difficulty fitting in?

97 CD: I don't know. I think it was just the circumstances. I think to some
98 extent, the other kids did try a little but I wasn't always interested in making
99 friends. I was quite happy to be alone. In fact I wanted to be alone. What
100 with all the other kids who were now at home. I just wanted things to go
101 back to how they had used to be. I once said that to my mum and she told
102 me I had to 'grow up and stop being so selfish'. I always remember her
103 saying that to me. It was like a kick in the teeth. She might as well have
104 said I meant nothing to her any more. Thrown me on the scrap heap.

105 MC: So you didn't fit in at school then?

106 CD: No. After a while they got fed up with me and started to play jokes on
107 me. Teased me. They used to nick my school-bag from me and throw it
108 round the classroom. It got to the point where I'd sit with my bag around
109 my leg to stop them from taking it. I used to get really panicked and scared
110 by that. It was almost as if they were trying to take everything away from
111 me. I suppose they just did it to see how I'd react. I suppose again, I didn't
112 do myself any favours. Because I dealt with it by thinking, and probably
113 showing, that I couldn't be beaten because I was too clever for them.

114 MC: What were your feelings towards the other children?

115 CD: They were just stupid. I couldn't relate to them. Particular people did
116 bully me. Two lads, Kevin Thompson and Hodgie, used to get me behind
117 the prefabs and punch me in the stomach. They'd say 'does that hurt?' and
118 punch harder each time. I'd just stand there and take it, just saying, 'no it
119 doesn't hurt'. I used to go home feeling really ill but not saying anything to
120 anybody. I did actually tell my mum when it had been going on for some
121 time but she just said I'd have to 'toughen up a bit' and learn to stand up
122 for myself. She told Terry what they'd been doing but he just laughed and
123 said it would make a 'man of me'. He stood there and gave me a punch to
124 see if I could take it and then offered that I could do the same to him. I just

125   turned and walked away. It felt like they were all torturing me. I just felt
126   like a useless object.

127   MC: Could you give a title to this chapter?

128   CD: You know, I just felt really angry and frustrated. I was very unhappy.
129   In many ways I wanted to be happy but there was no way out because I
130   was stuck in my shyness. I couldn't get out. I was trapped by it. I got very
131   angry at home and started doing things to get attention. I became really
132   possessive of my mother. I was jealous whenever she did things with Terry,
133   and especially if she paid attention to the other kids, which she seemed to
134   do more than ever because that pleased Terry. At first I used to cry a lot
135   when she went out with Terry but when I realized they were just laughing
136   at me I started to get aggressive instead. I used to go round the house
137   punching walls and kicking doors. My knuckles got all bruised and it really
138   hurt, but I denied myself the experience of pain. I think I was desperate.

139   MC: Why did you punch walls and kick doors?

140   CD: Because I wanted attention. I think the only attention I knew was pity.
141   I wanted desperately for my mother to love me more. I began to feel sorry
142   for myself and became really selfish. I didn't really care any more about my
143   mother's feelings. I mean, she had her own problems so she probably
144   didn't have time for me.

145   MC: What sort of problems?

146   CD: Well she was having to adjust to a new life in a new town with a new
147   husband and three kids added into the bargain. I don't suppose it could
148   have been easy.

149   MC: So you didn't think about that at all at the time?

150   CD: I didn't care. I hated Terry. I hated his kids. I saw them all as
151   intruders. I wanted them to get divorced. Better still, I wanted Terry to die.
152   I never even got to know him and when he used to kick me around I just
153   felt he was a total bastard who was there to make my life a misery. And I
154   couldn't cope with the feeling that my mother had betrayed me.

155   MC: So how would you characterize this chapter?

156   CD: Anger, really angry with the world, with family, school. Wondering
157   why I was ever born and if life was always going to be like this. I felt I had
158   never been given a chance . . . I suppose the next chapter didn't really have
159   much to do with any particular 'external' event, but more to do with what
160   was happening inside me. I began to notice myself more, both physically
161   and mentally. I realized that, despite everyone else, despite how everyone
162   treated me at home, despite how everyone at school laughed and
163   teased me about my height, especially now the girls, who just didn't seem
164   to find me attractive at all; despite all that, I still had me. I was a
165   person, had substance, a personality. I continued to spend more or less all

166   my time on my own.

167   MC: So what age are we talking about here?

168   CD: I suppose all of this took place from about 13 to 16. I would
169   have to include going into the sixth form in this chapter because I think I
170   changed a lot during those years. I think it was my first week when I
171   decided I wasn't going to let people walk all over me any more. I thought,
172   'I'm not going to hide any more, I refuse to. I am a person. I do have
173   feelings.' I've felt a lot of times that I didn't want to be alive but I realized
174   that I have something as a person and I should respect that. I began to
175   dream of better times, perhaps a future. For the first time in my life I
176   became ambitious.

177   MC: So how would you characterize this chapter?

178   CD: Realization. Definitely. Realization that I wasn't going to allow myself
179   to be a doormat all my life. And I think that's what prompted me to work
180   hard and study to get my A-levels – more or less as a route out. I realized
181   if I wanted to get out, to start a new life, I needed to get my education. I
182   suppose that would lead me on to my final chapter so far. Probably
183   university and leaving home. I've become so independent since then,
184   grown up a lot. I do try to keep optimistic but I'm still very much that
185   small child. You can't just leave the past behind and forget it never
186   happened.

187   MC: Let's now move on to peak experiences. What would you describe as
188   the most wonderful experience of your life?

189   CD: Passing my A-levels, knowing I was going to university. I was so
190   happy. I'd achieved something for the first time in my life. I never thought
191   I would do as well as I did. When I had that piece of paper in my hand
192   telling me how well I'd done I felt so wonderful. I always doubted
193   everything, my intelligence, everything, and there it was written in front of
194   me. I was right. I was who I said, I'd done what I said I'd do. I wasn't a
195   lie. I was me and I did this. I could be someone in this world. It was
196   brilliant. I was so happy and I was moving.

197   MC: And what about the worst experience in your life?

198   CD: Oh God, there are lots of those. Let me think. Yes. The one that comes
199   immediately to mind is one Sunday when we'd just moved to the new
200   house. So I must have been about 10 years old. I was so jealous of Terry
201   and his kids. We were all supposed to be going out for a day trip and I
202   didn't want to go. I'd refused and made a big scene about it, so they'd
203   just said, 'OK, if you don't want to go it's your loss not ours'. But the
204   thing is, I didn't want to go, but I didn't want my mother to go either. So
205   what I did is I got up early on the Sunday morning, when nobody else was
206   up, and went and punctured the front tyre of the car by breaking a milk
207   bottle and pressing it into the tyre. Just after I'd done it I felt totally

208   panicked; I think I had a kind of panic attack because I couldn't breathe or
209   anything. I knew I was going to get absolutely killed for it. So I went
210   down to the end of the road and I waited, it must have been for a few
211   hours because it was early on Sunday morning, for a bus to come. I got the
212   bus into town and just spent the whole day wandering around. Obviously
213   no shops were open so I just kept walking up and down working myself
214   into more and more of a frenzy. I didn't have any money for food or
215   anything so I was really starving as well. I was absolutely shitting myself
216   when I eventually plucked up courage to go back home. When I walked in
217   the front door I thought I was going to faint. Of course, I did get into
218   trouble but it was nothing out of the ordinary. Just a few clips round the
219   earhole and a few kicks. But it was one of the worst days of my life. I
220   remember it so clearly. I was so upset because they were all going out and
221   although I didn't want to go I didn't want to be left out. I wanted to run
222   away but I had nowhere to go.

223   MC: Now, what about a turning point in your life, an episode which
      changed your life?

224   CD: I think that must be the first week in the sixth form when this girl who
225   I actually thought I got on with quite well – if I'm honest, I actually fancied
226   her – she said to me in front of her mates, 'How tall are you anyway, twenty
227   foot? You must have had your feet in the greenhouse', and they all started
228   laughing hysterically at me. As I say, I thought she quite liked me and we
229   got on quite well together, but she just said that and wouldn't even look
230   me in the eye when she said it. It was that day I went home and thought,
231   why do I let people taunt and hurt me? Because I'm too sensitive. After so
232   many years I'm still so sensitive, it's unbelievable. I was really upset. I had
233   gone into the sixth form thinking things would be different and my first
234   week there things were the same. So I said to myself 'No, I don't want this
235   any more. I'm not that little lad any more. Why shouldn't I have some
236   respect?' At some point you have to say to yourself 'this is not my fault'.

237   MC: Did this make any changes in your life?

238   CD: I just decided inside and I think it did change me a little. Before I
239   always just accepted it – it was me, I was the problem and then it came to me
240   that other people were the problem. No one could do that to me any more.

241   MC: What about your earliest memory?

242   CD: I don't know, I can't pinpoint my earliest memory. It's all muddled. I
243   remember reaching for a packet of chocolate cookies in the top food
244   cupboard one day when my mother was out at work. I must have been
245   fairly young. I had to climb on to the work surface and then to cling on to
246   one side of the cupboard and try and tease the cookies out from behind the
247   sugar. As I did that, I knocked down a glass jar with some dried beans in it.
248   They went all over the floor and I had to try and tidy them up before she
249   came home.

250   MC: Did that have any impact on you?

251   CD: No. I don't think so. Just one of those little memories.

252   MC: What about an important childhood memory?

253   CD: I think it might be one day at infant school when I was having school
254   dinners. I hated school dinners. Mainly the atmosphere I think, and having
255   to sit there eating on a big table with loads of other kids watching you. I
256   wasn't used to that. And I just hated the mashed potato they gave us. I
257   literally couldn't swallow it. It made me gag. And I told my mum one day
258   that I couldn't eat this stuff, it made me ill. So, she must have been joking,
259   she said to me 'Well, stuff it in your hankie and then throw it away later'.
260   Anyway, not realizing she was joking, I actually did this at the dinner table.
261   And the headmistress, Miss Cuts they called her, caught me. I had to
262   stand in front of assembly next morning as she told everyone what I'd
263   done. I felt really ashamed. I thought I was going to be sick. I was
264   absolutely petrified and I was too scared to tell my mother about it.

265   MC: What kind of impact did this have on you?

266   CD: I hate big crowds even to this day. I hate standing up in front of a
267   group of people and talking. I detest mashed potato. Just the feel of it
268   going down my throat. Whenever it's put before me on a plate I feel like
269   that 5-year-old child again about to be hauled before assembly.

270   MC: What about an important adolescent memory?

271   CD: There was this other girl, Jane, who I got on quite well with in the
272   sixth form. I fancied her as well. We sometimes chatted together on the
273   way back from our Economics class, which was based at a different campus
274   to our other classes. There were about seven of us altogether – all the
275   others were lads. Me and Jane often ended up walking on in front because
276   the lads had a football and used to kick it around and generally arse around
277   on the way back. They would shout and jeer to us, reckoning that I
278   fancied her and all that. I mean, they all fancied her actually so they were
279   probably just jealous of the attention she was paying me. But it used to
280   make me feel a bit of a dick-head because they all knew she had a
281   boyfriend anyway and wasn't really all that interested in me, or any of us.
282   She called us immature. Anyway, one day, they were all being a bit rude
283   with her. This one lad, Simon, started saying things to her like 'Have
284   you had sex yet?' 'Who do you want to have it with?' 'Have you been
285   fingered?' – all kinds of stuff like that. We were all sitting in the sixth-form
286   common room and she looked really embarrassed and didn't know what to
287   say. All the lads were just laughing and egging Simon on, and I didn't want
288   to look like the odd one out, so, although I felt really uncomfortable, I just
289   went along with it and laughed and jeered. She ended up running out in
290   tears. Everybody jollied each other up then, saying 'what's up with her,
291   can't she take a joke?' But I think we all felt a bit bad about it. But then

292   Jane came to me the next day and said 'I thought you were my friend. I
293   didn't think you were like the others. I thought you would have stuck up
294   for me'. She said I'd betrayed her and didn't want to talk with me
295   any more. All I had wanted was to be accepted as part of the group. Not to
296   be the odd one out. I didn't even find it funny what Simon had said to her.
297   I felt obliged to laugh and just go along with it all.

298   MC: Do you often find yourself in positions where you are doing things
299   you don't want to do?

300   CD: Yes. Because I feel I have no choice or control.

301   MC: Would you say that is something in you or do other people take
302   advantage of you?

303   CD: In the past people have walked all over me and it's left me feeling I
304   don't have a choice, but I do. So yes, sometimes it's my fault.

305   MC: Any other important memory which stands out?

306   CD: No, not really. I can't really think of anything.

307   MC: What I would like you to do now is to discuss four of the most
308   significant people in your life.

309   CD: It might seem odd to say this but Terry, my stepfather, has played a
310   very significant role in my life. I wouldn't say it was a positive role but,
311   nevertheless, it has been very significant for me. He was always very harsh
312   with me, as I say, both physically, but I think, more important, mentally. He
313   never seemed to understand me, or even try and get to understand me. I
314   was only ever there for him as a burden, something that just came along
315   with my mother. And so he never made any effort. I guess he didn't think
316   there was any point because there was nothing in it for him. But that has
317   been important for me because it hardened me up. I think I always believed
318   when I was young that it was partly me that caused other people to tease
319   and make fun of me at school and treat me badly. But Terry made me
320   realize that it wasn't just me. Because whatever I did, however hard I tried
321   with him, it just made no difference. He still treated me like a piece of shit.
322   And I think that gave me a hard shove in life. It taught me a hard lesson.
323   People aren't nice and decent. They're only like that with you if there's
324   something in it for them. Terry made me realize that if I was going to get
325   anywhere in this life, I had to stick up for myself. Not let people walk all
326   over me. And then, of course, there's my mother. Despite everything that's
327   happened, I still love her very much. I mean, for a long time, I felt very
328   betrayed by her. But more recently I feel I have come to understand her a
329   bit more. She didn't have an easy life after my father died. I suppose she
330   felt lonely and needed a bit of company. I think she made a terrible mistake
331   marrying Terry, who, for all intents and purposes, is a total bastard. But I
332   suppose he supports her financially, takes her on holidays. I don't know.
333   It's not for me to say. I still wish she wasn't with him. I still can't see that

334 he's made her life anything but more difficult. But my mother, she was the
335 centre of my life as a child. I suppose I was too possessive. I couldn't have
336 her all to myself.

337 I think I can only think of one other person. My sixth-form teacher Mr
338 Howard. He helped me a lot and never judged. I think he has been the only
339 person who I would class as a friend who didn't walk all over me. I don't
340 think I would have got to university without him. He brought me out of
341 my shell a bit and made me have more confidence in myself. He made me
342 realize that I can forget the past and get on with my own life. He made me
343 believe I had a future.

344 I can't think of anyone else.

345 MC: Do you have any heroes or heroines?

346 CD: I admire people with strength who have endured suffering and still
346 kept their spirit like Braveheart [William Wallace] and Rob Roy. I admire
347 courage and talent such as Van Gogh and Dostoevsky.

348 MC: Do you have any plans or dreams for the future?

349 CD: I wish that I can learn about myself and other people. I hope other
350 people will learn something from me.

351 MC: Do you have any plans as to how you could actually achieve this?

352 CD: I don't know. I sometimes want to work with other people, but then
353 sometimes I hate people. I'd like to have lots of money and live in luxury.
354 That would be nice. But possessions only make you happy for a while.

356 MC: What are your short-term ambitions?

357 CD: I want to get a good degree.

358 MC: And what will that mean to you?

359 CD: Everything. I will have achieved something and it will stay with me for
360 life. It should give me more confidence. I believe a life is wasted if you
361 don't make anything of it. I want to make a contribution, change people's
362 views.

363 MC: Can you describe for me your outlook for the future?

364 CD: I would like a good career that I find fulfilling and challenging. I'd like
365 it to pay well. I'd like a home, a wife and a family eventually, some
366 security. I do have dreams, ambitions. I'm quite optimistic. The past has
367 taught me a lot and given me understanding. I empathize with outsiders. I
368 want to help people because living isn't easy.

369 MC: Could you describe two areas of your life in which you are currently
370 experiencing stress, conflict or a problem?

371 CD: Yes. I still have problems with getting on with people, especially

372   women. I try and be friendly and outgoing with people, rather than just
373   retreating into my own shell, but I find if I do become friendly with
374   someone, I start to get really jealous and possessive. All of my mates have
375   got girlfriends but I just put them off. I think I'm too selfish. And on the
376   other hand, although I do long for a girlfriend, there's some part of me that
377   just feels it's easier to be on my own. They're too much hassle. I
378   sometimes feel that I really hate and despise women. They always seem to
379   betray you and go off and talk about you behind your back with their
380   friends. I'm not sure they're worth it. They take the control out of your
381   own hands. That's why I just bury my head in my studies all the time.
382   Studying is the centre of my life. I plan and control when I'm going to
383   study and feel guilty if I don't follow it. It's a kind of control, the only
384   thing probably in my life that I can control.

385   MC: How do you plan to deal with this?

386   CD: I don't really have any plans because I just hope as my confidence
387   grows I will feel more in control. My real problem is my jealousy and
388   possessiveness because it damages the friendships and relationships I have.
389   It's because I'm so insecure. I'm scared of losing people. It's a problem
390   because it drives people away. It's scary sometimes. I realize my jealousy is
391   irrational but I don't know what to do about it. There's no direct thing I
392   can do, only wait until the time I do feel happy about myself.

393   MC: Let's now discuss some of your fundamental values and beliefs. Do
394   you believe in the existence of God?

395   CD: I believe in a God but I wouldn't really use that word because I don't
396   believe in God like the religions define. I believe in something, maybe it's
397   just a force or spirit. I like to believe there is something there that helps
398   you and that you can ask for forgiveness or say 'please help me'.
399   Something that when you pray it gives you strength. I like to believe there
400   is a God but it's my God, no one else's. I believe in God, not in religion if
401   that makes sense. God is a personal thing within you, you don't have to
402   prove this in any way.

403   MC: Do you believe in any kind of force that controls your life?

404   CD: No. I pray but it affects me in no way. I'm free to make my own
405   decisions.

406   MC: Does this differ from other people's beliefs around you?

407   CD: Mine is a more spiritual belief. For a lot of people church and God are
408   inseparable. You have to belong to a religion to believe in God. I've not
409   been christened and have no intention of doing so. I wanted to once, but
410   that was just so I would belong.

411   MC: Do you have any political orientations?

412   CD: To be honest I'm not really all that interested at the moment. I

413 wouldn't say I belong to any particular group. I just feel that this society
414 needs a lot of changes made to it and politics should incorporate more
415 socialist ideas.

416 MC: How would you sum up your politics?

417 CD: Fairness.

418 MC: What do you think is the most important value in human living?

419 CD: To make a difference to other people, to die and know you've done
420 something and not die and think your life was a waste. To make a valuable
421 contribution.

422 MC: Is that how you see your own life turning out?

423 CD: I'd like it to. If I died knowing I'd never made a difference I'd wish
424 I'd never been born.

425 MC: Do you think you do that now?

426 CD: I hope to help people and make a contribution. People I come into
427 contact with sometimes say I make a difference. If they listen to me they
428 think about it. I believe if you think something is wrong you should say so
429 and not be afraid. I've always been an outsider and feel that society does
430 not provide enough support for children growing up. Then when they have
431 problems people blame them for it instead of dealing with it. We have to
432 start looking at ourselves for problems we create in others, instead of
433 condemning them. And I don't think an unequal society benefits anyone, it
434 causes a lot of problems and is limiting and dysfunctional.

435 MC: How do you account for that belief?

436 CD: It's just the conclusion I've come to from my own and others'
437 experiences. As I've said, I know what it's like to be stuck in a life you feel
438 you have no choice in. I still feel the same way now.

439 MC: Looking back over your entire life story so far, can you see a central
440 theme running through your life?

441 CD: Yes. I think basically there is a strong theme of loneliness and
442 abandonment, jealousy and possessiveness. But I've only felt like that
443 because I wanted to belong. I think I have been mistreated in the past. But
444 I'm not the only one. And I do have the power now, to change things. I'm
445 not a victim of my past. I think that's about it really. That's how I'd sum it
446 up.

447 MC: OK, thanks. I think we can finish there.

Chapter summary

Before moving on to the next chapter, in order to be in a position where you can identify and analyse your own 'personal narrative', you should have done the following things:

- Chosen a person who will serve as your 'listener'.
- Taken part in an interview where your listener broadly follows the questions outlined in the McAdams interview protocol and you take on the role of storyteller.
- Tape-recorded and transcribed the interview.

You should, therefore, have a copy of the interview transcript like the one reproduced in this chapter.

Finally, there is a fourth step which is optional:

- Reverse roles with your listener and conduct an interview in which *you* become the listener and your partner takes on the role of storyteller.

Although this fourth step is not necessary for the identification and analysis of your own personal narrative, you may find that it enables you to come to a better, more empathic understanding and appreciation of the interactional dynamics involved in the interview encounter. This will add depth to your analysis and, ultimately, to the final version of your research report. In addition, you and your listener may just find that the exercise is interesting and insightful in its own right, and that your relationship and understanding of each other is enhanced simply by taking part in this process. This, after all, is what psychology should be all about!

Discussion points

- What is a personal narrative? Think of some of the different ways a personal narrative could be explored.
- Divide yourselves into groups of three or four and discuss some of the problems/issues that arose for you in choosing a listener, conducting your interview(s) and transcribing the data.

Key further reading

*Langellier, K. and Peterson, E. (1996) Family storytelling as a strategy of social control, in D. Mumby (ed.) *Narrative and Social Control*, Vol. 21 pp. 49–75. London: Sage Annual Review of Communication Research.

McAdams, D. (1993) *The Stories we live by: Personal Myths and the Making of the Self*, (Chapter 10). New York: Morrow.

Smith, J. (1995) Semi-structured interviewing and qualitative analysis, in J. Smith, R. Hare and L. Van Lagenhove (eds) *Rethinking Methods in Psychology*, pp. 9–27. London: Sage.

Wiener, W. and Rosenwald, G. (1993) A moment's monument: the psychology of keeping a diary, in R. Josselson and A. Lieblich (eds) *The Narrative Study of Lives*, pp. 30–58. London: Sage.

Notes on further reading

The McAdams and Smith chapters are helpful additional resources in terms of advice about conducting interviews and transcribing interview materials. On thinking about alternative ways of exploring yourself and your life history (for example, keeping a diary), Wiener and Rosenwald's paper is interesting.

*Langellier and Peterson's article is interesting in terms of encouraging you to think about the 'stories' told in your own family, and the way in which stories serve as a form of personal and social control.

5 | Analysis and writing up the project

Clarifying some of the assumptions of narrative psychological analysis

In this chapter we will be concerned mainly to sketch out in more detail how to go about conducting an analysis of your own 'personal narrative'. Before doing so, however, it is necessary to clarify some of the assumptions involved in the pursuit of such an endeavour. What are we actually interested in learning about from the autobiographical interview encounter, and what does this reveal about our conception of the relationship between 'self', 'life' and 'narrative'? How do these assumptions relate to other 'newer' approaches in psychology and how, if at all, are they different from more 'traditional' theoretical orientations?

As we saw in Chapter 2, the range of theoretical orientations available for studying selves and identities incorporates different 'realist' and 'constructivist' assumptions. These theoretical orientations affect how the process of interviewing is conceived and what exactly it can be used for (see Smith 1995). For instance, more traditional 'realist' approaches assume that the interview can be seen as a tool which elicits information about the respondent's beliefs, perceptions or accounts of a particular topic, in this case, stories and narratives of the self. By contrast, social constructivist approaches, such as discourse or rhetorical analysis, view the interview as a place where specific social and interactive functions are being performed. So, rather than taking an interviewee's reponse to a certain question as representative of how they think or feel, the discourse analyst is interested in the social functions achieved by particular responses, for example, the presentation of a 'morally worthy' self, the allocation of blame and so on. The discourse analyst is not at all interested in how this response may 'reflect' on the psychological or social reality of events 'outside' the interview context.

Between these two positions, however, as we argued in Chapter 2 and as Smith (1995: 10) argues, there is a 'middle position'. It is possible to consider that what repondents say does have some significance and 'reality' for them beyond the boundaries of the specific interview context, and that this is part of their 'ongoing story' which represents a manifestation of their psychological and social worlds. This is not to suggest that people are not also performing particular social and interactional tasks in the interview situation. But this is not all we are interested in. We can also work on the assumption that what people are telling us does bear some relationship to the reality they are experiencing in their psychological and social worlds. This is the position endorsed by this book, made clear when McAdams argues that the verbal accounts people produce in the autobiographical interview situation 'hold the outline of internalized personal' narratives (1993: 20). Again, this is not to suggest that 'everything people say is important' or to deny that some things are told just to make us 'look good' in the eyes of others. But it is to imply that an individual does not suddenly invent a personal narrative in the course of an interview. Rather, the narrative or story: 'is there all along, inside the mind. It is a psychological structure that evolves slowly over time, infusing life with unity and purpose. An interview can elicit aspects of that [narrative], offering me hints concerning the truth already in place in the mind of the teller' (McAdams 1993: 20).

Analysing personal narratives

The assumption in a narrative psychological analysis, then, is that we are interested in learning something about our own and others' personal narratives and, in turn, the light those narratives throw on psychological and social realities. Understanding the content and complexity of meanings produced in the autobiographical interview situation is therefore crucial. As we saw in Chapters 1 and 2, understanding such meaning is no easy task. It involves interpretation and this involves the investigator (you) engaging in an 'interpretive relationship' with the transcript (see Smith 1996: 18). Meaning is not just 'transparently' available in the interview or transcript. Rather, it has to be achieved through a 'sustained engagement with the text and a process of interpretation' (p. 18).

You are now faced with a transcript (like the one reproduced in Chapter 4) which you are required to analyse in detail. How do you do this? Although there is no one correct way to conduct a narrative psychological analysis, in the blueprint that follows, drawing further on McAdams' theoretical and methodological approach towards personal narratives, I will suggest some of the concepts you should be looking for. In order to illustrate what this kind of analysis should look like, I will draw on the interview conducted with CD (reproduced in Chapter 4).

Step 1: Reading and familiarizing

The first step in the analysis consists of repeatedly reading through the whole interview transcript about five or six times in order to familiarize yourself with the material and to get a general gist of emerging and significant themes.

Step 2: Identifying important concepts to look for

The second step is to get a grasp of the principal elements of the 'personal narrative' that you need to identify. According to McAdams, there are three of these: (a) narrative tone; (b) imagery; and (c) themes. Each of these is discussed in more detail below.

(a) Narrative tone

This is perhaps the most pervasive feature of a personal narrative in adulthood and is conveyed both in the *content* of the story and also the *form* or *manner* in which it is told. For example, the tone can be predominantly optimistic or pessimistic. An optimistic story can be optimistic because good things happen or because, even though bad things happen, one remains hopeful that things will improve. Similarly, a pessimistic story can be pessimistic because of a series of bad events or because good things are perceived in a negative light (see McAdams 1993: Chapter 2). Drawing on a range of developmental psychology studies, McAdams argues that the most formative influence on narrative tone derives from the achievement of secure or insecure attachment relationships during the early childhood years. It may be insightful to explore this hypothesis in relation to your own case.

(b) Imagery

Every personal narrative contains and expresses a characteristic set of images. In order to understand our own narratives we must explore the unique way in which we employ imagery to make sense of who we are. Pay careful attention to the kind of language used in describing and characterizing your life chapters and key events. It may provide a clue to personally meaningful images, symbols and metaphors. Like our identities, imagery is both discovered and made. We make our own images but the nature of that making is strongly dependent on the raw materials (such as language and stories) made available in our culture. When you have identified the characteristic set of imagery employed in your own case, try to explore the genesis of that imagery. How has it developed? Is it related to your family background (some psychologists argue that an adult's personal imagery is largely established in the complex family dynamics of the first three or four years of life)? Or can it be located more widely in the dominant discourses (incorporating morals, values and belief systems) of the society in which you live?

(c) Themes

What are the dominant themes in your personal narrative? Underlying the many events reported in your account, can you see any pattern with regard to what has motivated you or been particularly important to you? McAdams, again drawing on numerous psychological theories, argues that power (the desire for agency and independence) and love (the desire for connection and dependence) constitute two of the most important themes of stories because they correspond to two of the central (and often conflicting) motivations in human life (for a critique of McAdams see McLeod 1997, Chapters 2 and 3). In interpreting your autobiographical account you should look carefully at what it tells you about your own motivational themes. To what extent are you driven by power or love? More importantly, in what particular ways do the needs for power and love express themselves in your story? These needs often become especially apparent during times when we experience our identities as 'in crisis', for example during adolescence, when experiencing illness, bereavement and so on. We notice inconsistencies between who we once were and who we are now. This disparity may be so striking that we summon up questions never asked before: 'Who is the real me?'; 'Who am I'? We may begin to take seriously the possibility of alternative lives never before seriously entertained. Such 'episodes' in our lives provide clues to what drives, motivates and is important to us in our lives.

Step 3: Identifying 'narrative tone'

In order to identify narrative tone you need to look at both what you have reported in relation to your own past experiences, and also the way in which you have done so. For example, in relation to CD, the tone of his account is predominantly pessimistic. He reports the early years of his life as being full of fear, lack of control and insecurity. This may be related to the events he underwent as a child, such as his father dying and his mother remarrying a man who treated him very harshly. This negative legacy accompanied him into his adolescent years and to the present day, made apparent in his still very insecure standing and his desperate need to control his feelings of jealousy and possessiveness. Although he is trying to overcome the negative influence of his past by getting an education, moving away from the parental home and his determination not to remain a 'victim of the past', the tone of CD's account is still predominantly subdued. This is apparent, for instance, in the way he recognizes the difficulties of 'forgetting the past' and still perceiving himself internally as that small, vulnerable child.

Step 4: Identifying 'imagery' and 'themes'

It is useful to look for both imagery and themes together. This is because they overlap and the use of certain images and imagery tends to point towards, and be indicative of, particular themes. I have found that the easiest way to identify imagery and themes is to work through the transcript in a systematic fashion, starting first with the 'life chapters' question, and then proceeding separately through each of the interview questions. Imagery and themes should be identified in relation to each question. At this stage of the analysis you are still really only trying to get a general overview of the data, and the aim is to draw up a kind of 'rough map' of the picture emerging from the interview. In the brief overview that follows, I want to provide some indication of what this map should look like.

Starting with the 'life chapters' question, having read through CD's response a number of times, it became apparent that CD's life so far could be divided into three main 'phases' which he himself characterized as 'Innocence', 'Anger and frustration' and 'Realization'. Each of these phases incorporated distinct, though related imagery, which, in turn, pointed to certain themes. Table 5.1 indicates this in more detail.

The next step is to go through the 'key events' question in the same way, identifying images and themes. This is shown in Table 5.2.

The same procedure should then be used in relation to the 'significant people' and 'heroes' question. It should be noted that important people will figure over the course of the whole autobiographical encounter but they will become most apparent in this section of the interview where you describe in greater detail the four most significant people in your life. Why are these people important to you? Do they represent positive or negative images? Table 5.3 depicts the images and themes emerging from CD's characterization of the most important people in his life.

Symbols and themes should next be identifed in relation to the question 'future script'. What does our response to the question regarding our plans and dreams for the future reveal about motivational themes, our basic wants and needs in life? Does your vision of yourself in the future follow on in a meaningful way from how you see yourself in the present and how you now see yourself in the past? Table 5.4 shows how these questions can be summarized in relation to CD's autobiographical account.

And what about the question on current 'stresses and problems'? What does this tell us about our motivational themes, our issues of conflict that need to be resolved in the future? Table 5.5 depicts this relationship in the case of CD.

And finally, what of the question 'personal ideology'? What does CD's response to this question reveal about the importance of various motivational themes in his life? This is shown in Table 5.6.

Table 5.1. 'The life chapters' question

Identification of phase	Imagery	Themes
Phase 1: 'Innocence' (up to age 10)	Separation between 'good' home and 'bad' 'outside world (including school), for example 'good' home = 'mum and me', 'happy', 'sitting at home in front of the TV', 'peace and quiet', 'safety', 'security'; 'Bad' 'outside' world = 'other lads', 'rough', 'rowdy', 'big', 'fathers', 'fear', 'scared'	Safe vs unsafe
Phase 2: 'Anger and Frustration' (age 10–13)	'Infiltration' of 'bad' 'outside' world into 'goodness' of home. Vulnerability, powerlessness and attempt to maintain some sort of security, for example 'small bit of security … was lost', 'stranger took away my mother', 'brought three other kids into the house', 'intruders', 'trying to take everything away from me', 'panicked', 'scared', 'betrayed' by mother, 'jealous', 'possessive', an 'outsider'. CD felt: 'as if I was a dog', like 'unwanted baggage', a 'useless object', 'tortured', 'trapped', 'kicked in the teeth', like 'people walked all over me', like 'a doormat'.	Control vs non-control Possession vs loss/betrayal
Phase 3: 'Realization' (age 13 to present)	Coming more to a realization of who 'he' is. The real 'inner' me vs the 'external' 'non-me', for example 'external' 'non-me' = 'gawky', 'stupid', needs to be 'toughened up', 'made a man of', 'withdrawn', 'outsider', 'stuck out like a sore thumb', 'alone', 'stuck in shyness', 'denial of pain'. 'Real me' = a 'person who does have feelings', 'not hiding any more', 'dreaming of better times, perhaps a future', 'not allowing myself to be a doormat all my life', 'optimistic', 'a route out'.	Recognition vs non-recognition

Table 5.2. The 'key events' question

Key events	Imagery	Themes
(1) Peak experience – passing A-levels	Achievement – 'there it was written in front of me', 'I was right, I was who I said', 'I wasn't a lie. I was me and I did this' 'I could be someone'.	Recognition, agency
(2) Worst experience – 'the terrible Sunday'	Fear, jealousy, panic, isolation, 'loneliness' – 'spent the whole day wandering around', 'working myself into a frenzy', 'I didn't want to be left out', 'I wanted to run away but had nowhere to to go'.	Betrayal and possessiveness, need to belong
(3) Turning point – 'the girl in the sixth form'	Humiliation, victimization – 'they all started laughing hysterically at me', 'she wouldn't look me in the eye', 'why do I let people taunt and hurt me?', 'why shouldn't I have some self-respect?', 'this is not my fault'.	Betrayal, need to belong, also the need to assert agency
(4) Important adolescent memory – 'Jane'	Humiliation – 'I didn't want to look like the odd one out', 'I just went along with it and laughed and jeered', 'she said I'd betrayed her', 'all I wanted was to be accepted as part of the group', 'not to be the odd one out'	Betrayal, need to belong

Step 5: Weaving all of this together into a coherent story

Having constructed a rough, 'working' map of the various images and themes emerging from your interpretation of the interview data, your next step is to weave all of this together into a coherent story. In the example that follows, I will imagine that I am CD, constructing the kind of account that you will be expected to produce in relation to your own autobiographical account.

Table 5.3. The 'significant people' question

Significant people	Imagery	Themes
(1) Terry – stepfather	Negative – 'harsh', 'a burden', 'hardened me up', 'hard lesson', 'hard shove', 'treated me like a piece of shit', made CD realize 'if I was going to get anywhere in life I had to stick up for myself', people only want you if 'there's something in it for them'.	Lack of control, need to assert self, agency
(2) Mother	Ambiguity – 'loves' her but feels 'betrayed'. Makes CD realize he was 'too possessive', he couldn't 'have her all to myself'.	Betrayal, need to feel loved and as if he belongs
(3) Sixth-form teacher	Positive – 'the only person who didn't walk all over me', 'brought me out of my shell', 'made me believe I had a future'.	Control and recognition, need for agency
(4) Heroes – Braveheart (William Wallace), Rob Roy, Van, Gogh, Dostoevsky	Positive – 'people with strength', 'courage' and 'talent', 'who have endured suffering and still kept their spirit'.	Control and recognition, need for agency

Example

McAdams (1995) suggests that narrative tone is the most pervasive feature of a personal narrative in adulthood. This is conveyed in both the content of the story and also the form in which it is told. Interpreting my own account, I find that it can be summarized as predominantly pessimistic in tone. The early years of my life are characterized as being full of fear, lack of control and insecurity. This negative legacy accompanied me into my adolescent years where I was similarly fearful and afraid of other people's reactions and feelings towards me and felt that I had constantly to 'protect' myself from the 'badness' inherent in the world. Even to the present day, this negative tone is still largely apparent in relation to my insecure standing and my desperate need to control my feelings of jealousy and possessiveness. Obviously, I am trying to overcome the negative influence of my past by moving away from home and I feel a strong determination not to remain a 'victim' of my

Table 5.4. The 'future script' question

Future script	Imagery	Themes
Short-term plans – 'to get a good degree'	Achievement – 'something that will stay with me for life', 'more confidence' 'a life is wasted if you don't make anything out of it'.	Recognition, agency
Outlook for the future – 'career and family'	Achievement and security – 'a good career that I find fulfilling and challenging' and 'a wife and family . . . some security'.	Recognition, agency and a need for security and belonging
Plans or dreams – 'making a contribution'	Contributing – 'I wish that I can learn about myself and other people', 'I hope that other people will learn something from me', 'I want to help people because living isn't easy', 'I empathize with outsiders'. And yet ambiguity, for example 'I sometimes want to work with other people but then sometimes I hate people'.	Need to belong and yet fear and hatred of others

past. However, even having said this, my determination is tempered by my knowledge and feeling that it is extremely difficult just to forget the past because I still feel very much like that small child who was vulnerable and received little love.

It is important at this point to note that McAdams argues that the most formative influence on narrative tone derives from the achievement of secure or insecure attachment relationships during the early childhood years. This may be confirmed in my own case because I feel that although at the time I had little awareness of the impact that my father's death had on me, it introduced a strong element of insecurity (both financial and psychological) into my mother's life. Although for a time this meant that my mother and I had a very close relationship, to some extent this may not have been healthy because I think we clung and became too dependent on each other. For me,

Table 5.5. Current 'stresses and problems' question

Current problem	Imagery	Themes
Getting on with women	Inability to connect and need to retain control, for example 'I retreat into my own shell', find it 'easier to be on my own', women are 'too much hassle', they 'betray you'. CD 'hates and despises women'. They 'take the control out of your hands', make him feel 'jealous and possessive' because he is 'insecure' and 'scared of losing people' which 'drives people away'.	Betrayal and possession, need to be loved and belong but also conflicting need to be in control and to assert own agency

Table 5.6. The 'personal ideology' question

Personal ideology	Imagery	Themes
(1) Belief in God	'It is my God, no one else's', 'God is a personal thing within you'. CD once wanted to be christened but 'just so I would belong'.	Recognition, agency
(2) Most important value	'To make a difference to other people', 'to die and know you've done something', 'to help people and make a difference', 'I've always been an outsider and don't think society provides enough support'.	Need to belong

this meant that when she later remarried, I experienced great difficulties in 'letting her go' and I feel that my present-day feelings of jealousy and possessiveness may date back to this time.

The imagery used in my account is interesting in terms of what it reveals about my state of mind and what is important to me in my life. My response to the first 'life chapters' question is perhaps most important in revealing imagery and dominant motivational themes. As is apparent in the transcript, I divide my life into three separate phases: the first phase, 'Innocence', spans my early years up until the age of 10; the second phase, 'Anger and frustration', charts the early years of my mother's remarriage; and the third phase, 'Realization', begins at about the age of 13.

In the first phase I appeared to have a strong sense of distinction between what was 'good' and what was 'bad'. I split these two domains into radically different compartments in my mind, as is apparent when I talk about my memory dividing 'home and school' into distinct parts and 'hating' the idea that there would be 'any connection' between the two (L15–16, L19–21). This chapter is all about maintaining that distinction and separating the two worlds. For example, I experienced my life at home as full of 'peace and quiet' (L8), feeling contented and 'safe' as I sat 'in front of the TV' (L21, L23–4, L26). I felt 'happy' in a world where there was just 'me and my mum' (L33). She 'catered for all my needs' (L42) and 'made me feel important, like I was the centre of the world' (L43–4). By contrast, the 'bad' world was the outside world, 'school' (L44), 'other lads' (L24), 'playing out' (L30, L47). There, 'outside of home' (L53), I felt 'small' (L45), 'vulnerable and powerless' (L52–3), 'scared' (L46, L49) and out of control. I 'hated and resented' (L30–1) my mother when she tried to persuade me to go out into this world. My main need was to keep the two worlds totally separate. This points to the main theme of this chapter: safety and unsafety. My main motivational desire was to render the world reasonably safe, to feel loved and secure, to feel as if I belonged (mainly with my mother).

In the next chapter this attempt to preserve the safety of the 'good' world was rudely shattered by the 'entry' of Terry, my stepfather, into my life. Here begin the feelings of loss and a real fear of lack of control over the events that were happening in my life. Terry epitomized the 'infiltration' (L67) of 'badness' from school to home. He was a 'stranger' (L70) who 'took away' (L70) my mother and 'brought' (L70) three other 'intruders' (L151) 'into the house' (L71) (the sacred place of safety). The fear and anxiety I felt at school was all a continuation of this. There, I also felt a total sense of 'panic', having to sit with my leg around my bag because I felt they were 'trying to take everything away from me' (L110–11). It was at this point that I really began to feel like an 'outsider' (L95), 'sticking out like a sore thumb' (L86–7) 'weird and withdrawn' (L94–5), 'gawky' (L89) and 'stupid' (L89). I felt totally powerless, degraded and vulnerable, as is apparent in the metaphors I used to describe myself, for example, 'as if I was a dog' (L74), 'unwanted baggage' (L93), a 'useless object' (L126) a 'doormat' (L179), someone thrown 'on the scrap heap' (L104). Added to all of this fear was a real sense of betrayal and jealousy. I felt that my mother had 'betrayed' (L78, L154) me and 'kicked me in the teeth' (L103). I felt 'physically sick' (L77) when I saw them with their arms around each other. And that is not an exaggeration. The feeling was totally guttural and I can still feel it in the pit of my stomach as I think about it now. I felt 'desperate for my mother to love me' (L141) but instead, 'they were just laughing at me' (L122, L135–6). In all of this, what comes across most strongly in terms of motivational themes is my strong need again to experience a sense of safety, love and control. My feeling that these were being 'lost' set in motion powerful feelings of jealousy and betrayal which have since remained a constant theme in my life.

The final phase to consider in the life chapters section came about when I was about 13 and here the imagery used builds up a strong distinction between things that happened 'externally' (L159) and those going on 'inside me' (L160). At this point, I began to realize that whatever 'everyone else' (L161) thought, however much 'they' laughed and teased (L162–3), 'I still had me' (L164–5). I began to realize that there was 'something' (L174) to me, I was a 'person' (L165) in my own right. It was at this point that I began to allow myself to imagine I had 'a future', 'to dream of better times' (L175). I think it is clear here that a new motivational theme was beginning to take over. I became sick of this longing to feel part of other people and to feel that they accepted me. All that had ever got me was 'people walking all over me' (L171) and 'using me as a doormat' (L179). Instead, I felt the need for greater agency and independence, a need for people to recognize me for who *I* was, or was becoming. I felt a sense of indignity that people could have treated me as they had. It was time for action and change.

To summarize, the life chapters question reveals my strong need to feel a sense of connection and belonging, for love, with significant other people. Having said that, however, my experiences have taught me to be wary of this need because it has often led to my exploitation and betrayal. Hence, my conflicting and perhaps heightened need to assert myself independently in order to protect myself against such exploitation.

Moving on to other questions in the interview schedule, it becomes apparent that these themes are continuously repeated in my recollection of 'key events', 'significant people', present-day 'stresses and conflicts', 'plans and dreams for the future' and my 'personal ideology'. For example, if we first consider my response to the question 'key events'. I described my 'peak experience' as passing my A-levels. Why? What did that experience reveal to me about myself? It made me feel that *I* had 'achieved something for the first time in my life' (L190). Whereas I had 'always doubted' (L192) everything about myself before, this was proof that 'I was right', 'I was who I said' (L194), 'I wasn't a lie', 'I was me' (L194–5) and 'I could be someone' (L195). It was my 'route out' (L180) and I was 'moving' (L196) to a new, independent life. This was my peak experience because it appealed to my strong need to prove myself, in the light of my victimizing experiences, as an agential, independent individual. By contrast, my recollection of my worst experience speaks strongly of my fear of loss of love, of being left alone, of not belonging. I felt so bad that day, wandering alone without food or money, because I was afraid that they were going to reject me when I got home. Or perhaps it was more because of my imagined fear of the enjoyment they were experiencing without me. If I wasn't there, I didn't want my mother to feel happy. I wanted her to need me, not anyone else.

McAdams (1995) argues that our motivational needs often become especially apparent during times when we experience our identities as 'in crisis', for example during adolescence. It is then that we notice inconsistencies between who we once were and who we are now. This disparity may be so striking that we summon up questions never asked before: 'Who is the real me?'; 'Who am I'? It is such 'episodes' in our lives which provide clues to what drives, motivates, and is important to us in our lives. This is apparent in my recollection of an important 'turning point' in my life which took place during the phase I have previously characterized as 'Realization'. This episode involved a girl in the sixth form who laughed cruelly at me and made me look a fool in front of her friends because of my height. I remember it so clearly because I had thought this girl quite liked and fancied me; at least she had made it seem that way. Her response just exacerbated my feelings of insecurity and brought up all the old feelings of jealousy and betrayal. It made me determined not to let myself be exploited any more. I felt that I had to have some dignity and independence, some 'respect' (L236). If people were constantly going to hurt me in that way, then I should protect myself against it more, become harder and more independent and less sensitive.

But then another important adolescent memory made me realize that things were not quite so black and white as they used to appear. My experience with Jane, when I laughed at her along with the other lads and then she said she didn't want to speak to me any more because I had betrayed her, made me see things from the other side. Maybe all the people who I have always experienced as betraying *me* did so only because they wanted to be 'accepted as part of the group', 'not to be the odd one out' (L295–6). I remember resenting Jane because her response to me made me feel guilty and as if she was dependent on me. I felt like saying that it wasn't at all personal and she shouldn't have taken my actions so seriously. I think this memory is important because it was one of the first times I began to understand the role I had played in my own victimization by allowing myself to become upset by other people's actions, by reading more into them than they meant. In some senses that was quite liberating because it meant that I could be less hard on other people, and maybe it will eventually mean being less hard on myself and allow me to open up to other people a bit more without such a high risk of being hurt.

Having said that, however, my response to the question about current stresses and problems indicates that the conflict between my need for love and my need to assert myself and to retain control, still remains quite central to my life. This is apparent in the fact that I find it 'easier to be on my own' than with women because they are 'too much hassle' (L377). I know that this derives from my feelings of insecurity and my need to protect myself against betrayal and loss. Consequently, I tend to 'retreat into my own shell' (L373) and 'bury my head in my studies' (L381). Reading over the transcript, however, I am surprised at the strength of my feelings and shocked by the realization that I really do sometimes 'hate and despise' (L378) women because of their ability to 'take away' (L380–1) the control I have strived so hard to gain over my life. Once again, I think this indicates how important my need to belong actually is, and that is why I have built up such strong defences against such a need being disappointed (the problem is, of course, that my defences also militate against me ever satisfying this need).

The same ambiguity and conflict between my competing motivational needs is also apparent in my response to the questions about 'future script' and 'personal ideology'. I think it becomes clear here that my predominant need is to connect with other people insofar as I repetitively talk about my desire to achieve something by 'making a valuable contribution' (L361, L420–1), 'making a difference to people' (L419, L426–7), 'helping other people' because 'living isn't easy' (L368) and 'empathizing with outsiders' (L367). But at the same time I am struck by the old fears that make me aware that in giving myself to others I am opening myself to further hurt. This is clear when I say that although I want to work with people, 'sometimes I hate people' (L353).

I think my ambivalence towards love on the one hand, and my need to assert myself, on the other, is manifest in my description of the most significant people in my life. These people seem to epitomize the central conflicts that are going on in my life. For example, Terry, my stepfather, comes across largely as a very negative, but nevertheless significant, figure in my life. I think the advent of my strong feelings of inadequacy and victimization can be attributed largely to him. It was Terry who always made me feel like a 'piece of shit' (L321) and who treated me badly. But simultaneously, my gradual awareness that this had very little to do with me per se, and that some people would treat you like this regardless, played an important role in 'hardening' (L317, L322) me up. Maybe this 'hard lesson' was not a wholly negative one. Maybe I needed this 'hard shove' in order to provide me with sufficient motivation to work hard to get out of that life? Maybe he was the origin of my strong need for agency and independence?

Having said that, however, the intense battle I frequently feel with regard to balancing my need for love and affection with that of independence and control, makes me wonder whether the version of agency I picked up from Terry was the right kind required for healthy psychological and emotional development. I cannot help but feel the strong positive emotional pull back to the feeling of intimacy and connection I experienced with my mother as a young child. This is what my mother represents for me. A positive image, the 'centre of my life', my 'possession'; I had her 'all to myself' (L336). And yet she also represents danger. The danger of getting too close. The danger of 'betrayal' (L328). She was everything to me and then she threw me away. Perhaps she is the origin of my strong need for a sense of love and connection? But perhaps this version of love that I picked up from my mother was not entirely healthy either? Because this is also the origin of my strong feelings of hatred and fear of other people, especially women.

A more positive and less ambivalent image of agency and independence is represented by Mr Howard, my sixth-form teacher. He never 'walked all over me' (L339) and allowed me to 'develop more confidence in myself' (L341). From him, I was able to begin to believe that 'I had a future' (L343). My image of Mr Howard is a very positive one because I think this is the kind of sense of agency a young person needs in order to enable them to grow and mature into a healthy adult individual. The independence he taught me, in contrast to Terry, was not rooted in a sense of fear, hatred and victimization, but one of care and affection. It is the kind of agency that can be developed while still recognizing our need for affection and love from others. This is the kind of vision I have for myself in the future. It is a vision idealized in the heroes I mentioned such as Braveheart (William Wallace) (L346), who was able to be independent and courageous, and yet wasn't afraid to love at the same time.

Step 6: Writing up – the research report

At this stage you should be in a position to move from your identification, analysis and construction of a coherent account of your personal narrative, to the process of writing this up. It may be that this write-up will take the form of a research report to be submitted as part of the coursework assessment for your degree. To some extent, in this kind of qualitative analysis, the division between analysis and writing up is arbitrary because analysis continues during the process of writing (Smith 1995: 23). How do you transform your narrative analysis into a research report? There are a number of different sections to be included in a research report and in most cases this will be about 2500 words long. These sections should be constructed in the following order: (i) Introduction; (ii) Method; (iii) Results (not included in the word count); (iv) Analysis/discussion; (v) Reflection; (vi) Bibliography (not included in the word count). Each of these will now be outlined in more detail.

(i) Introduction (about 300 words)

In this section you should make clear the rationale for your narrative psychological project by outlining some of the theoretical and methodological issues and questions underlying this approach. A coherent overview of some of these issues and additional reading is provided in Chapters 1–3 of this book. You should address issues regarding the constructive inter-relationship between self, identity, stories, language and morality and the methodological implications of such concerns. You should make reference to previous research that has been conducted in this area.

(ii) Method (about 100–150 words)

Here you should provide a brief account of how you conducted your study. Outline issues such as how you selected your listener, how, where and when the interview was conducted, problems which arose, and how the interview was recorded and transcribed.

(iii) Results (not included in the word count)

The results or 'raw data' for this project consist of the tape-recording of the interview and its transcription. The transcription should be included at the end of the report in a section clearly marked 'Appendix', along with the audiotape of the interview.

(iv) Analysis/Discussion (about 1300–1350 words)

This is probably the most important part of the report, where you demonstrate your ability to analyse and put together into a coherent whole the material derived from the interview process. An example of how this should be done has already been provided under 'Step 5: Weaving all of this together into a coherent story'. You should refer back to this section now in order to familiarize yourself with what is required at this stage. As you will see, this section takes the form of an argument interspersed with extracts or references to the transcript to support your case. This process of analysis often develops in the process of writing. Keep thinking as you write because your interpretation is likely to become richer as you do so (Smith 1995: 24).

(v) Reflection (about 750 words)

In this section of the report you should reflect back on what you have been trying to achieve in the course of this project. In the light of having collected and analysed your material, you should be in a position to reflect critically on some of the issues that arose and connect these to some of the methodological and theoretical questions related to the pursuit of a narrative psychology inquiry. Some suggestions of the kinds of questions appropriate to address in this section are listed below.

(a) The link between personal and cultural narratives

Having identified and analysed your personal narrative in the 'analysis' section (see step 5) you should now reflect back on the way in which this narrative fits into your familial and social environment. For example, in this section, CD may address himself further to the genesis of the characteristic set of images and themes that manifested themselves in his interpretation of his autobiographical account. He has already suggested that these may derive from the lack of stability in his own and his mother's life after his father's death when he was only 2. But there are also wider considerations to address here, concerning the way in which the kind of analysis produced by CD, and also the autobiographical technique we have used, endorse certain assumptions about the nature of self and identity.

For example, it seems 'natural' and 'logical' when using this kind of technique to look back into history and memory, back to our childhood years, in order to gain understanding of our current sense of self. However, as we saw in Chapter 1, this prioritization of the past and the primacy of memory in making sense of ourselves and our identities, is indicative of a more general cultural shift in contemporary society. Charles Taylor (see Chapter 1) characterized this as an 'inward' turn in which we are implicitly motivated to turn towards forms of self-exploration such as that endorsed by McAdams' autobiographical technique. This search for self has become one of the fundamental themes of modern culture, as is manifest in the widespread and increasing popularity of various forms of therapy and counselling. It is not without its problems, in terms of moral, ethical and political considerations, as will be discussed further in Section III of this book (see also Landrine 1992; Omer 1993; Cushman 1995; Simonds 1996; McLeod 1997, especially Chapter 3). You need to read this section and think about the way in which the return to the 'inner' or 'core' sense of self and identity endorsed by these kinds of contemporary techniques is potentially problematic. Some of these problems should be addressed in this section. They also relate to another issue, that of the 'plausibility' of the narrative, which will be discussed in more detail below.

(b) Establishing the validity of narrative psychological research

The narrative psychological researcher, as in other qualitative and discursively oriented approaches, believes that the material used in any kind of analysis is deeply influenced by the researcher. This is in contrast to more scientific approaches, which aim to achieve a state of objectivity and neutrality in which the analytic material exists and can be interpreted in isolation from the researcher (see also Chapter 1). Rather than collecting 'neutral' data, the narrative psychological researcher frames the question, picks the participants and interacts with them to produce data that are then used for analysis. Further processes of selection and interpretation shape the conclusions and presentation of the analysis. It is therefore hypocritical to attempt to 'withdraw from the picture and treat the material or the findings of the research as an objective record of "reality" ' (Yardley 1997: 35–6). Having engaged in this process of data selection and interpretation in relation to your own autobiographical account, you will now be in a position to address some of these issues in a more detailed fashion.

One of the important issues here is the question of 'representativeness' and 'generality'. Quantitative approaches often assume that the sample on which their data and analysis are based should be sufficiently typical of a particular population, in order that any conclusions drawn from the sample can be generalized to the population as a whole. However, narrative psychological research, again along with other qualitative approaches, does not work with the same concept of representativeness. The aim of these kinds of approaches, by contrast, is to produce detailed, 'information-rich' data, which are impossible to separate from context if their full meaning is to be appreciated and understood. Accordingly, these approaches often use case-study-type methods (as we have used in this project), whose aim is to create a 'detailed and profound insight into a particular, perhaps unique, account or experience rather than a set of broad generalisations about commonalities between different people' (Yardley 1997: 36). The rationale of this approach is to 'fully exploit one of the principal merits of qualitative methods, the analysis of meaning in depth and in context' (p. 36). As we have already discussed in Chapter 1, narrative psychological approaches can be characterized as a hermeneutic inquiry in which parts of the individual's self and identity can be understood only in relation to the whole (across the life span, in the context of a particular family biography, history, society and moral perspective and so on). The aim is therefore to produce in-depth analyses and insight into individual case-histories which appreciate the complexities and ambiguities of these interrelationships.

These considerations regarding selection, interpretation and representativeness also have implications for the way in which qualitative researchers go about justifying, or, in other words, validating, their analyses. If we relinquish any conception of 'objective' truth, of a truth existing in isolation from our own selective and interpretive practices, then on what basis do we claim that our analysis is correct? How do we make claims for the authority of our account? In narrative research, the concept of validity generally means being 'well grounded and supportable' (Polkinghorne 1988: 175). Hence, in order to support his/her analytic findings, the researcher has to build up arguments and present evidence from the data set in front of him/her (as in the 'analytic' example provided earlier in this chapter where illustrative examples from the interview transcription are continuously used). The argument does not produce certainty, rather, it produces likelihood. Most researchers therefore justify their account by 'asserting only a limited authority based on a combination of thorough and conscientious exploration and reporting, intellectual excellence, consensus of opinion and productive utility' (Yardley 1997: 40). For example, an interpretation may be justified on the grounds that it is 'comprehensive and coherent', 'meaningful to both participants and peers' (otherwise known as being 'plausible' or 'persuasive') and 'consistent with the data and theoretically sophisticated' (p. 40). All of these considerations are important in establishing the validity of narrative psychological research.

For example, we have already touched on the first criterion, the comprehensiveness and coherence of the account in Chapter 3, when we addressed the issue of 'historical' and 'narrative' truth in relation to psychotherapeutic endeavours. There we realized that we cannot just construct any old story or narrative in relation to the events that have happened in our past or of the vision we have for the future. In order to be effective and psychologically adaptive, the narrative has to entail a commitment to 'historical' truth insofar as it contains a realistic assessment of both where we have come from (economically, psychologically, emotionally, morally) and, relatedly, where we are going in the future. It is necessary to explore this question in relation to your own analysis of your autobiographical account. Does it contain a commitment to historical truth? Or is it imprisoned in historical truth, failing to allow any leeway for the liberating potential of narrative truth, the envisioning of alternative possibilities? This will help you to address the question of whether your analysis of your account is comprehensive and coherent.

It is perhaps not surprising that one of the criteria for justification, being 'meaningful to both participants and peers' (otherwise known as being 'plausible' or 'persuasive'), is particularly important to a narrative psychological approach. As we saw in Chapter 3, at the heart of this book is an attempt to create liberating and transforming ways of experiencing ourselves. It is not much good, therefore, if you go through the whole of this project and produce an account of your narrative that you find meaningless, implausible or totally unpersuasive. This all connects into your own assessment of the narrative you have lived by so far in your life and whether or not your analysis reveals it to be a 'good' or an adequate narrative. These issues regarding what constitutes a good narrative or a good story, are addressed in more detail in Section III. For the time being, however, you need to reflect on whether or not your narrative seems to have worked well for you so far. Does it make for a believable, vitalizing and satisfying narrative? Are there problems with your narrative? Is it too accepting of certain ways of seeing the world, for example your parents' perspectives? Does it allow sufficient room for your own independent thoughts and feelings? Or maybe it seems too tied to a certain political perspective such as feminism, which, on re-reading your narrative, strikes you as inauthentic and implausible because it fails to capture reality as you have lived and remembered it? (see Chapter 6). What are the moral and ethical implications of the way in which you have construed your narrative? (see Chapters 6–8).

The final criterion for justifying your argument is that it is 'consistent with the data and theoretically sophisticated'. At all times during your analysis (step 5) you should have been building up your argument by continuously referring to the transcript to support your case. In addition, in this 'reflection' section of the report, you should be establishing connections between your analytic findings and the debates and issues ongoing within the narrative psychological literature. For instance, you may want to address what your analysis reveals about the theoretical issue of the narrative configuration of time and identity discussed in Chapter 3. CD, for instance, could demonstrate the way in which the beginning of his belief of himself as a 'person' during his early adolescent years was linked to his conception of himself as, for the first time, 'dreaming of better times, perhaps a future' (L175) and no longer seeing himself as a 'victim' of his past (L445). Similarly, you may want to show how an identity crisis you experienced at a particular stage in your life, revealed the link between identity and time, insofar as your conception of the relationship between past, present and future totally disintegrated, leaving you bereft of meaning and direction (see Chapter 7).

(c) Interactional dynamics of the interview situation
The whole point of conducting this autobiographical research in an interview context has been to explore the way in which selves and identities are

constructed in dialogue with another person. In conducting this research, you have been placed in the position of being an interviewee, someone who tells your story to the interviewer (NB: if you took the step of reversing these roles as was suggested in Chapter 4, you will have served as both interviewer and interviewee). In this section you should discuss how the dynamics of the interview situation affected the kinds of stories you told about yourself, or the kind of self you presented to the other person. You should be able to do this both from studying the transcript and also from your recollected observations of the interview (to aid in this process it is useful to jot down your feelings about the interview immediately after it has been completed). Rennie (1994) has conducted some interesting work on how clients experience the telling of their stories in therapeutic encounters. This work may be of use to you at this reflective stage of your analysis. These considerations are extremely important in the research report because the rationale behind narrative psychological research is that narratives are context-sensitive and their form and content are responsive to the aims and conditions of the interview setting. How is the form and content of your narrative influenced by the particularities of the interview situtation you found yourself in? What kind of a self were you trying to portray? What about the interview transcript reproduced in Chapter 4 between CD and me? Carefully examine the transactions taking place in this transcript. What kind of dynamics do you think affected the interview situation and the kind of self produced by CD? (on the dialogical nature of interview situations see Silverman 1993; Lucas 1997; McLeod 1997; Crossley and Crossley 1998).

(vi) Bibliography (not included in the word count)
This is the final stage of the research report and should include references to all texts and sources used in producing the document.

Chapter summary

By the end of this chapter you should be clear on the following things:

- 'Realist' and 'constructivist' assumptions about personal narratives and the implications for how data from an interview situation can be used in analysis.
- How to conduct an analysis of your transcript. This always involves interpretation and can be subdivided into six steps:
  (1) Reading and familiarizing
  (2) Identifying important concepts to look for
  (3) Identifying narrative tone
  (4) Identifying imagery and themes in relation to each interview question

(5) Weaving all of this into a coherent account
(6) Writing up the research report.
- Writing up the research report can be further subdivided into six main steps:
(1) Introduction
(2) Method
(3) Results
(4) Analysis/Discussion
(5) Reflection
(6) Bibiliography.

Discussion points

- How did the interactional dimensions of the interview situation affect how you presented yourself to your interviewer?
- How is your 'personal' narrative connected to the culture in which you live? Which dominant narratives do you use? How have these framed your experience of yourself and the ambitions you have for the future?
- Does this kind of method reify the conception of a 'unitary' or 'core' self? Is this problematic? How does this connect to other dominant cultural methods of self-exploration? (see Simonds 1996).

Key further reading

*Crossley, N. and Crossley M.L. (1998) HIV, empowerment and the sick role: an investigation of a contemporary moral maze, *Health*, 2(2): 157–74.

Kohler Riessman, C. (1990) Strategic uses of narrative in the presentation of self and illness: a research note, *Social Science and Medicine*, 30(11): 1195–1200.

Lucas, J. (1997) Making sense of interviews: the narrative dimension, *Social Sciences in Health*, 3(2): 113–26.

McAdams, D. (1993) *The Stories we live by: Personal Myths and the Making of the Self*. New York: Morrow.

McLeod, J. (1997) *Narrative and Psychotherapy* (Chapter 3). London: Sage.

Silverman, D. (1993) *Interpreting Qualitative Data* (Chapter 5). London: Sage.

Simonds, W. (1996) All consuming selves: self-help literature and women's identities, in D. Grodin and T. Lindlof (eds) *Constructing the Self in a Mediated World*, pp. 15–29. London: Sage.

Notes on further reading

McAdams' book is essential for further background reading in terms of narrative processes and the construction of self. The McLeod and Simonds readings provide further exploration of the way in which contemporary society, through psychotherapy and self-help materials, may encourage forms of self-exploration, discussing the potential positive and negative implications of this. The Kohler-Riessman, Lucas, and Silverman references all look at the way in which interviewees do not just orient passively to an interview situation, but actively construct themselves, revealing the important moral and cultural foundations of identity-related processes.

The *Crossley and Crossley reading explores issues related to the morally value-laden nature of processes of identity construction in the context of interviews with HIV-positive individuals.

Contemporary applications

Preface

By the time you have reached this point in the book, you should have just completed a narrative psychological analysis of your own autobiography. Over the course of the next two chapters, we will be looking at further application of the narrative psychological method. In particular, we will focus on two of the main types of materials to which a narrative psychological style of analysis is most applicable. These include texts such as published autobiographies, biographies and diaries, and life-history-type interviews. More specifically, Chapter 6 shows how a narrative psychological approach can be used to analyse published autobiographical accounts such as those written by 'survivors' of childhood sexual abuse. Chapter 7 then goes on to show how the same approach can be used with interview material, in this case from interviews conducted with HIV-positive individuals.

A note on trauma narratives

Chapter 6 draws on previous research I have conducted in relation to autobiographical accounts of childhood sexual abuse written by female 'survivors' (see Davies 1995a). This research took place in the context of a rapidly proliferating collection of personal accounts of incestuous abuse and the need for testimony in relation to traumatic events more generally. Indeed, some authors such as Frank (1995: 71) have argued that this need to 'find one's own voice' is not just limited to traumatizing experiences, but that it is a feature characteristic of postmodern contemporary culture in which subordinated peoples (such as women, the working class, ethnic minorities, disabled people) have been 'written on from the outside' and have therefore 'lost their voices'. Hence, 'speaking in a voice recognisable as one's own becomes increasingly difficult', 'speech proliferates in search of that voice' and 'self stories proliferate' (Frank 1995: 71; see also Priest 1996).

One of the predominant themes in the literature of various kinds of trauma is the 'urge to bear witness', of the need for 'survivors' to testify to other people the truth of their experience (Tal 1996: 120). As Elie Wiesel, a writer on the Holocaust, reported,

> The only role I sought was witness. I believed that, having survived by change, I was duty bound to give meaning to my survival, to justify each moment of my life. I knew the story had to be told. Not to transmit an experience is to betray it.
>
> (Wiesel, cited in Tal 1996: 120)

Jill Morgan, a victim of childhood sexual abuse, explained her desire to speak in similar terms:

> A close personal friend has asked repeatedly, 'Why do you have to rehash it? It happened. It's over. Now forget it and go on'. Only by owning myself and my past, by affirming and confirming my innocence in the whole, sordid drama, can I rest and feel comfortable with myself.
>
> (cited in Tal 1996: 121)

Each of these authors, in relation to very different experiences, articulates the belief that he or she is a storyteller with a mission. Their responsibility as survivors is to 'bear the tale', and the process of storytelling is viewed as a 'personally reconstitutive act' (Tal 1996: 121). As Frank (1995: xii) argues, wounded people need to be cared for, but they can also become healers because 'their injuries become the source of the potency of their stories'. Through such stories, 'the teller not only recovers her voice; she becomes a witness to the conditions that rob others of their voices' (p. xiii). In this way, by telling their personal stories, individuals who have undergone trauma 'define the ethic of our times: an ethic of voice, affording each a right to speak her own truth, in her own words' (p. xiii).

We often experience the narratives told by people who have suffered various illnesses and traumas as gripping, emotive and powerful. The power of such stories, according to Frank (1995: 48), derives from the implicit link we make between the 'truth' of a story and the suffering attending the telling of that story. This link has a long history which can be traced back to the ancient Greeks who set in place the 'relation of truth and suffering that remains dominant in our thinking' (p. 48). In duBois' (1991) study of the bodies of slaves in Ancient Greece, for instance, she found that Greek slaves were tortured to force them to give evidence against their master. Thus, torture was seen as an ordeal out of which truth could be produced. It is from within this same philosophical tradition that we believe truth can be produced from the suffering of the ill body and/or mind, and that the illness narrative is the expression of such truth. Hence, 'the hearing of both the tortured slave's narrative and the ill person's narrative rests on a belief that at the extremes of suffering the body produces a truth' (Frank 1993: 48).

The power of such illness and trauma narratives, however, is not without its problems, as I soon came to realize in my analysis of personal accounts of childhood sexual abuse. Much of the research conducted in the field of trauma studies takes place under the influence of a humanistic paradigm (see Brody 1987; S. Taylor 1989) and tends to assume a certain 'transparency' with regard to the illness story, seeing it as a simple reflection of the individual's experience. However, as we argued in Chapter 2, this kind of approach fails to take sufficient account of the social construction of individual experience and the way in which such stories are embedded in social and political relations of power. In Chapter 6, therefore, we see how my detailed case-study of a specific autobiographical account of childhood sexual abuse attempted to retrieve the 'worldliness' of subjectivity and elucidate the social structure of personal experience. As we will see, however, this project is not without its own difficulties and we end this chapter by wondering if we have fallen into the same trap as discourse analytic and postmodernist approaches. Have we 'lost' the 'personal' dimension of individual experience? Is a more hermeneutic perspective required? Is it the case that 'we cannot simply discover the world and ourselves through . . . an analysis of language and its structures' (Pucci 1992: 209). Do we, as Ricoeur suggests, need a 'prior and more originary notion, starting from our experience of being-in-the-world and in time, and proceeding from this ontological condition towards its expression in language' (Ricoeur 1984: 78)?

It is in the wake of these considerations that we turn, in Chapter 7, to address the 'lived' experience of being and time in the context of HIV infection. Drawing on my research with people who have been diagnosed HIV positive for a relatively long period of time, we seek to explore how such a diagnosis affects a person's life. It is argued that one of the main problems faced by HIV-positive individuals is the disruption of their routine (future) orientation towards time, which has drastic ramifications in many areas of their personal and social lives. One of the main ways in which people have to cope with such disruption is by developing alternative ways of conceiving and living in time. In this chapter, these orientations towards time are connected to a number of dominant cultural stories or narratives that people have available to them in contemporary society for dealing with illness and trauma. These are explored in detail in relation to a number of case-studies. The aim of this chapter is to present an example of how a narrative psychological approach is capable of exploring both the 'personal' and 'social' dimensions of experience. In Chapter 8, we return to address in more detail the relationship between narratives, power, society and morality.

6 Surviving childhood sexual abuse

> Feminists have an ethical as well as an intellectual responsibility to ask tough questions about the current narratives of illness [and] trauma. . . . We can lead the way in making distinctions between therapeutic narratives and destructive hystories.
>
> (Showalter 1997: 13)

Introduction

In this chapter we will look at how a narrative style of analysis can be applied to contemporary issues of trauma such as childhood sexual abuse and the construction of subjectivity and identity. The focus will be on autobiographical accounts which, since awareness of childhood sexual abuse began to emerge during the late 1960s/1970s, have become increasingly prolific. The women who have written these accounts have used very different 'narratives' to make sense of their experiences, with radical implications for the construction of identity, memory, health, illness, blame and responsibility. These narratives are related to particular socio-historical climates and offer different, sometimes conflicting, 'moral visions' of the events under consideration. Consequently, they have important implications for the way in which both the victims and perpetrators of sexually abusive events are understood and 'treated'. These issues will be addressed in more detail by focusing on one particular case-study based on an autobiographical account of sexual abuse written by Sylvia Fraser entitled *My Father's House: A Memoir of Incest and Healing* (1989). A more detailed account of some of the issues raised in this chapter can be found in my earlier book, based on my PhD thesis, entitled *Healing Sylvia: Childhood Sexual Abuse and the Construction of Identity* (Davies 1995a).

Why is it important to deconstruct survivors' autobiographical accounts of childhood sexual abuse?

The aim of this chapter is to address the way in which self, subjectivity and identity are constructed in autobiographical accounts of childhood sexual abuse. This process of 'deconstruction' is important on a number of inter-related substantive, theoretical and practical/moral levels.

At the first, substantive level, is a concern with the recent increasing pro-liferation of autobiographical writings related to childhood sexual abuse and the kind of portrayal of experience evident in those accounts. The first written autobiographical accounts of childhood sexual abuse which began to appear during the 1960s and 1970s were related to the explicitly femin-ist 'political' project of making the 'personal political' and locating the indi-vidual 'private' experience of childhood sexual abuse within the larger 'public' domain of a patriarchal society (for example, Angelou 1969; Brady 1979; Allen 1980; Bass and Thornton 1983; Ward 1984; Armstrong 1987, 1996). Many of these accounts were committed to the political importance of writing and reading strategies for the creation of (feminist) identity, com-munity and political solidarity (Martin 1988: 80). The activities of telling, writing and reading such accounts were linked to the important task of countering representations that made women and children silent, invisible, deviant, perverse and marginal. Such storytelling was thus conceived as part of the larger struggle for self-determination among oppressed and silent groups (see Davies 1995a: 4).

However, the profile of events documented in these earlier narratives has not been sustained in contemporary first-person accounts emerging during the late 1980s and 1990s. These accounts are more influenced by what can be characterized as 'healing' or 'therapeutic' narratives (Davies 1995a: 4). For example, Kitzinger (1992) points to academic textbooks, journals, pop-psychology and self-help manuals as indicative of this movement. Among such manuals she cites: *Reclaiming Our Lives: Adult Survivors of Incest* (Poston and Lisbon 1989); *The Healing Way: Adult Recovery from Child-hood Sexual Abuse* (Kunzmann 1990); and *Reach for the Rainbow: Advanced Healing for Survivors of Sexual Abuse* (Finney 1990). Although Kitzinger does not include first-person accounts as part of this movement, I have previously argued that the very same move towards strategies of heal-ing is apparent in autobiographical accounts of childhood sexual abuse. Among such examples are Sylvia Fraser's *My Father's House* (1989); Jacque-line Spring's *Cry Hard and Swim: The Story of an Incest Survivor* (1987); and Cathy Anne Matthews' *Breaking Through: No Longer a Victim of Child Abuse* (1990). The important point to note about these more recent accounts is their presentation of a very different 'profile' of the experience of child sexual abuse to that found in the earlier accounts (Davies 1995a: 5). This relates to the second practical, moral and ethical level; the concern to highlight the way in which certain conceptions of personal experience have practical implications for the victims and perpetrators of incestuous crimes, especially in light of contemporary debates around issues such as 'false memory syndrome' (see Davies 1995a: 15).

On a more theoretical level, the project of exploring narratives involved in the construction of identity is related to some of the aims, objectives and concerns of the 'social constructivist' movement discussed previously in Chapters 1 and 2. To recall, analytic approaches such as postmodernism and discourse analysis are sceptical about the 'realist' assumptions embedded in more traditional approaches towards the study of self and identity. They are critical of the assumption that 'subjective' processes such as self, identity and memory can be characterized as 'internal' or 'pre-existent', existing 'beyond' the confines of language and narratives. For example, in Chapter 3 we made use of the social constructivist approaches in order to critique popularized Freudian images of the psyche which encourage us to view the process of retrieving memories from the past as a kind of 'archaeological' dig. By contrast, therapeutic approaches drawing on narrative theories tend to construe the process of memory retrieval as a more 'dialogical' process; memories are not simply 'retrieved' but are actively constructed in the process of therapeutic interactions between therapist and client. As will become clear over the course of this chapter, such issues are especially pertinent when considering contemporary autobiographical accounts of childhood sexual abuse informed by 'healing' approaches. This is because many of these approaches are informed by the popularized Freudian model of the psyche and tend, therefore, to present an image of personal 'memories' and 'experiences' as if they were untainted by cultural narratives, practices and ideologies. Pursuing the narrative psychological approach, however, we will demonstrate how the identity constructed by 'survivors' of childhood sexual abuse post-trauma is inextricably tied to interpretation, language and narratives.

The case-study

In more detailed terms, *Healing Sylvia* provides a case-study of the narrative practices incorporated in one woman's story of her incest survival. It is based on Sylvia Fraser's (1989) autobiography entitled *My Father's House: A Memoir of Incest and Healing*. The study charts the production of the personal story across the whole of the autobiography. Fraser's book describes the sexual abuse she suffered as a child at the hands of her father. In order to cope with the abusive situation Fraser characterizes herself as having 'split into two'. Thus, from the age of 7 she acquired an 'other self' who performed the sexual activities required of her by her father. As an adult, Fraser originally had no recollection of these events as she suffered from amnesia. Recovering the memory of traumatic scenes from her childhood enabled her to progress from the experience of mental disintegration towards a 'healed' state.

The psychoanalytic/therapeutic narrative

My Father's House is divided into five main sections: (1) Remembering; (2) Rescue; (3) Retreat; (4) Revelation; and (5) Resolution. Over the course of my analysis of the text, it soon became apparent that these sections were based on the typical pattern of psychoanalytic procedure set out by Freud in his infamous 1914 paper entitled 'Remembering, repeating and working through' (Freud 1956: 145). This psychoanalytic model or narrative provides the basis for the whole of the text and serves to construct Fraser's experience in a certain way. For instance, concepts derived from psychoanalytic theory such as the 'unconscious' dominate in the construction and portrayal of her experiences (Davies 1993).

Voices and selves

In the process of telling her story, Fraser uses a number of different 'voices'. It is important to understand that these voices are all interconnected in the text; each of the voices (which are supposed to represent various aspects of Fraser's 'self') takes on meaning only in relation to the various 'other' voices around it. It may be useful here to recall the way in which we understood the process of interviewing and therapy in Chapters 3 and 5 as a 'dialogical relationship'. The voices in Fraser's text interactively animate one another in the same way as the questions and responses of the interviewer/interviewee, therapist/client mutually determine one another. Another useful analogy can be taken from Chapter 1 where we looked briefly at the work of Mead and his analysis of the concept of self, which showed us the inextricable connection between identity and time. I can experience myself as 'I' only when I see and experience myself in the past tense as a 'me' (Mead 1967: 174).

There are basically three of these voices in Fraser's text, all of which use the first-person pronoun 'I'. These can be characterized as the 'interpretive voice' (IV), the 'narrative voice' (NV) and the 'unconscious voice' (UV) (Davies 1995a: 32). As I have already suggested, these voices reflect certain aspects of the self and, in doing so, reflect the influence of a psychoanalytic model on the formulation of events in *My Father's House*. This is because they can be seen as representative of the tripartite model of the mind set out by Freud. For example, the IV represents the integrated and balanced ego or psyche. It basically represents Fraser as she is at the point of writing, looking back over her past experiences and bringing them all together in the context of an integrated whole. This is the 'healed' Fraser who has gone through many traumatizing experiences and managed to 'survive'. It is the voice which speaks in the Author's Note right at the beginning of the text, telling us: 'The story I have told in this book is autobiographical. As a result of amnesia, much of it was unknown to me until three years ago . . .' (Fraser 1989). The authority of this voice derives from its 'reflective' stance towards past events. Here, Fraser acts as the historian of her own life who can look back and offer an overall perspective that was inaccessible to her at the time in which she was actually living those events.

The narrative voice, by contrast, represents the 'persona' aspect of the psyche, the 'public' aspect of the self which is shown to others and responds to externally imposed social rules. This voice uses the present tense and, throughout the text, portrays Fraser at various stages of chronological development. At each stage of the story the vocabulary and style are those that would have been available to Fraser herself at that point in her biographical development. For instance, in the first chapter, which portrays the author's early childhood, this voice begins: 'I sit on my daddy's lap playing ticktacktoe' (Fraser 1989: 3). And then in a later chapter portraying adolescence: 'We walk to Hamilton High, hugging our loose-leaf notebooks to our chest in the female style, thus squelching any rumour we might have breasts . . .' (p. 66). Thus, the narrative voice portrays an ongoing stream of action – the 'here and now' which is still in the process of being made as the text progresses. Hence, the characterization of events in this voice, unlike that of the interpretive voice, is confined to the partial temporal field associated with the particular stage of biographical development being portrayed (Davies 1995a: 33).

The third, 'unconscious voice' represents the Freudian 'unconscious'; the part of the mind which is inaccessible to the conscious mind but which affects behaviour and emotions (sometimes called the 'id'). The UV is marked off in the main body of the text through the use of italics. Like the NV it uses the present tense, which creates the impression that events are being narrated from an experiential, subjective viewpoint. The UV is repeatedly interspersed into the NV in order to give the impression of spontaneity, of the seepage of knowledge from unconsciousness into consciousness. For example: 'My father calls me into his bedroom. *Since my mother is also in the house my other self understands it is me he is calling and not her*' (Fraser 1989: 95).

Narratives and the portrayal of experience

I have already suggested that the psychoanalytic or therapeutic narrative frames the whole of Fraser's text. However, this is not the only narrative in evidence in the text; there is also a narrative which could be characterized as typically 'feminist', one which promotes a version of events connecting the 'personal' victimization suffered by Fraser as a child to the more 'political' question of treatment of women more generally in a patriarchal society. One of the main aims of *Healing Sylvia* was to show how these two narratives co-exist together in *My Father's House* and how, ultimately, the therapeutic narrative manages to usurp and dominate the feminist narrative, thus resulting in a particular presentation of the experience of childhood sexual abuse with profound practical and moral implications. In the analysis that follows, we will explore briefly how this process takes place.

The 'primary narrative'

The first section of Fraser's text entitled 'Recollection' consists of a kind of 'free association' process whereby the narrative chronologically pursues Fraser's development from her early childhood years to her marriage during her early 20s. This section is quite lengthy and takes up more than half of the text as a whole. The material presented in 'Recollection' is crucial because it contains material which could be characterized as a 'primary narrative'. What I mean by this is that at later stages of the text (representing the psychoanalytic procedure of 'working through'), certain parts of this 'material' will be selected and 'worked' on in order that Fraser can achieve an adequate understanding and grasp of her history. As we shall see, this process of selection and interpretation is of the utmost importance in terms of constituting the definitive version of events in *My Father's House*. There are basically two agendas, two timetables, presented in this early section of the text. These can be characterized as: (1) the 'private' biographical timetable; and (2) the 'public' biographical timetable. We shall now address each of these in more detail.

The 'private' biographical timetable

This 'private' timetable is largely related to the early years of Fraser's childhood. As the narrative voice portrays the world of Fraser as a child, a whole range of symbols and themes are built up; these are important for the significance they take on later in the text in terms of the world of the unconscious 'other self'.

The first theme is that of inheritance, signified by the symbol of the 'fairytale princess'. For example, when 5-year-old Fraser walks around the supermarket one day with her mother, a lady remarks: 'What lovely golden curls, just like a fairytale princess' (p. 5). These curls also connect the child to her daddy who plays with her blonde hair and tells her he had curls just like that when he was a baby. Fraser's paternal grandmother, known as 'Other Grandmother', removes a pearly comb from her own hair and puts it into Fraser's 'as if she were looking into a mirror . . . "You get your blonde hair from your father and me. . . . Just like a fairytale princess" ' (p. 18). Another signifier of the theme of inheritance is 'Aunt Estelle', the sister of Fraser's father. Throughout the text there are vague allusions to the fact that Aunt Estelle and Fraser's father had an incestuous relationship when they were younger. And more family connections are drawn when the child panics at the thought of kissing her Grandmother goodbye, 'Why this revulsion for an old woman's kiss? I do not know. I cannot say. *This truth belongs to my other self and it is a harsh one: Other Grandmother's caved-in cheek is the same squishy texture as daddy's scrotum*' (p. 19). As the text progresses it becomes clear that these symbols representing the theme of inheritance are built up in order to suggest that the incest taking place between Fraser and her father is the product of an unfortunate family history.

Events are further located in the context of family history in terms of the life of the unconscious 'other self'. Just as people such as Aunt Estelle and Other Grandmother are characterized in terms of their relationship to family history, places are similarly described in 'relational' terms. For example, rather than locating events in some 'publicly' identifiable place, events taking place in the 'other self' are located in the private space of 'my father's house', more specifically, in 'a single room' of that house. Additionally, 'Other Grandmother's House' comes to represent one of the 'spaces' associated with the 'other self'. For example, comparisons are drawn between the two houses: '*Just as everyone is deaf at Other Grandmother's house, everyone is blind in my father's house* (p. 21). The themes of blindness and deafness point to another important symbol; the ornamental 'see-no-evil, hear-no-evil, speak-no-evil monkeys on the radio console' (p. 9). These ornaments represent the family's turning away from recognition of the abuse, a well-known 'symptom' of incestuous 'dysfunctional' families.

Tied into the theme of inheritance are interrelated themes of mental illness, death and suicide. One symbol which is quite important in carrying these themes throughout the text is that of 'cats'. This symbol is introduced as Fraser's father threatens her in order to silence her about the abuse: '*If you say once more that you're going to tell I'm sending that cat of yours to the pound for gassing!*' (p. 12).

Alongside the themes of decay, decadence and inheritance is also the 'glamorous', unpredictable, exciting and 'romantic' aspect of the life of the 'other self'. It is in relation to such themes that the influence of Freud's theory of the Oedipus complex becomes most apparent. Such 'glamour' is represented by the 'Lawson family', the family of Fraser's schoolfriend, Lulu. Lulu's grandmother was an actress and both her parents 'look like movie stars' (p. 29). Paul Lawson, Lulu's father, is a lieutenant in the navy. Holding up a silver-framed photo of her father in his white uniform, Lulu asks Fraser if she thinks 'Paul' is 'the deadspit of Clark Gable?' (p. 31). She then kisses her father's photo and refuses to go to sleep until she finds an old tattered handkerchief which has her father's smell on it. Fraser is portrayed as feeling jealous; she waits until Lulu has gone to sleep and then takes the handkerchief, pretending it is hers.

Links between the Lawson and Fraser families are drawn on a number of occasions. Lulu's 'big white house on Delaware Avenue' reminds Fraser of Other Grandmother's house where Aunt Estelle lives, the only difference being that everything is dusted at the Lawsons' (p. 30). Comparisons are also drawn between Mrs Lawson and Fraser's mother. For instance, Mrs

Lawson does volunteer work like Fraser's mother, but, unlike her mother, Mrs Lawson 'gets her picture in the paper wearing a hat with a veil'. The significance of these connections becomes clear at later stages in the text when the theme of the Oedipus complex becomes more fully articulated.

For the time being, it is important to note that the comparison between Mrs Lawson and Fraser's mother brings forth issues of mother–daughter rivalry, competition and jealousy. This theme of the mother's jealousy of her daughter is evident throughout the text and is symbolized by the mother's 'disapproving and scolding lips'. For example, when Fraser's mother finds her touching herself between the legs, she strikes her across the cheek, shouting 'Don't ever let me catch you doing that again!' (p. 7). In defiance, Fraser lies in the dark, her hand between her legs, singing 'Don't ever let me catch you!' and 'twisting her lips like her mother's' (p. 7). Similarly, when Fraser lies on her father's bed being sexually abused, she stares at the scroll on the headboards and thinks it looks like her mother's scolding lips.

It is extremely difficult to provide an overview of all the themes and symbols pertaining to the 'private' life of the 'other self', both because there are so many of them and also because they are inseparably tied together. The important point to grasp here, however, is the *way in which* these symbols and themes serve to locate the child's experience of sexual abuse as a product of family inheritance and thus, of 'private' childhood biography.

The 'public' biographical timetable

As I have already suggested, in the first section of the text, a coexisting 'timetable' is also developed. By contrast to the 'private' familial world of the 'other self', the narrative also portrays the chronological development of Fraser in terms of the 'public' social and historical context, specifically in terms of patriarchy. This kind of portrayal presents a typical 'political' feminist version of the events going on in Fraser's family; it is concerned to connect the 'personal' with the 'political'.

For example, the first 'persona' developed in the narrative is of Fraser as a child. Here, it is clear that the portrayal of the experiential world of the child is solidly located in the 'public' context of the patriarchal nuclear family. Both Fraser and her mother are characterized as subordinate to the authority of the father. For example, 'My father sits in his fetch-me chair. . . . He grunts: "Fetch me a paring knife" . . . My father sharpens his pencil. "Take this back"' (p. 13). The mother is portrayed mainly as a subservient housewife dependent on her husband for his economic support. This is made explicit in a scene when the child rebels against her father's sexual demands:

> *Desperation makes me bold. At last I say the won't love me words: 'I'm going to tell my mommy on you!' My father replaces bribes with threats: 'If you do you'll have to give me back all your toys'. I tot up my losses: my Blondie and Dagwood cutouts, my fairytale colouring*

*books, my crayons. 'My mommy gave those things to me. They're
mine'. 'I paid for them. Everything in this house belongs to me. . . .
Your mother will do what I say'* (p. 11).

As one reads about the experiences suffered by the young child at the
hand's of her father, one is made increasingly aware of the child's growing
sense of panic, fear and helplessness as she is locked further in her father's
power. For example, near the beginning of the chapter the reader hears the
innocent voice of the child as she tells us: 'My daddy squeezes my legs
between his knees. I count my pennies, already imagining them to be black-
balls and liquorice from the Candy factory. . . . *My daddy and I share
secrets*' (p. 6). As the chapter progresses, however, so, too, does the child's
heightening sense of fear and frustration: '*His sweat drips on me. I don't like
his wet-ums. His wet ums splashes me . . . I'm afraid to complain because
daddy won't love me won't love me won't love me*' (p. 11). And, '*Now when
daddy plays with me I keep my eyes tightly scrunched so I can't see. I don't
want his pennies or his candies or his cookies. Mostly I leave them by the
pillow while he swallows me and I hold my breath to keep me from crying
because daddy won't love me love me love me*' (p. 11). It is in relation to
scenes such as the above that the child is clearly portrayed in a manner
which emphasizes her subordinate position relative to the powerful position
occupied by the father as head of the family.

Moreover, as Fraser gets older and begins to attend school, it becomes
apparent that the sexual abuse perpetrated on her by her father is not simply
an anamolous event, not simply an idiosyncratic feature of her own deviant
father or family. At school, she comes into contact with another sexually
abused child, Magda Lunt, who is classed as a reject by the other children:
' "Magda's father beats her up. Phew! Magda stinks of fish" ' (p. 20). Fraser
stands on the sidewalk: 'Magda doesn't stink of fish. I know that smell. I've
smelled it on myself. It's the stink of . . . *fear*. It's the stink of . . . *daddy won't
love me love me*' (p. 20). These two young girls are locked in partnership by
virtue of the abusive events perpetrated on them by their fathers. The experience of childhood sexual abuse is not simply a 'private' experience; rather,
the narrative implies a growing awareness of the fact that such private
experiences may reflect a more collective phenomenon. This interpretation
of events is further buttressed by the fact that Fraser is not only sexually
abused by her father but also by Mr Brown, a lodger who stays in her
father's house during the summer of 1944.

This emphasis on the collectivity of girls' and women's experiences continues throughout the portrayal of the adolescent years, expressed in the
form of a critique of the hypocrisy of the moral values of the 1950s which
revolved around the 'cult of the virgin'. This is a world dominated by male
power. Such power is thematized in terms of male violence and male ownership and possession. For example, Fraser's adolescent experiences are totally
dominated by boys and men engaging in sexually insulting behaviour. She is
sexually assaulted by two boys in the cinema as hands 'claw' at her sweater

and 'dive' under her skirt (p. 50). Fraser is also verbally assaulted as one boy tells her: ' "Next time you'd better be wearing tin pants because we're going to work you over so good you'll . . ." ' (p. 57). Sexually abusive language is also directed towards Fraser and other cheerleaders as they support the school football team. As they cheerlead at the side of the football pitch, obscenities 'unroll like used toilet paper': ' "That's right Blondie. Get those tits moving!' The crowd gives a nervous guffaw. Other voices chime in: "Crotch! Crotch! Give us CROTCH" ' (p. 88). As cheerleaders, Fraser describes the girls as having 'a self mocking awareness of the colossal hypocrisy of which we are the eager butts' (p. 70).

Further examples of sexual harassment take place at school. Fraser sees a 'defaced school election poster' on which 'My lips have been reddened, my hair painted gold. The caption, EXPERIENCE COUNTS has been altered to read EXPERIENCED CUNT' (p. 91). Fraser also receives dirty phone calls and poison-pen letters. It is in relation to such widespread practices of objectification that the narrative draws an analogy between the father's abusive acts and those existing in society at large. For example, when Fraser's father first attempts full penetrative intercourse, Fraser feels '. . . *used, not as one person exploited by another, but as a condom is used then discarded in the gutter. . . . She is old enough now, to understand how completely she had been betrayed*' (p. 43).

Connections are also drawn between economics, sex, possession and freedom. Waiting to go into the cinema, Fraser remembers 'the first rule of dating: loss of economic freedom equals loss of personal freedom' (p. 48). At a raided pyjama party, boys huddle along the wall looking on while the girls are 'humiliated at having to hang around like merchandise when nobody is buying' (p. 61). And at the school dance Fraser feels as if she is 'possessed' by her date as his arms coil around, constricting her like 'clamps'. When she dances with someone other than her date we are informed this is not usual practice because the 'financial investment' is so high. After having being 'returned' to her date she feels guilty, *'like Daddy's naughty girl who's failed to please'* (p. 86). Moreover, Fraser feels an obligation to 'give her services' to her date as he takes her home after the school dance: 'This shouldn't be first date stuff but I've been adding up the gasoline and the corsage . . . and I find something owing which, being an honest tradeswoman, I feel obliged to deliver' (p. 86).

Ideological power, the power to determine language, thought and reality, is also portrayed as inextricably bound up with economic power. From this perspective, men have the power to determine reality. This reality is the reality encountered by Fraser's adolescent self called 'Appearances'. 'Appearances' is geared towards the satisfaction of male-defined standards. Fraser and the other girls see themselves and others through the 'male gaze' (p. 64). Because 'Hollywood agrees' that gentlemen prefer blonde hair, for Appearances, blonde hair is 'standard equipment' (p. 75). Because dating is the standard by which Fraser's high school, Hamilton High, judges a girl's popularity, Appearances fills her date book 'like a junkie' (p. 65).

Over this part of the text a resounding theme is that the reality experienced by each girl or woman in a male-dominated world takes on an increasing form of artificiality or non-reality. Fraser is characterized as feeling weary owing to the constant pressures of presentation required by Appearances; she feels as though she is continuously preparing for a part in a play. Her friend Lulu is characterized as 'always playing a part. Like me' (p. 81). As is to be expected with people who feel they have no stake or share in the dominant version of reality, such experiences result in a confused mixture of rage, anger, guilt and fear. Anger and frustration are expressed in the form of self-harm as the adolescent Fraser claims she can burn her arm with a cigarette and not feel anything. She can wrap her arm around the pain 'till it smothers in its own scream'. Fraser also ceases to menstruate and her weight goes down to 98 lbs. And Fraser is not alone in such experiences. Her friends are also characterized as suffering from the same kind of 'hysteria'. Babs has anorexia and bad nerves; Lulu, pregnant but trying to deny it, has worn the same box-pleated skirt and blazer for a month, holding books against her stomach to hide the bulge.

The fear and frustration deriving from male social, economic and ideological power, results in hysteria and almost leads to Fraser's total mental breakdown. Just as this is about to happen, however, Fraser meets Danny, her future husband, and falls in love. Danny, her 'prince', 'saves' and 'heals' her, leading her away from confusion. At this point, the text, tongue in cheek, suggests that 'love' has the power to heal; to bring forth the 'real truth', the real 'reality' of the world: 'And so the handsome prince kissed the sleeping princess and . . . and. . . . No, it doesn't quite work that way. This is real life after all' (p. 113). By contrast with such fantastical romantic images, the text then proceeds to document the nature of women's 'real life' experiences of love. As Fraser leaves school and takes a part-time job in her vacation prior to entering university, she learns a 'new vocabulary' – of 'failed rescue' and 'unmet hopes' (p. 112). Single women yearn for the 'right man' to rescue them but fail to notice that the married women remain 'unrescued'. The married women dream of buying the 'right house' so they can rescue their marriages and children.

When Fraser enters university, 'the cult of the virgin' still lies heavily upon female undergraduates. 'As always, sex has to do with "them", "their needs and our reactions" ' (p. 129). Once more, male power is linked to economic status. The faculties of medicine and business administration are viewed as 'hunting grounds for male selection' because a 'good catch' must include 'guaranteed upper-middle-class income' (p. 122). By contrast, most girls take arts subjects and secretarial science courses which reflect the belief that 'a girl's happiest role is as wife and mother' (p. 121). This belief is espoused by Professor Wynne from the philosophy department when Fraser discusses with him her career options. He tells her she has been living in a 'fool's paradise'. No one, he tells her, takes a woman scholar seriously, especially not in philosophy. Luckily, he comments, Fraser is engaged. Professor Wynne has always told his wife that the 'simple example' of her sitting before their children reading scholarly material in the original Latin is a better advert for classical education than all of his preaching (p. 136).

From the above overview, it is clear that over the course of the first section of *My Father's House*, two different agendas co-exist. The first is the 'private' world of the unconscious 'other self' in which themes of inheritance and incest as the product of a dysfunctional family history predominate. The second is the more 'public' agenda in which the 'personal' experiences of girls and women are located within the public social and historical context of patriarchy. The second section of the text, 'Retreat', represents the psychoanalytic procedure of 'working through'. As I have already suggested, the way in which material from the primary narrative is selected in this section is crucial in determining which 'agenda' will predominate in the final version of events put forward in *My Father's House*. The analysis that follows demonstrates how this process of selection takes place.

'Working through the primary narrative': prioritizing the 'private' biographical world

The second section of the text begins with the narrative portraying Fraser in her late 30s, being taken over by depression; it seeps, 'like a poisonous fog', through the 'cracks' in her life. Fraser becomes obsessed by the image of a 'hangman's noose': 'It's the last thing I see before falling asleep at night. . . . It fills my dreams. . . . It hangs before me' (p. 146). Links to family history are made: '*Though I don't yet know it, my maternal grandfather hanged himself, age forty four, and a maternal aunt soon would*' (p. 146).

The depression experienced by Fraser forces her to regress, to return to an earlier stage of psychic development. This is indicated by the return to symbols and themes found in the first three chapters of the text narrating the early childhood years. For example, Fraser is characterized as being 'lured by memories' and finds herself attracted to childhood haunts with 'a sense of mission' (p. 148). When Fraser goes back to her parental home and searches through her father's attic, she finds disturbing pictures of a pregnant Satan-like teddy bear that she drew as a child. Connections between pregnancy, suicide, death and evil are developed, as when she finds herself doodling in a meeting. She looks down and discovers 'Teddy Umcline [her childhood teddy bear] with a pregnant belly. His jaunty tie eventually transmogrifies into a hangman's noose. Full circle' (p. 148).

The major focus of the narrative voice in this chapter is on Fraser's writing of an earlier novel *Pandora*. Under the force of the unconscious 'other self' this becomes a novel based on the first seven years of her life: '*My other self has learned to type. She presses my keys, throwing up masses of defiant memories – stream of consciousness stuff*' (p. 149). And as the 'other self' takes over the writing of *Pandora*, Fraser loses all track of chronological time: 'Days melt into weeks. Weeks slide into months. Fall hardens into winter then lightens into spring' (p. 149). Danny informs Fraser that she does not seem to notice that time is passing. Fraser explains that the manuscript is more than 2000 pages long, written in the 'first person hysterical . . . like a gush of primordial pain' from a part of her she never knew existed (p. 151). 'One day in 1971', the narrative voice tells us, *Pandora* is finished and 'at 255 pages, it exists as an entity separate from me, with its circumstances of creation still more or less a mystery to me' (p. 151). It is important to note, however, that the 'other self', although 'acquiring a voice' through *Pandora*, had stopped short of revealing its most damning secret; this is to remain repressed until a later date.

The title of the next chapter, 'Triangles', points the way towards themes of the Oedipus complex, family relationships and 'private' biography. The force and power of the unconscious is made explicit from the start with the statement: 'It seems to be a law of human nature as compelling as Newton's that whatever is hidden in the psyche will struggle to reveal itself' (p. 153). The agenda of the private 'other self' now begins to take over Fraser's life with full force. What is that agenda? The reader is informed that it consists of the 'other self's' 'nostalgia for her first love' who now wants to 're-unite with daddy' (p. 153). Fraser, in typical psychoanalytic style, elaborates thus, 'My other self required a daddy substitute, attractive to me as well as to her. The man she chose was, like most kings, married. This was not incidental. A triangle allowed her to hate his queen as a projection of the jealous fury she felt for the mother-rival who failed to protect her' (p. 153).

Here, the use of terms such as 'first love', 'daddy substitute', 'triangle', 'projection', 'jealousy' and 'mother-rival' are clearly resonant of the psychoanalytic narrative. It is this narrative which sets the scene for one of the most important events in this section – Fraser's committing of adultery.

Throughout this chapter, in preparation for the adultery scene, there is a return to significant symbols and themes associated with Fraser's early 'private' biography; the 'relational' world of her 'other self'. For example, the adulterous acts take place at the house of Fraser's childhood friend, Lulu Lawson. The Lawson house, you will recall, is the house that has previously been connected with Other Grandmother's house, which is associated with themes of inheritance, decay and death. It 'reminds me of Other Grandmother's house where Aunt Estelle lives all boarded up' (p. 30). Immediately prior to the adulterous scene, the narrative is concerned to build up links to past family history. Fraser, along with her mother and sister, visits her father, who is now old, infirm and in hospital. The scene is clearly reminiscent of the child's weekly visits to Other Grandmother reported during the early stages of *My Father's House*. Indeed, this link is made in the narrative as Fraser finds herself remembering Sunday visits to Other Grandmother's house. In the hospital scene, a connection is drawn between Sylvia and Aunt Estelle (who, it is suggested, Sylvia's father previously had an incestuous relationship with). When Sylvia's father opens his eyes, he looks directly into Sylvia's face and says: 'Thanks for coming Estelle' (p. 170). Sylvia's 'other self' shrieks inside her: *'It's not Aunt Estelle. It's me'* (p. 170). As has previously been suggested, the character of Aunt Estelle serves to advance the theme of repetition of past events in the present and thus to account for the incidence of abuse in terms of family history.

In the adultery scene, people who took on a significant role in Sylvia's early childhood biography are brought to the forefront. For example, we encounter Paul Lawson, the father of Lulu Lawson, with whom the adult Sylvia now has an affair. He serves as the substitute father figure. Recall again the early stages of *My Father's House* when Sylvia felt jealous of Lulu because of her handsome father. In this chapter, Paul now tells Sylvia that he has not been able to 'get her off his mind': ' "How do you feel about that" ', he asks, ' "the father of your high-school chum . . . a dirty old man"?' (p. 161). Over the course of the adultery scene and during the actual act of sexual intercourse, the 'other self' takes over. This is made clear by the use of italics (the unconscious voice). For example: 'Paul opens the door wearing a white terry bathrobe, his gray hair wet and tufted as if from the shower. *My daddy sits on his bed in his undershirt*' (p. 176). And: 'Gazing into my eyes, Paul announces: "Amazing! Wasn't that amazing? I haven't done anything quite so impulsive since I was seventeen". *My daddy and I share secrets*' (p. 171). It is also important here to note the way in which the actions of the 'other self' are characterized in a childish fashion. For example, the unconscious voice uses language typically associated with a child such as 'daddy', 'Teddy' 'granny', 'little girl', 'trapped princess', and her actions are characterized as 'giddy', 'babbling' and with 'childish bravado'.

From this brief overview, then, it becomes clear that the 'working through' stage of *My Father's House* carefully selects material from the early stages of the text where the timetable of the 'private' biographical self, with its emphasis on inheritance and private family history, predominates. The selection of this narrative framework of meaning will have a strong influence on the rest of the text that follows. As part and parcel of this process of selection, the 'public' timetable, influenced by the feminist narrative, is subordinated and figures little in subsequent sections of the text. In addition, not only is the psychoanalytic narrative now prioritized, it also operates in such a way that it presents a *reinterpretation* of events previously understood in relation to a feminist narrative (such as childhood sexual abuse, love, marriage and mental illness). The effect of this is to present a psychoanalytically informed version of these events, which serves to individualize and depoliticize them. The following analysis demonstrates how this is achieved in relation to the themes of childhood sexual abuse, love and marriage.

Usurping the feminist narrative

Infantile sexuality

The first way in which the psychoanalytic narrative brings forth a reinterpretation of the feminist account presented in the first section of the text is in terms of the issue of 'infantile sexuality'. By portraying the 'other self' as being in charge of her actions during the adultery scene, Fraser forces a question regarding the 'motivation' and thus the innocence of the young child who originally engaged in sexual intercourse with her father. For example, immediately after having sex with her, Paul apologizes for 'jumping' her as soon as he opened the door. Then he asks, 'For the record, why did you come?'. Sylvia begins her 'covering statement' but then breaks off. 'For this', she answers. As we have already seen, the adultery scene takes place during the process of regression. This means that it is supposed to be a direct repetition of events that took place during childhood. Indeed, the text tries to create this impression through its heavy use of italics. Given this notion of repetition, therefore, it is clear that the reason Fraser gives for visiting Paul (that is, for sex) also has implications for her 'visiting' her father's bedroom in earlier childhood scenes. The implication is that she also desired sex as a child.

But the important point to note here is that the focus on childhood motivation or desire (deriving from the psychoanalytic narrative), fails to take into consideration the 'public' social and historical context of the situation. Recall the young child's desperation at the hands of her father's abuse, '*Now when daddy plays with me I keep my eyes tightly scrunched so I can't see. I don't want his pennies or his candies or his cookies. Mostly I leave them by the pillow while he swallows me and I hold my breath to keep me from crying because daddy won't love me love me love me*' (p. 11). By drawing a direct analogy between sexual events occurring in the adult world (between Fraser and Paul), and those occurring in the child's world (between Fraser and her father), there is no recognition of the different rights and duties, and thus the differing degrees of exploitation in the two situations. This is evident by the way in which 'sexually abusive' events between the child and her father now become 'sanitized' and variously referred to as a 'sexual relationship' (p. 15), an 'incestuous relationship' (p. 120) and 'our affair' (p. 39).

Love and marriage

A second way in which earlier feminist interpretations of events is usurped is in relation to the issue of love and marriage. We have already seen that compulsive, unconscious forces are portrayed as causal factors motivating Fraser to commit adultery. In order to present this portrayal as convincing, it is important that the reader should not be able to find any other reason to account for Fraser's committing of adultery. If an 'external' factor (such as problems with the marriage) cannot be found, then the act of adultery can more convincingly be portrayed as the product of 'internal' psychological forces. This is precisely what Fraser does in the text. She constructs an image of her marriage as one of contentment and happiness. Adultery, she tells us, is characterized as a 'large word' beginning with a 'scarlet letter'. Over the course of 15 years of marriage she had 'never considered it' (p. 153). She had no need to because her marriage consisted of 'romance', 'fun' and 'glamour'. This perception of the 'perfect marriage' is sustained in terms of both Fraser's and other people's perception of the marriage. For example, prior to the adultery scene, Paul asks Fraser: 'Am I being entirely absurd or do you suppose we could have an affair?' Fraser replies rather 'starchily' that she has never been unfaithful to her husband. In a similar vein, Fraser's friend tells her that as far as she is concerned Danny and Fraser have got the 'perfect marriage' (p. 167). When Fraser eventually separates from her husband she tries, unsuccessfully, to explain her reasons for leaving. In some ways, she ruminates, a good marriage is more vulnerable than a bad one because the expectations are so high. She ends up by saying 'I left because I left'. All of this lends credence to the fact that the unconscious workings of the mind caused Fraser to commit adultery: 'Like a sleepwalker, I watched askance while someone who looked like me cast aside everything I valued' (p. 154).

It is important to point out that this conception of love and marriage is very different from that encountered in the first section of the text. As we have already seen, there the experience of 'love' was tied into the economic, social and ideological context of patriarchy; themes of male possession and dominance prevailed. Given the fact that the break-up of Fraser's marriage begins to take place in 1971, the historical period witnessing the emergence of the feminist movement and women's liberation, 'the beginning of a period when domestic conflict seemed just part of all the other terrible things that were happening in the world' (French 1987: 573), one would expect the foregrounding of this type of feminist analysis. However, this is clearly not the case. Rather, the alternative psychoanalytic narrative takes over.

This is made explicit in a reunion scene in which Fraser meets up with her old school friends. The women talk about 'the usual' – love and marriage. One of the women reaches the conclusion that marriage is 'a great institution for men but it sucks for women' (p. 178). Rather than elaborating on such themes, however, Fraser 'detaches' herself from the conversation and goes into the wharf for a swim. In this scene, Fraser is portrayed as increasingly losing her grip on reality; she is losing control, something irrational is taking over her life.

In another scene which takes place after Danny and Fraser have split up, the narrative touches on earlier themes of male possession. As they discuss their separate lives Danny says that he is miserable living alone; all the plants are dying. Fraser suggests he may be overwatering them, to which Danny responds with a 'wry smile': 'That sounds like me'. Here, the implication is that Danny is overpossessive and this is buttressed by the next question which is asked with 'clenched knuckles': 'Is there someone else?' Fraser answers in the negative and uses this question as a means of deliberating further on her 'reasons' for leaving the marriage. Again, the issue is diverted from the context of male ownership and placed under the aegis of the now dominant psychoanalytic narrative. 'By now', Fraser tells us, she is sure she had to leave Danny but she still fails to understand why: 'Why? It makes no sense. Only that I am compelled. Why?' (p. 189).

Implications – adopting the 'psychoanalytic/therapeutic' narrative

The practical implications of adopting the psychoanalytic narrative as the dominant mode of interpretation in *My Father's House* become clear towards the end of the book when Fraser reflects back on her experiences, having undergone mental illness and therapy, in order to make further sense of the actions of her mother, father and herself. To cut a long story short, Fraser continues to appropriate Freudian theories and concepts in order to account for these experiences. The end result is that the mother is construed as an active agent in her suppression of knowledge about the abuse, and thus, as responsible for failing to protect her child. By contrast, the father is portrayed as a passive victim of his own childhood and rendered largely non-culpable for the crimes he perpetrated against his daughter. Finally, Fraser, as adult victim of incestuous crimes, is encouraged to accept responsibility for the part her 'other self' (the 'unconscious' infantile sexual part of the self) played in the 'games' with her father. The acceptance of responsibility in this way is portrayed as instrumental in Fraser's ability to 'forgive' both herself and her father, and thus to move on in the 'healing' process.

The 'healing' story is all about achieving integration, adaptation and closure. For this reason, when the 'healed' Fraser ends the text of her 'survival', she is concerned to produce explanations which leave her at peace with herself and the world. In order to do this, she appropriates explanations which connect the events that have happened in her life with events that happen in the world more generally. Hence she makes 'universalizing' comments such as 'All of us are born into the second act of a tragedy in progress'; 'All of us are haunted by the failed hopes and undigested deeds of our forebears' (p. 253). This understanding of human life is expanded into a wider understanding of the nature of the universe and the forces of time and space. Fraser tells us that in the place of her narrow world of cause and effect – in place of her 'rational' understanding of the world, she has burst into an 'infinite world full of wonder'. The whole mystery of the universe now has her reverence (p. 253). She now understands 'life as a journey' in which she has travelled from 'darkness into light'. 'Things do add up', speculates Fraser, 'life does have shape and maybe even purpose' (p. 253). It is this conception of the universe that allows her to 'resolve' her problems and advocate the necessity of expressing empathy, love and forgiveness for her father. It is only by doing this that Fraser is able to express hope for the future. Hence, she claims: 'I also forgive my father because I love him. This is the biggest shock of all. Not only that I once loved him but that I love him even now. For hope, read love' (p. 241).

In my analysis of Fraser's text, I emphasized that the purpose of such vague and general statements regarding the nature of individual humanity and the relationship between human beings and the universe, is to achieve closure with regard to the search for an explanation as to why she suffered such traumatic events as a child (Davies 1995a: 138). Moreover, I argued that 'the move towards closure in the search for explanations indicates the way in which the 'healing' solution advocates a passive adaptation and adjustment to social norms and values' (Davies 1995a: 139). This was allegedly in contrast to earlier accounts which had been written under the impact of feminist struggles for conceptual and political unity and therefore produced an entirely different picture of events from that emerging in and through the 'healing' narrative. Drawing on feminist criticism I argued that 'feminisms grappling with the personal as political promises to degenerate into absorption with the personal as personal' (Cocks 1984: 48).

I also argued, along with other feminist researchers, that making incest a topic of public discourse has resulted in the 'medicalization' of incest and the creation of an 'incest industry' (see Armstrong 1987: 19; Kitzinger 1992; Tal 1996). The effect of medicalization has been to reduce incest from a 'crime' to a 'disease'; a psychological illness which involves the entire family. Armstrong, for instance, argues that contemporary psychology places an inappropriate amount of responsibility on the mother of the abused child: 'From the outset, all the heavy artillery was aimed at this mother. The entire construction of the "family disease" model depended on her existence . . .' (Armstrong 1987: 266; see also Walters (1996) and Woodward (1997) on cultural constructions of the mother). Hence, by looking at incest as a 'family' problem, the 'status quo could be preserved' and the problem explained in such a way that it 'lay in the dysfunctional nature of a particular family rather than the abusive behaviour of one man' (Tal 1996: 196). 'Psychology', argued Kitzinger, has 'devised a framework for processing our personal experiences which erase feminist questions about the implications of sexual violence for relations between men and women' (Kitzinger 1992: 400). Thus, I argued, in the 'healing' narrative emphasis is shifted away from the social, moral and political context on to an explanation of the psychological facets of power. That is to say, the analysis of power is reduced to an analysis of the complexities of an inner psychic life (Davies 1995a: 141).

The issue of narrative 'plausibility'

My analysis of Fraser's autobiographical account of the sexual abuse she suffered as a child and her subsequent recovery, raises some tricky questions regarding the issue of 'narrative plausibility' which I originally failed to address in *Healing Sylvia*. We have already discussed the concept of narrative plausibility in Chapter 5 when considering our analysis and interpretation of our own life histories. For the moment, let us just pause to ask the question: Is Fraser's rendition of the events which happened to her in the past 'plausible'? Freeman (1993: 162), who also analyses Fraser's autobiography, suggests that such plausibility would include elements of 'coherence' and whether or not the narrative is 'fitting' of the events it is attempting to portray. Acknowledging that Fraser's narrative is 'a clear instance of someone who is offering an explicitly theoretically based (psychoanalytic) account of why her life came to take the strange twists and turns it did' (Freeman 1993: 161), Freeman asks: Is the narrative she uses one which enables us to make better sense than other possible narratives?

Clearly, the implicit thrust of my analysis and argument in *Healing Sylvia* is that Fraser's use of the psychoanalytic narrative results in an account of her past experiences which are, to a large extent, implausible, insofar as an alternative 'feminist' narrative would have enabled us to make 'better sense' of those events. Such an account would, allegedly, have presented a more coherent 'plot' in which the abusive events of Fraser's childhood were more fully integrated into the social and historical context in which she found herself. But it could be argued, by contrast, that this traditional 'political'-style feminist analysis is implausible insofar as it fails to adequately address the individual particularities of Fraser's experience. The very fact that Fraser has previously used such a feminist narrative to understand her own and others' experiences (in her earlier novel *Pandora* and in the 'Recollection' section of *My Father's House*) may, in itself, be testimony to the fact that it proved 'implausible' *to her*. Maybe she felt that the 'old-style' feminist narrative failed to provide a sufficiently coherent understanding of her own life and didn't allow her to go far enough in developing her understanding of herself?

Indeed, looking back on my own analysis of Fraser's text now, I am unsatisfied and unconvinced that the method I used allowed sufficient leeway to help us understand the nature of such personal, traumatic experiences. In this sense, it could be said that *Healing Sylvia* is guilty of the very same criticisms that were made of postmodernism and discourse analysis in Chapter 2. Namely, it produces an account of the way in which personal experience is constituted through linguistic and cultural narratives, but in the process of so doing, 'loses' any concept of the lived nature of such experiences. In this way, by failing to address the 'personal' dimension of Fraser's experience, this kind of analysis serves to 'objectify' her. Although my intention was never to belittle the traumatizing consequences of child abuse, or the need to heal and recover, I am not too sure that the kind of analysis presented in *Healing Sylvia* does not do precisely that. Perhaps Fraser thought that the feminist narrative 'objectified' her own experience in much the same way; it seemed too neat and gave no space for her to appreciate the messiness of her own personal psychology? Perhaps that is why she needed another narrative, a psychoanalytic narrative, to help her achieve such self-understanding?[1]

This brief consideration of the issue of narrative plausibility forces us to address the question, what constitutes a 'better' story? And here we see that this is an inextricably moral question. If we grant that there is no possibility of simply speaking of 'objective' historical facts, a historical 'truth' which exists independently of the way we construe it, then we are left with the fact that this question cannot be separated from the 'moral visions' with which we operate (MacIntyre 1981; Freeman 1993: 174). If I argue that the 'old-style' feminist narrative constitutes a better way of understanding what happened to Fraser, then I am betraying the fact that my moral vision is one which advocates the need for a more 'collective' or 'sociological' view of events taking place in society. By contrast, if I argue that the psychoanalytic narrative constitutes a better version, then I am more likely to appreciate the need for a more 'individualistic' or 'psychological' viewpoint. Linked to this question is a consideration of the way in which different narratives serve different purposes. A 'better' story for therapeutic purposes, for instance, may be the psychoanalytic narrative. Likewise, in terms of offering a social and cultural critique, the 'old-style' feminist narrative may be 'better'.

We have already discussed some of these questions regarding what constitutes a better story in relation to our own narratives in Chapter 5. And in Chapter 2 we also saw how such issues tie into considerations regarding the sexual practices of HIV-positive individuals. As we shall discuss further in Chapter 8, such questions regarding the prioritizing of the psychological or the sociological tie into larger issues related to the moral and political structures of the narratives we use to make sense of ourselves and the world.

Chapter summary

By the end of this chapter you should understand the following concepts and issues:

- Why it is important to 'deconstruct' survivors' accounts of traumatic experiences (substantive, theoretical and moral/practical).
- The way in which the construction of 'voices' and 'selves' in *My Father's House* connects to a 'psychoanalytic'/'therapeutic' model.
- The co-existence of 'feminist' and 'therapeutic' narratives in *My Father's House* – each offering contrasting 'moral' visions of childhood sexual abuse.
- The way in which the therapeutic narrative is prioritized to create an authoritative version of events, for example infantile sexuality, love and marriage, mental illness.
- The depoliticizing implications of the therapeutic narrative.
- The potential pitfalls of using the kind of analytic approach adopted in *Healing Sylvia*, for example the tendency to 'objectify' and lose a sense of 'personal subjectivity.

Discussion points

- Why is it important to 'deconstruct' survivors' accounts of traumatic experiences?
- Do you agree that the therapeutic narrative prioritized in Fraser's autobiography results in a depoliticization of the issues around childhood sexual abuse?
- In what ways do the portrayal of the mother in Fraser's *My Father's House* link to historical and contemporary narrative constructions of the mother–daughter relationship? Discuss some of the problems with such portrayals (see Walters 1996; Woodward 1997).
- Does this kind of discursive/linguistic analysis achieve what we have earlier suggested a narrative style of analysis should achieve?

Key further reading

Davies, M.L. (1993) Healing Sylvia: accounting for the textual 'discovery' of unconscious knowledge, *Sociology*, 27(1): 110–20.

Davies, M.L. (1995) *Healing Sylvia: Childhood Sexual Abuse and the Construction of Identity*. London: Taylor & Francis.

Showalter, E. (1997) *Hystories: Hysterical Epidemics and Modern Culture* (Chapters 10 and 11). Basingstoke: Picador.

Warner, S. (1997) Review article of Davies' *Healing Sylvia*, Orr's *No Right Way* and Reder *et al.*'s *Beyond Blame, Feminism and Psychology* 3: 377–83.

*Woodward, K. (1997) Motherhood, identities, meanings and myths', in K. Woodward (ed.) *Identity and Difference*, pp. 7–63. London: Sage.

Notes on further reading

The Davies and Warner references constitute important further background to the material covered in this chapter. Likewise, the Showalter reference is interesting in terms of its coverage of narratives related to various 'epidemics' associated with contemporary culture such as childhood sexual abuse.

The *Woodward article constitutes a useful extension of ideas covered in this chapter with particular regard to social representations of motherhood found in contemporary society.

End note

1 It is important, however, to note that psychoanalytic narratives are not without their 'objectifying' tendencies, as has been shown throughout the course of this analysis of Fraser's text, and as will be discussed further in Chapter 8 (see Crossley 1998c).

7

Terminal illness: Surviving with a long-term HIV-positive diagnosis

The destination and map I had used to navigate before were no longer useful.
(Judith Zaruches, cited in Frank 1995: 1)

Introduction

This chapter focuses on the potentially traumatic effect that serious chronic or physical illness can have on a person's life. Research is reviewed which demonstrates how physical illness can shatter basic 'ontological' assumptions (related to time and routine narrative configuration) that a person holds about him/herself and the world around him/her. In particular, this chapter draws on research I have conducted with people living long term with an HIV-positive diagnosis. Although living with such an illness can have potentially devastating effects, the primary challenge for the individual is to reascribe a sense of meaning to his/her life. This is achieved through the use of different forms of narrative which enable the individual to make sense of his/her experience. The various forms of these narratives are documented in this chapter. The research is discussed in the context of more general work on 'illness narratives' in the social psychological and sociological literature.

Background

In recent years the fact that HIV infection provokes a multidimensional biological, psychological and social crisis for many of those affected has been
recognized (Adler Cohen 1990). Not only do those diagnosed HIV positive
face the impending possibility of severe illness, neuropsychiatric disorder
and death, they are also likely to suffer psychological problems related to
lack of self-esteem, loss of sense of control and meaning and depression,
exacerbated by a whole range of problems in interpersonal and social
relationships, including housing, financial and employment prospects (Beckham 1988; Weitz 1989; Sandstrom 1990; Viney 1991; Hildebrand 1992;
Cherry and Smith 1993; Schwartzberg 1993). In this chapter attention will
be focused mainly on the existential dimension of the HIV-positive person's
experience, with a view to exploring in more detail one of the fundamental
themes underpinning the mixture of psychological and psychosocial dilemmas confronting him/her, namely, the relationship of time to the HIV-
positive experience.

The material on which this chapter is based derives from research com-
missioned by the European Commission as part of its 'Europe Against AIDS'
programme on the psychological, emotional and service delivery needs of
long-term HIV-positive individuals (see Davies 1995b). This chapter draws
on in-depth semi-structured interviews I conducted between 1994 and 1996
with people who had been living for at least 5 years with an HIV-positive
diagnosis in Britain who belonged to a group called the National Long-Term
Survivors Group (NLTSG).

The disruption of routine
temporal orientation

As we have seen in previous chapters, our assumptions and orientations
towards time have a crucial impact on our psychological and social life,
affecting our sense of identity, self-concept and moral responsibility (Carr
1986; C. Taylor 1989; Elias 1992; Davies 1995a). Living life projecting into
the future provides us with a sense of basic (sometimes called 'ontological')
security insofar as it encourages the belief that events and actions can be
influenced and controlled and, relatedly, that our thoughts, actions and
behaviour are not simply fruitless or meaningless. It also encourages us to
live our lives in a more responsible fashion because we know we will be held
accountable for our actions, both by ourselves (in terms of our conscience),
and by others. It is important to make clear, however, that we are not necessarily consciously aware of the fact that we project into the future in this way.
Indeed, our taken-for-granted assumptions about and towards time are
made visible only when a 'shock' or a 'disruption' occurs, throwing them
into sharp relief (see Schutz 1962; Garfinkel 1984). An HIV-positive diagnosis constitutes a paradigmatic example of such a shock and thus presents

us with an opportunity to explore in more detail our routine temporal conceptions and the psychological consequences (both negative and positive) associated with their breakdown.

Many phenomenologically and existentially oriented writers have highlighted that time is basic and fundamental to an understanding of human existence. More specifically, the normal, routine temporal orientation of human beings has been characterized as one predominantly projecting into the future. Frankl (1984: 84), for instance, claimed that 'It is a peculiarity of man that he can only live by looking to the future – *sub specie aeternitatis*'. Ortega y Gasset (1953) similarly argued that 'Life is an operation which is done in a forward direction. We live towards the future, because to live consists inexorably in *doing*, in each individual life *making* itself' (p. 52, my emphasis). And the philosopher Jean-Paul Sartre wrote that 'Man is constantly outside of himself; in projecting himself, in losing himself outside of himself, he makes for man's existing . . . it is by pursuing transcendent goals that he is able to exist; man, being this state of passing beyond . . .' (Sartre 1947: 31). The implication of such a future orientation is that human beings generally care little for the present:

> Man cares nothing for the present, anticipating the future, finding it too slow in coming, as if one could make it come faster. Or calls back the past, to stop its rapid flight . . . so frivolous are we that we dream of the days which are not, and pass by without reflection those which alone exist. . . . The present generally gives us pain; one conceals it from one's sight because it afflicts one, or if it is pleasant there is regret to see it vanishing away. The present is never our end; the past and the future are our means, the future alone is our end. Thus, we never live, but hope to live. . . .
>
> (Pascal 1889: 24)

Much of the traumatic psychological impact associated with a serious, potentially terminal diagnosis such as HIV positivity, can be traced back to the disturbance and disruption of this fundamentally experienced sense of 'lived time'. When a person receives a terminal diagnosis they are immediately shocked out of the complacency of the assumed futurity of their existence and their whole conception of themselves, their life and their world is likely to undergo radical changes. As Van den Berg (1972: 4) explains, 'The beginning of every serious illness is a halt. Normal life ends. Another life takes its place. One suddenly becomes uncertain about things most taken for granted: faith and integrity of the body, of one's role in other people's lives and their role in one's own life, and faith in the future'.

In the face of imminent death, one's whole previously unquestioned orientation towards the future and related devaluation of the present is brought to light, appearing absurd in the new life context. What is the point in orienting towards and 'planning' for the future when one will not be alive to see the plans' fruition? Why not just live in the present rather than 'hoping to live' in the future? Hence:

> The horizon of time is narrowed. The plans of yesterday lose their meaning and importance. They seem more complicated, more exhausting, more foolish and ambitious than I saw them the day before . . . the past seems saturated with trivialities. It seems to me that I hardly ever tackled my real tasks. . . .
>
> (Van den Berg 1972: 28)

With such thoughts and feelings, the routine sense of lived time is reversed and the experience of the present is likely to become an end in itself, rather than simply a means to an end (one's future life), the reality of which has become increasingly uncertain. Hence, an HIV-positive diagnosis has the capacity to fundamentally disturb one of the central characteristics definitive of the contemporary human being's existence; the fact that s/he lives in and for the future.

It is, however, important not to be too pessimistic about the situation of the HIV-positive individual. This is because current scientific research findings and developments in triple combination therapies seem to bode well in terms of retarding the progression of HIV infection to AIDS (see Davies 1997). Having said that, however, such developments do not detract from the disturbing psychological situation faced by the HIV-positive individual. Indeed, it is not difficult to imagine how the vacillations of scientific endeavour may exacerbate the psychological trauma experienced by the individual, at one moment offering the prospect of success and hope for the future, at the next cruelly dashing those hopes with the apparent failure of 'another trial' and another 'new' form of treatment. The main aims of this chapter are to clarify the existential dimension of this experience and to explore some of the narratives which people use to manage and rationalize their situation.

Subjective experiences of long-term HIV positivity – losing a future?

The fact that an HIV-positive diagnosis, at least in the early years, condemns the individual to the present, disallowing the freedom of future projection, was evident in most accounts of the experience given by HIV-positive individuals. Many people mentioned that one of the main ways that being HIV positive had affected their lives was that it made it difficult to make any plans beyond 6 months, whether they were career, financial, family or more general plans. As one man explained:

> . . . [One of the] main things . . . that epitomises a person with HIV . . . (is that) as soon as you are diagnosed instantly your future is gone [clicks fingers], you have no normal existence of making plans, you can't even think about it, but it is just a reaction, your future is gone'.

> When you are a young man – the idea of dying of old age at 70, suddenly you've got the situation where you think, I might not make it to 30, suddenly your horizon becomes much closer, you just don't make

any long-term plans any more, everything is short-term, just in case. . . .'

The situation among people who have been living for 5 years or more with an HIV-positive diagnosis is, however, somewhat more complicated than this. What seems to be very disturbing in this situation is the uncertainty associated with the diagnosis. The average amount of time that people I researched had been living with an HIV-positive diagnosis was 9 years, which meant that most of them were diagnosed HIV positive in about 1985. At that time, very little was known about the progression of the disease and most people were led to believe that the diagnosis was terminal and that they were likely to die in the near future, between 1 and 2 years, although some doctors told their patients that they did not know how long they were expected to live. A large part of the problem for the HIV-positive individual is that s/he does not know what stance s/he should take towards the diagnosis. Is it best to 'realistically' accept 'the fact' that s/he will die in the very near future? But how near? In the words of one man, '. . . the doctors have been proved wrong once. They told me I would die within the year, but I am still here 10 years on. . . .' In addition, given the seemingly promising advances in scientific research regarding the identification of mechanisms mediating immune response to HIV infection, acceptance of the assumption of imminent death may seem premature and overly pessimistic.

On a more personal level, most people living with an HIV-positive diagnosis have a story to tell about a friend or a person whom they have known who simply 'gave up' the fight against the virus and was dead within a matter of months. They frequently claim that they are 'certain' that this is one of the main reasons why their friend or acquaintance died. Simultaneously, however, I got the impression that a nagging doubt prevails in the HIV-positive individual's mind. 'Does the way in which I think about this illness, my attitude towards it, really affect its course? Can I really exercise any control over whether I live or die?' Is this belief simply a 'delusion of reprieve', like the condemned man who, immediately before his execution, has the illusion that he might be reprieved at the very last minute (Frankl 1984). The following quotes capture some elements of the dilemma of uncertainty that the HIV-positive individual finds him/herself trapped in:

> . . . it is really weird because also *you don't have a direct OK*, you are HIV, you have AIDS, you know . . . you have a terminal illness, but, 'we *don't know when you are going to die* or *if you are going to die,* we don't know that'.

> You are given a death sentence . . . you realize you don't have as much time to waste, *that is not necessarily true but you get the feeling that is the case.* . . .

> I think every year is going to be my last, it is *not knowing* that is frightening more than nothing, not knowing if you are going to die in 6 months, or 6 years, or . . .

> . . . well *you don't know how long you are going to be*, but *there again nobody does*, you don't know how long, *nobody knows how long we have got, which is the most annoying thing.*

As is clear from these individuals, although they have received what is commonly considered to be a terminal diagnosis, at the same time they are also aware of the possibility that this might not be the case. In their words, one does not have a 'direct OK . . . you are going to die', or a 'death sentence' because, although it feels like this, it is not necessarily true. It is the uncertainty, the 'not knowing' whether one's death will be in '6 months or 6 years or . . .' that is 'more frightening than anything', or, in another man's words, 'the most annoying thing'. In this sense, the disrupted temporal orientation is analogous to other traumatic experiences such as imprisonment in a concentration camp. For example, recording his experiences in a death camp, Frankl (1984) wrote that '. . . the most depressing influence of all was that a prisoner could not know how long his term of imprisonment would be. He had been given no date for his release'. In other words, he 'lived a provisional existence of unknown limit'. As one of the quotes above points out with regard to the uncertainty of time and death, however, the HIV-positive individual does not really differ from the rest of the population, insofar as 'nobody knows how long they've got'.

Given this observation, in what sense *does* the individual living with an HIV-positive diagnosis differ from the rest of the population, particularly with regard to his/her orientation towards time and death? Few of us know when we are going to die but we all know *that* we are going to die at some unforeseen point. So, in what respect is our existential situation any different from that of the HIV-positive individual? Don't we all live 'a provisional existence of unknown limit'? It could be argued that the situation of the HIV-positive individual is analogous to people who are diagnosed as genetically predisposed to illnesses such as cancer and heart disease (although the predisposition is statistically far greater with regard to HIV infection), a situation that will become increasingly common in the future with the advance of the human genome project and the availability of genetic testing (see Nelkin and Tancredi 1990; Shapiro 1991; Wertz 1992; McLean 1994). All of these people live with a heightened awareness of the threat of serious illness, suffering and early death. Indeed, some authors such as Frank (1995: 9) have argued that this heightened consciousness of our own vulnerability is a characteristic feature of the contemporary 'postmodern' age in which the technical achievements of medicine have made it possible to live far longer with serious chronic illnesses (such as cancer, heart disease and so on). What people also have to learn to live with in these situations is the insecurity and heightened fear of death and the unknown that such illnesses introduce into their lives.

All of these experiences have the capacity to impose a permanent veil of what existentialist writers have called Angst (a kind of intense anxiety or dread) over a person's life. As we discussed in Chapter 3, Angst is often characterized as being like the experience of vertigo and the experience of groundlessness. In his classic work *Being and Time*, Heidegger (1962) explored how the prospect of death occasions Angst towards one's routine existence in the world, potentiating a new way to be, or a new mode of existence for the individual, namely, as a Being-Towards-Death. In the experiencing of Angst all 'entities within the world . . . sink away' (Heidegger 1962: 182) and the familiar world becomes 'uncanny' (*unheimlich*). The individual is no longer able to understand him/herself and his/her world in the previously familiar terms of 'how things have been publicly interpreted' or of how the individual him/herself interpreted them before. The individual feels that none of the values and commitments with which s/he finds him/herself embroiled in everyday life makes sense any more. Such a sense of Angst or crisis is evident in the following quotes from HIV-positive individuals:

> I think the most difficult thing to come to terms with in living with HIV, if you are going to be honest with yourself and acknowledge it, is that there are so many uncertainties. Suddenly you discover *things which you have been led to believe were certainties* can't be taken for granted any more, not just issues around health or relationships or your career or your economic position. *Suddenly they all become uncertainties* and that is the nearest I have come to feeling that *these supposed rules*, like set in stone or whatever, *no longer apply to you* and somehow you still kind of feel that *it is legitimate for the rest of the population to claim it is true for them, but suddenly it isn't for you*. . . .

And:

> . . . *absolutely everything*, everything that you have had in life *just breaks down, becomes dust*, powder, you know, and you become *completely naked and utterly lost*, you do not know what to do, *where did you come from, where do you go* and *where are you standing at that moment*, this is something indescribable and nobody can help you. You have to build up by yourself, it is an extremely difficult and helpless situation, it is very traumatic.

Both of these quotes refer to the relatively early 'crisis' stages of living with an HIV-positive diagnosis, a stage which generally falls within the first 2 to 4 years, after an early period of denial and prior to a more stable form of adaptation to living with the diagnosis. As is clear from the above comments, at this stage, the experience of Angst is very clear as these individuals attempt to adjust to the overwhelming knowledge that death is imminent. This overwhelming experience of Angst is probably a universal human experience and most individuals will face similar existential anxiety in the face of imminent non-being. In this respect, the HIV-positive individual's experience of this kind of anxiety is not unique and probably displays a typical response to the threat of impending disaster.

On the other hand, however, it has already been suggested that a characteristic experiential feature of the individual who has been living with an HIV-positive diagnosis for a substantial period of time, is that the imminent possibility of death is supplemented with the possibility that the death may not be as imminent or as inevitable as it at first seemed. The confusion and trauma resulting from this dilemma stem from the difficulty of sustaining two mutually contradictory life orientations or two 'ways of being'. The first involves an orientation towards death, a closing off from the future, a retraction from the 'busy-ness' of life and a reconciliation of oneself towards the end. The second, an orientation towards life, involves an opening and expanding on to the horizonal future, throwing oneself into the business of life and battling against the obstacles blocking one's path. Given that more or less every situation faced by individuals involves some element of orientation towards the future – whether in 'objective' reality – a future date for one's diary, or in subjective reality – thoughts, feelings or fantasies about the future – the trauma inflicted by the HIV-positive 'in-between' position is immense. This is why I referred earlier to the fact that an HIV-positive diagnosis imposes a semi-permanent veil of Angst on the individual's life. It is not as if such Angst is experienced in the fully blown, dramatic manifestation provided in the descriptions above. Rather, it exists in a more latent state, as a kind of festering sore or wound. The radical disturbance of the assumption of futurity introduced into a person's life with an HIV-positive diagnosis means that every event or situation may be experienced as a kind of jolt in which the natural orientation towards the future is suddenly perceived as illegitimate and inapplicable to the individual. It is with respect to the permanency, the latent ever-presentness, the intensified awareness of the experience of Angst that the HIV-positive individual's experience differs from that of the physically and psychically healthy population. Although such people may have occasional pangs of anxiety with regard to their potential non-existence, such Angst can, to a large extent, be 'anaesthetized' and kept at bay by various kinds of diversions. By contrast, the impact of an HIV-positive diagnosis (and other chronic, life-threatening illnesses such as cancer and heart disease) may have such an overwhelming effect on a person's life that diversions become less and less possible and merely another manifestation or painful reminder of the imminent non-existence that cannot be 'forgotten'.

Temporal orientation of people living with an HIV-positive diagnosis for more than 5 years

Although it is important to recognize the specific problems introduced into a person's existence with the advent of HIV infection, particularly their increased psychological vulnerability, it is also important to recognize that people develop various ways of thinking and dealing with their situation which enable them to adjust with varying degrees of effectiveness. One of their main tasks in this respect is to learn how to live in the face of their impending demise without allowing the anxiety and uncertainty to overwhelm them to such an extent that all meaning and happiness are robbed from their current existence. From my interview data, it was possible to characterize three different forms of temporal orientation adopted by individuals as part of their way of dealing with HIV positivity, some potentiating more healthy adaptation than others. These forms of temporal orientation can be categorized as 'living with a philosophy of the present', 'living in the future' and 'living in the empty present' (see Davies 1997). These temporal orientations form part and parcel of three more general narratives or stories that HIV-positive individuals make use of in telling the tale of their illness experience. These include: (1) the 'conversion/growth' story (sometimes also called the 'Internal' story); (2) the 'normalizing' story (sometimes also called the 'External' story); and (3) the story of 'loss' (Crossley 1999a). We will explore each of these in more detail later in this chapter.

Before doing so, however, it is important to reiterate that when people describe their stories in an interview context, they are not just doing so 'for the sake of description' (Frank 1995: 55). Drawing on the social constructivist approach outlined in Chapter 2 and as discussed in Chapter 5, we will work with the assumption that the interview transcripts from which these concepts are derived are not naïve 'receptacles' of meaning, as if the interviewees were simply providing an 'accurate' description of their feelings and adaptations. Rather, in the process of description, the individual is actually doing things such as presenting and constituting a certain identity with all the implications that has for related issues of responsibility and morality (see Williams 1984; Potter and Wetherell 1987; Silverman 1993; Davies 1995a; Crossley 1997b, 1998b, 1999a; Lucas 1997; Radley 1997; Yardley 1997; Crossley and Crossley 1998). As Frank (1995) makes clear, when a person tells the story of their illness, a 'self is being formed in what is told', both for themselves and for others. 'The act of telling is a dual reaffirmation. Relationships with others are reaffirmed and the self is reaffirmed. Serious illness requires both reaffirmations' (Frank 1995: 56). As we shall see in this chapter, each of the different stories told by HIV-positive individuals incorporates a characteristic set of themes, images and metaphors which serve to construct the experience of HIV infection in very different ways, with radical implications for the individual's adaptation to life with an HIV-positive diagnosis.

'Living with a philosophy of the present' and the 'conversion/growth' story

Many existentialists have written about the way in which a human being's consciousness of the finiteness of their life (the fact that they are going to die) constitutes a precondition for their appreciation of its unique value and meaning. According to Sartre, for example, a person's finitude is a necessary condition of his/her freedom and individuality:

> Death is the limit, but also a constituent of freedom. . . . If a being were endowed with temporal infinity, he could realise all his possibilities . . . he would disappear with respect to both individuality (the realisation of some possibilities to the exclusion of others) and to freedom (dangerous and irremediable choice of certain possibilities).
>
> (Sartre 1947: 135)

How would things be if we were to live for ever?: 'Death is a quality of life, *the* quality of life, the index of value of human existence. As a march is completed by the last milestone, so is life completed by death . . .' (Van den Berg 1972: 54, original emphasis); 'From this nothingness [i.e. death] alone can I obtain my assurance of true existence' (Jaspers, cited in Cooper 1990: 133). From this perspective, the suffering and pain inflicted on me by my awareness and fear of the inevitable end to my existence, my primordial sense of insecurity, is necessary for my development: 'Life is our reaction to the basic insecurity which constitutes its substance. It is, therefore, an extremely serious matter for a person to find themselves surrounded by apparent securities, for consciousness of security *kills life* . . .' (Ortega y Gasset 1953: 303–7, original emphasis).

It is in this sense that the 'provisional existence' of the HIV-infected individual and the loss of a hold on the securities of 'routine life', may lend an opportunity for some individuals to achieve spiritual growth and an appreciation of new values and meaning in the context of learning to live with HIV. For example, looking back over his life prior to HIV, the individual may feel that he was far too future-oriented, to such an extent that he never enjoyed the present and therefore never experienced any sense of real meaning or value in his life. He may feel that he was previously totally preoccupied with matters of career, learning, esteem, making money and, as a consequence, was inclined to forget the 'little things' in life that are actually important. In this sense, the illness of the body can be a condition for a soundness of mind which the healthy person easily misses (Van den Berg 1972: 72–3).

Twenty-one of the people I interviewed (out of a total of 38), had experienced this kind of renewed understanding of their concepts of time, meaning and values. Some examples are provided below:

> . . . Before this diagnosis I think *I would have lived in the future*, looking to the future, but I think since I have had this diagnosis I'm much more *living in the present, here and now, today and tonight*. . . . I think it is [a good thing] because it means I am getting the most from every moment as it is actually unfolding rather than, oh next week I will be feeling much better or next month I will, you know, I will have to save X amount of money. . . . I don't think like that any more, *I just live in the here and now*. Or I try to live in the here and now, I think *it is a struggle every day*. . . .

One of the things that I do now which I didn't use to do was that every morning when I wake up I look out of the window and I say, thank you God or whoever, what a lovely morning. It wasn't something that I ever did before but I think each morning, I have to *take each morning as it arrives* . . . so, do you know any of Sartre's writings, you know, Jean-Paul Sartre, the existentialist, so each sort of section, each day, each sort of time is measured in that way I suppose, I say 'well, I've got today'.

. . . We're brought up in a culture which says there *will be another tomorrow* in which you might experience something which is either *bigger or better in some kind of way,* or further away or you will earn more or whatever. And therefore, it seemed to me that . . . *a lot of today was wasted* and I am, I am much more into a philosophy which is about, *I couldn't guarantee there was going to be a tomorrow for me,* I did actually become aware that *the now* often had *tremendous qualities and tremendous potential* that *I previously ignored in my haste to be tomorrow before it arrived* . . . talking to somebody once, they said, 'but isn't that the philosophy that Buddhists hold dear?' and that was a revelation to me at the time . . . somehow, amazingly, it hasn't affected my ability to work for things which obviously require that I have an immediate and long-term future. So, I kind of feel like it has been a productive experience in the sense that I now get the best of both worlds, where before there was just one world on offer. . . .

I think it is up to each individual to make their own meaning and I think the meaning is very simple and I think we look for it to be some amazing kind of, we look for very complex answers to why we are here and I think it is very simple. It is just about *moments of connecting with somebody,* moments of love being reciprocated or moments of beauty that you share, or a child's first steps, or whatever. It is *those moments that I really feel now* . . . just like, I actually enjoy the moments when I am miserable now *because I know they don't last,* just like those moments of happiness don't last and . . . *that is why they are special really, because they don't last. Because if they are there all the time they wouldn't be special* . . . and I think *you can live a whole lifetime and maybe you can have just two moments of whatever and it is worth it.* And I feel really lucky because it feels like I have a lot of those moments now. . . .

As is clear from these quotes, for these people the HIV-positive diagnosis has, in a curious sense, provided a certain feeling of liberation from the shackles of everyday existence in which one is always fighting towards the future. This sense of freedom derives from the fact that the HIV-positive individual is, to a certain extent, freed from the responsibility of having to construct a meaningful long-term plan for his/her life and, subsequently, is enabled to enjoy the present for what it is, rather than being totally preoccupied with distant future possibilities.

This temporal orientation 'living with a philosophy of the present' was associated with a more general cultural story used by HIV-positive individuals to make sense of their illness experience. This is the story of 'conversion/growth'. In order to illustrate some of the characteristic features of this story, we will look briefly at the case-study of Stephen, a 48-year-old gay man who can be seen as a paradigmatic example of the 'conversion/growth' story. Stephen had been living with an HIV-positive diagnosis for 10 years at the time of his interview. He built up an image of himself as a person who had recently 'seen the light' and was in the process of converting himself into a different kind of person as a consequence of this. A number of interrelated themes formed part and parcel of this story.

The first theme centred around a heightened awareness of the connection between the physical and psychological dimensions of HIV disease. For example, Stephen was insistent throughout his interview of the importance of 'your own level of stress and your own physical and mental health exercise as a joint exercise other than treating one side or the other'. A related theme was the connection (in Stephen's perception, the 'disjunction') between 'emotional needs' on the one hand, and 'material satisfaction'/ 'societal definitions' on the other. Stephen felt that he had been far too oriented in the past to the latter aims and goals, with the consequence that he had failed to respond adequately to his 'emotional needs': 'I was an accountant', he said, 'or I was *this* or I was *that*'. He had 'objectified' himself in terms of social definitions. Hence, 'my stress levels began to increase enormously'.

The emphasis placed on emotional and psychological needs from within the 'conversion/growth' story is linked to the influence of therapy. For instance, using imagery resonant of psychotherapy, Stephen built up a direct analogy between the early days of his HIV-positive diagnosis and his childhood. He characterized his childhood situation as one which was without 'love and safety and compassion' insofar as he had to live with a mother who was 'an enemy as opposed to a friend'. Stephen illustrated this with the poignant image of his mother taking away his asthma inhaler and his subsequent feeling of rising panic and stress which led to the onset of attacks. These events were important, according to Stephen, because they left an 'imprint of denial' on his brain. When he was diagnosed HIV positive he 'immediately felt there was an enemy inside my body'. But this analogy with his disturbed past led to Stephen's determination to convert his experience into something new, rather than simply repeating past patterns of destruction. He expressed this resolve when he said to himself: 'no, I am not going to live with this . . . and the minute I started to think like this I began to behave differently'.

A third, related theme was also important; the link to 'consumerism' or 'empowerment'. In a curious mixture of self-care and military imagery, Stephen constructed a picture of a battle in progress. 'I am trying', he said, 'to find a different approach . . . trying to find out number one . . . arming myself with information which empowers me and making choices to suit my own personality'. This theme of empowerment also linked back to Stephen's distinction between his emotional and material needs. His story once again took on a strong tone of 'conversion' in which it became apparent that Stephen perceived things radically differently from the way he did in the past. He used to define his 'importance in life' by 'the title I held in my working position', but that led to an 'empty mental tool box' and parts of himself that he had 'locked and hidden away from'. His 'dreams and hobbies' had been 'put in a bag', 'stored on a shelf' in 'a little backroom in your mind, the unconscious'. As part of his empowerment, Stephen felt the need to retrieve those aspects of himself.

These three interrelated themes, the connection between mental and physical (holism between mind and body), the disjunction between psychological/emotional and material/social needs, and consumerism/empowerment, predominated in Stephen's narrative and are representative of the 'conversion/growth' story more generally. Stephen lived out this story in relation to many areas of his life such as his approach towards managing and understanding his illness, his work and emotional life. His 'philosophy of the present' orientation towards time is one manifestation of this more general 'conversion/growth' story.

'Living in the future' and the 'normalizing' story

Seven of the HIV-positive individuals interviewed displayed a temporal orientation which, in contrast to the above 'philosophy of the present', embodied a strategy of minimization or 'active denial' insofar as they were determined not to let their HIV-positive diagnosis 'ruin' the plans that they held for the future. The following quotes are examples of this orientation:

> As far as I am concerned *I am going to live as long as anyone else* . . . they were saying some people will probably live about 25 years . . . according to some research . . . it has only been around for about 14 years, who knows . . . some people might get infected when they are 20 and live till they are 80, they might, you don't know, who knows? . . .

> It has not affected plans for the future . . . *I plan for the future, I plan for retirement* and things like that, I have got my own pension schemes, *I have got no intentions of going*, you know, as far as I am concerned I shall, I am retiring early and enjoying myself . . . as far as I am concerned I am not going to, until somebody tells [me] different, *I am going to be here until, you know, until I am 90* or whatever, to my natural time . . .

> . . . *I am determined to live as long as I can* . . . I want to see the kid go to school, do all sorts of things and grow up, watch it pass a driving test and other things. Lisa said, you know, try and think of us having

children and then in years to come, grandchildren, and try and picture that . . . the last couple of years I am getting stronger each, all the time, doing more things, I am looking into more things, you know . . . if we have a baby I will need a bigger house . . . I might start my own business up next year or towards the end of next year or whenever . . . I am looking into that, if that all works out I will be pleased, one little sprog on my knee, getting the house all sorted out, there is always something to do anyway. . . .

As is clear from these examples, this way of being is totally different from the adoption of the 'philosophy of the present' as a mode of living. Rather than accepting the possibility that one is likely to die in the near future and compensating this acceptance by developing a philosophy and a mode of life which celebrates the present moment, these people refuse to relinquish their routine future orientation, thus refusing to entertain the possibility of the imminence of their death.

This temporal orientation 'living in the future', was associated with a more general cultural story used by HIV-positive individuals to make sense of their illness experience. This is the story of 'normalization'. Twenty-five-year-old John, a heterosexual, married man, a haemophiliac who was infected by contaminated blood products in 1983, can be seen as representative of this cultural story.

Throughout his interview John constructed an image of himself as a person who had been minimally affected by his HIV-positive diagnosis. He continuously made use of rhetorical strategies which enabled him to deny, minimize and normalize the effects that having an HIV-positive diagnosis had had on various aspects of his life. For example, he asserted that since being diagnosed he had had 'no problems', 'nothing' wrong with him and denied undertaking any specific actions to take care of himself and his health. He claimed that he didn't take pills and that his diet, like many other areas of his life, remained 'the same as it always has been'. John made clear his determination to continue minimizing the effects of being HIV positive in response to a question regarding whether he had ever been on medication. 'No,' he said, 'and I don't think I ever will be either.' He clearly resented the intrusion of medication and medical care into his otherwise 'normal' life.

John constructed a similar image of his sexual life. Given that HIV is a sexually transmissible disease, it is probably legitimate to expect that most HIV-positive individuals would feel some degree of emotional anxiety regarding sexual relationships. John's response served to shatter any such assumption. He said that he got 'pissed off' because he always had to have protected sex with his wife: 'it really gets on my nerves sometimes'. This response again served to normalize John's position with regard to his sexual relationships. In effect, his claim denied the seriousness of the situation by demonstrating that the main thing he was concerned about was the diminution of his basic sexual pleasures.

At first sight, John's orientation towards work appeared contradictory with regard to his attempt to normalize his situation because he talked about his determination to finish work. This may seem incongruent with the idea of continuing to live as normal a life as possible. When I picked up on this point during the interview John responded in a way that provided some insight into his moral vision by asserting the 'sort of person' he was. 'I won't stop working', he claimed, 'I don't intend to sit at home and waste away', 'I'm just not that sort of person'. Rather, he always has to be 'doing' things, always 'keeping busy'. His main concerns in contemplating giving up paid work were very practical. John assumed the stereotypical male breadwinner role. He was responsible for his wife and 'we can't move without my wage'. Consequently, John was forced to keep on working until such a time that they could afford to move. John's concerns were very much the concerns of the 'normal' working person. He hated his job and would give it up at the first opportunity, money permitting.

When John was asked questions about how being HIV positive had affected his plans for the future, a question which assumes that the HIV-positive individual will, in some way, whether for good or ill, be 'existentially' affected by the diagnosis, he asserted a denial of such assumptions. 'It hasn't', he replied. John proceeded to illustrate this by purposively listing all the things he had done or would be doing in the future: '*I plan* for the future'; '*I plan* for retirement'; '*I have got* my own pension schemes'; '*I have got* no intentions of going'; '*I am not* going . . . until I am 90 or whatever my natural time'. John's 'no-nonsense' philosophy was further highlighted when he was asked what he thought had kept him living healthily for so long: 'I haven't got a clue', he said, and clearly did not see the problem worthy of speculation. It 'must', though, he claimed, be something he was 'doing', so whatever it was, he would 'just carry on doing it' and 'hopefully, it will keep on working'. When John was asked about his feelings about death and dying he characteristically denied that he had 'ever' been scared: 'If I am going to die I am going to die, I just hope everybody enjoys the party afterwards'.

The predominant images and metaphors used by John, as representative of the 'normalizing' story, were those of 'doing', 'carrying on as normal', 'being sensible' about the whole thing, 'keeping busy', 'working', 'not letting it get to you'. This story was embodied and lived out in terms of John's attitude and orientation towards drugs and medications, his body, his sexual life, his relationship with his wife, his work life and his planning for the future.

'Living in the empty present' and the story of 'loss'

Ten people who were interviewed had not been able to compensate for the loss of their routine understanding of themselves and their place in the world by developing a 'philosophy of the present' or by 'minimizing' the impact of the diagnosis on their temporal perception and future plans. These people can be characterized as 'living in the empty present'. Examples of this approach are provided below:

> It makes you want to play each day as it comes to a certain degree . . . I never look much further than 12 months now which is really strange, *it just clouds my perception of time*. It makes me think, you know, *don't go any further* than a year, Jamie, just in case. You *could fall ill*, something could happen to *spoil it*, so just do it slowly. . . . It is not easy, especially when you are brought up to plan and sort of, you know, plan your life ahead of you. . . .

> All I have got there at the moment is worries and *my only plans are to really remain well* and they are not plans as a whole. . . .

> . . . I suppose *I am constantly mentally planning for the inevitable* . . . [I feel] . . . sadness more than anything . . . hurting the ones you love, *not being able to live as you have done, planning for the future*, having something to aim for, missing out on the nephews and nieces growing up. Silly things like planting the garden at the beginning of summer and thinking 'am I going to see it at the end?' . . . I mean I have never had a garden before, I wouldn't mind but I never before this last year did any gardening. I know to a degree it makes sense but to a degree doesn't, but it was important to me to actually go out and buy some daffodil bulbs, some tulip bulbs, some crocuses and get the garden planted and make sure the dog didn't dig them up. Putting them in and thinking, *'am I going to see them?'* . . .

> I don't think of the future as in what is going to happen in a year's time. *My future seems to have stopped when Mark died* because *I am on my own and just live from day to day* . . . it has affected me because *I know I am not going to get old*, I want to see the kids, I have seen the baby walk the first time, for instance, the best thing that could ever happen to me now is seeing him walking into the juniors, but it is, you know, you don't know if it is going to happen. So it's . . . *I try not to think too far ahead because if I build my hopes up too high* . . . you know, I just live from week to week.

In these examples it is possible to see the damaging effects of an inability to project into the future, to live with hopes, possibilities and aspirations. When this ability is shattered by trauma such as HIV positivity, the present is held on to tightly as if it were the only thing left; it seems vital, in the absence of a foreseeable future, for the individual to cling desperately to what is currently available and to build some sense of security around that. The main problem with doing this is that the security the individual builds for him/herself is comparable to that of a prison. The self-imposed limitations the individual places on him/herself mean that the potentialities of the individual are radically reduced in order to save what is left. This is clear in the above quotes in which numerous people state that they do not like to think about, plan or commit themselves to future possibilities because they are afraid of disappointment. The anxiety associated with such fears has the implication that they fail to commit themselves to various projects and possibilities, and therefore lose all sense of meaning and coherence in their lives. Their lives become a fruitless attempt to maintain the status quo, however futile that status quo may seem to be.

Another damaging aspect of the absence of futurity and projection is the increased focus on the past, a futile desire to 'have things as they used to be' and a dwelling on 'what could have been'. This perspective is evident when people speak wishfully in the past tense, of 'not being able to live as I have done', and of futile wishes such as 'I would love to have my three score years and 10'. Other studies of traumatic experiences such as internment in concentration camps (Frankl 1984: 48) and survivors of the A-bomb in Hiroshima (Lifton 1968) have illustrated how such an occupation with the past to the detriment of the future rapidly deteriorates into a loss of sense of meaning in life and subsequent mental and physical decay. It is perhaps not surprising that the few HIV-positive individuals who expressed suicidal thoughts all adopted the temporal perspective of 'living in the empty present', as is evident in the quotes below:

> Sometimes *I probably even hope for it* [death] . . . because the longer it goes on *the harder it seems to be.* Just *more of a struggle* each day. Sometimes *I don't think it is worth it.* I have actually attempted suicide twice . . . I just got really depressed about being HIV . . . and I just thought *it would be easier to end it all.* . . .

> *I just get so sad* and just think, please let me die, you now, *I don't care.* . . .

> I think really, I think really, I think I want to die, I think, you know, my life has shown me lots and many things, some have been very good, some of them have been very bad and I think I have had a good life actually but death . . . spiritually I think you know, that I just want to get to the other side as quickly as I can because I feel my life at the moment is just, *I have got nothing really to live for*, I feel I have, I don't know, I just feel, *I feel really sad*, yes . . . *I feel I have had enough, I am ready to go,* I feel I have had enough, you know when I get this feeling, I don't know, it is not very good. . . .

The temporal orientation 'living in the empty present' was associated with a more general cultural story used by HIV-positive individuals to make sense of their illness experience. This is the story of 'loss'. Craig, a 34-year-old gay man who had been living with an HIV-positive diagnosis for 9 years at the time of the interview, is a paradigmatic example of this cultural story.

Throughout his interview Craig presented himself as a person who had lost his way. He drew a stark contrast between what his life used to be like, the kind of person he used to be, and what his life was like now. This was evident from the very opening stages of the interview in response to questions about how being HIV positive had affected his health. He responded with comments such as: 'I have been feeling a lot worse *than I used to do*', 'I have been feeling very tired, lethargic and depressed' and 'basically, I am, I don't feel as well as I used to'. Craig repetitively reproduced this contrast between 'healthy past' and 'ill present' throughout the interview.

The predominant images built up by Craig were those of 'insularity', 'withdrawal', 'barriers' and being 'cloistered'. He created a picture of his life as one in which he had more or less been taken over by the disease, in which he succumbed to 'its' dictates. For example, when asked what he did to take care of his health, he said that he tried to 'eat and sleep well', did not 'drink to excess' and had basically 'slowed down' his lifestyle. (Note the contrast between Craig and John. John, 'normalizing' his life, claimed that he had not cut down on any of these things.) Craig saw his physician 'every month' for 'the blood test and any symptoms *there are*'. This phrase revealed a great deal about Craig's orientation towards his HIV infection. He did not go to the GP to check for the *possibility* of symptoms, that is to check *if* any symptoms were present; rather, his statement revealed his assumption that symptoms *will* exist ('any symptoms there are').

With regard to his social life, Craig said that he just wanted 'to hide away'. His cloistered existence was also revealed in his feeling that he did not want to tell people about the diagnosis: 'The moment you say something . . . you seem to be on a slippery slope down, the beginning of the end. . . .' Craig's lack of words, his inability to speak to other people about his diagnosis, formed part and parcel of his more general withdrawal from the world, into himself. His fear of the 'slippery slope down' into the realm of other people was also revealed in his need to continuously have 'the barriers' up around him. Craig claimed that he was 'far more insular than *I used to be*'. 'I don't', he said, 'have a wide circle of friends *any more*'. 'I think the KS lesions are probably the biggest thing now. If *I hadn't got them I might* have a little more confidence.' And in relation to his work life Craig once more drew contrasts between the past and the present: 'I think that *had I not got HIV I would be* more outgoing, a little more assertive than I am.'

From this brief analysis, then, it is clear that Craig lived out the story of 'loss' in relation to many areas of his life such as his approach towards managing and understanding his illness, his work and emotional life. His 'empty present' orientation towards time is simply one manifestation of this more general story of loss.

What do these experiences show us about the structure of our everyday experience?

So far in this chapter we have characterized the three main 'temporal orientations' of a sample of people living relatively long term with an HIV-positive diagnosis, and how they connect to three more general cultural narratives. To recap, these are: (1) 'living in the future' and the 'normalizing' story; (2) living with a 'philosophy of the present' and the 'conversion/growth' story; and (3) 'living in the empty present' and the story of 'loss'. These stories are similar to other forms of meaning documented in the literature on long-term HIV/AIDS survival (Schwartzberg 1993). There are also some interesting studies of narratives related to other illness conditions (see Early 1982; Brody 1987; Kleinman 1988; Robinson 1990; Viney and Bousfield 1991; Frank 1993, 1995; del Vecchio Good *et al.* 1994; Farmer 1994; Garro 1994; Good and del Vecchio Good 1994; Radley 1994).

Returning to the central concern of this book, in what way do these experiences of HIV-positive individuals shed light on the routine narrative configuration of human experience? They show very clearly, as we discussed in Chapter 3, that our experience as human beings is one in which we are constantly struggling to maintain coherence and order in the face of 'an ever-threatening, impending chaos at all levels, from the smallest project to the overall "coherence of life" ' (Carr 1986: 91). For example, those individuals who made use of either the 'conversion/growth' story or the 'normalizing' story were both attempting to retain some sense of creative meaning, project and aim, despite the realization that their demise may be imminent. Of course, they did this in very different ways, as is clear from the cases of Stephen and John described earlier in this chapter. John, for instance, retained a sense of coherence by just 'carrying on' as usual, 'doing' all of the activities he normally does, planning his and his family's future life ahead of them. Stephen, by contrast, felt that it was necessary to take on board the spiritual implications that his diagnosis had for him and change his life and orientation towards the future accordingly.

Although incorporating very different strategies, both of these modes of formulating positive meaning help the individual to retain, in Lifton's (1968) terms, a sense of 'symbolic immortality'. What this basically means is that the individual, in the face of inevitable biological death, needs to maintain an inner sense of continuity with what has gone before and what will go on after his/her own existence. This need is achieved through the various stories depicted in this chapter. Finding a way towards creative meaning despite the impending threat of death and the meaninglessness of life in the light of one's own demise, is perhaps what Heidegger meant by his claim that the anticipation of death creates the condition for authentic existence and the development of 'Being-as-a-whole' (Heidegger 1962: 264).

But these experiences also show us, as is clear in the story of 'loss', what happens when we find ourselves unable to sustain this fight for the maintenance of a sense of coherence. From these interviews, I got the distinct impression that people 'living in the empty present' had literally lost the 'will' to live. The threat of death had left them bereft of creative possibilities and the determination to sustain any coherent, positive sense of meaning and value to their lives. If the end is near what is the point in 'struggling', 'caring', 'hurting' or 'hoping'? It is in this sense that the group who 'live in the empty present' fail to achieve the dynamic sense of connection between past, present and future and thus their lives become locked in a prison closed to possibilities, simultaneously creating a hell of the present.

Personal experience and narratives

The concept of narrative and the three specific stories identified in this chapter are also broadly congruent with some of the findings in other studies addressing the way in which individuals adjust and make sense of illness. For example, these narratives are similar to the 'styles' of adjustment previously identified by Radley and Green (1987) in their study of chronic illness. The 'normalizing' story, for instance, is similar to Radley and Green's 'active denial' adjustment style, the story of 'loss' to the 'resignation' adjustment style, and the 'conversion/growth' story is analogous to the 'secondary gain' adjustment style. The conception of the process of adjustment captured by Radley's concept of 'style' is also pertinent to this analysis (Radley 1994, 1997). 'Styles' of adjustment, like 'narratives', are not reducible to individual qualities or personal traits. As Williams (1996: 33) argues, narratives 'exist in and through mouths, bodies and their techniques'. How the individual deals with illness also depends on the presence of significant others, how they respond to the illness, and other resources in the individual's specific life context. Hence, the concept of narrative used in this chapter attempts to convey, in the same way as Radley's concept of 'style', the idea that long-term adjustment to HIV infection incorporates a personal, experiential dimension which is embodied in terms of certain physical orientations to the world, as well as having a social dimension insofar as that experience is framed within cultural ways of making sense.

For instance, John's 'normalizing' response to his condition formed part and parcel of his life with wife, based on a traditional male-as-breadwinner model. His adaptations consisted of attempts to maintain this structure to as great a degree as possible. By contrast, Stephen's desire to achieve greater emotional and spiritual fulfilment, to 'find out number one', as he put it, took place in the aftermath of bereavement. Stephen's relatively long-term partner had died of AIDS two years previously and it was partly in relation to such events that Stephen felt the need to commit himself to the achievement of psychological growth. Craig's retreat into his cloistered and closeted world in the context of HIV infection remained consistent with the rest of his life, in which he had hidden the fact that he was gay from his parents and the community he currently lived in. These circumstances permitted him to retreat from the world of the 'healthy' into his 'sick' world of infection, rejection and guilt.

The connection drawn between narratives and the personal experience of HIV infection in this chapter bring us back to some of the questions of 'realism' that we first addressed in Chapter 2. Although in this chapter we have expressed a 'social constructivist' concern to examine the kind of selves and identities that people are constructing when using certain narratives, at the same time we have worked with the 'realist' assumption that these narratives also have the capacity to 'reflect' the realities of traumatizing personal experiences. In this sense, we have assumed that there is a congruent relationship between talking about life with an HIV-positive diagnosis and actually living that life. As we have previously argued, although such realist assumptions may seem problematic from a social constructivist perspective, they constitute a crucial premise for researchers interested in the social, cultural and psychological arena of health and are entirely necessary for the 'applied aspirations' of social scientists working within the health arena if they are to 'influence practices and policies outside research psychology' (Abraham and Hampson 1996: 226; Smith 1996).

Narratives and contemporary culture

Finally in this chapter it is important to look at the role played by more general social and cultural influences on the narratives available to individuals living with an HIV-positive diagnosis (and chronic illness more generally). Since the 1950s in Western societies much illness has become a 'political' issue insofar as the predominant biomedical paradigm underlying the conceptualization and treatment of various kinds of illness has been challenged. Patient rights groups and civil liberties organizations have campaigned against the 'passive' role allocated to patients by traditional medicine and have demonstrated for the right to be treated not just as patients, but as people too. This fight has been especially strong and vociferous with regard to HIV/AIDS, partly due to the marginalized and stigmatized nature of those groups whom the disease has mainly affected: gay men, blacks, drug users, haemophiliacs and prostitutes.

The narratives depicted in this chapter bear traces of this personal and cultural fight for patients to be treated as something more than a biological entity infected by disease. They also constitute different ways of expressing this fight, alternative forms of conceiving and dealing with the 'personal as political' in contemporary culture (see also Chapter 6; Davies 1995a). For example, linked to the 'normalizing' story's characteristic refusal to accept the limitations imposed by HIV infection is a politics of refusal; a refusal to accept HIV infection as a handicapping condition which is sometimes expressed in a commitment to traditional forms of 'active' politics whose aim is to achieve equality by campaigning against discrimination, changing legislation and policy, and improving the civil rights and liberties of HIV/AIDS-infected people.

This story of 'normalization' is analogous to what Frank (1995) calls a 'restitution' narrative. According to Frank, such 'restitution' narratives are characteristic of modernity and constitute the 'culturally preferred narrative' in contemporary culture. Basically, such narratives incorporate the 'modernist expectation that for every suffering there is a remedy' (Frank 1995: 80). This 'remedy' could be in the form of some sort of medical intervention which 'cures' the disease, or some form of political activism which 'solves' the problem by implementing a particular policy or vision. The important feature of such restitution narratives is that they incorporate the assumption that by *acting* on the world in some way, a 'solution' will be forthcoming. So John, for instance, believes that if he just keeps on 'working' and 'doing what he is doing', things will work out all right at the end of the day. Another example of such a 'restitution' narrative is the 'old-style' feminist narrative incorporated in certain parts of Fraser's *My Father's House* (discussed in the last chapter). Incorporated in this narrative is a belief that if women come together as a collective group committed to the diminution of patriachal power, a 'solution' to male exploitation will eventually be found and implemented. Frank (1995) is critical of such narratives and we will explore further in Chapter 8 why this is so. For the time being it is sufficient simply to note the connections between the narratives depicted in this chapter and those characterized by Frank.

The 'conversion/growth' story is linked to a more recent way of conceptualizing the idea that the 'personal is political' . Analogous to the dominant therapeutic narrative evident in Fraser's *My Father's House* (see Chapter 6), this involves more of a focus on the 'inner' or psychological dimension of experience and a commitment to achieving greater self-understanding, awareness and progression. The proliferation of psychological interventions such as psychotherapy and various kinds of 'healing' approaches into Western culture in recent years is testimony to the increasing popularity of this narrative. The 'conversion/growth' narrative is also analogous to what Frank (1995) calls a 'quest' narrative, in which illness is portrayed as a journey, the individual experiences crisis and change, and is able finally to open themselves to the contingency and mystery of life. We have already expressed some degree of scepticism with regard to such narratives in Chapter 6. In the next chapter we will return to address some of these issues in more detail.

Finally, it is important to note that the negativity and frequently suicidal thoughts and feelings expressed from within the story of 'loss' express an inability, or lack of desire, to appropriate the predominant forms of sense-making available in contemporary culture. This is analogous to Frank's 'chaos narrative' in which 'the modernist bulwark of remedy, progress and professionalism cracks to reveal vulnerability, futility and impotence' (Frank 1995: 97). Frank (1995) argues that 'If the restitution narrative promises possibilities of outdistancing or outwitting suffering, the chaos narrative tells how easily any of us can be sucked under'. Because of the chaotic sequencing of events and the lack of narrative configuration in the chaos narrative, Frank argues that this is not really a narrative at all but an 'anti-narrative'. And the 'anti-narrative', like the story of loss, is one 'of time without sequence, telling without mediation and speaking about oneself without being fully able to reflect on oneself' (p. 98).

Chapter summary

By the end of this chapter you should understand the following concepts and issues:

- Some of the basic facts regarding HIV infection.
- The way in which serious or terminal illness disrupts our routine, taken-for-granted temporal orientation, that is our continuous projection into the future and the implications that has for our sense of meaning and security.
- The subjective experience of living long-term with an HIV-positive diagnosis, for example the Angst and uncertainty.
- Potential similarities and differences between the subjective experience of being diagnosed HIV positive and other 'illness' conditions in contemporary society.
- The three main ways of adapting to 'shattered assumptions' regarding time and their relationship to dominant cultural 'stories' or 'narratives':
  (1) 'Living with a philosophy of the present' and the 'conversion/growth' story
  (2) 'Living in the future' and the 'normalizing' story
  (3) 'Living in the empty present' and the story of 'loss'.
- The link between personal narratives and life circumstances.
- The connection between personal narratives and wider cultural narratives.

Discussion points

- What does the HIV-positive experience (or experiences of other serious/chronic illnesses) reveal about our routine orientation towards time? What are the implications, both positive and negative, of this routine orientation?
- Do you think one of the ways of adapting to the HIV-positive experience is likely to be more beneficial than others? In what ways? Why?
- How might a person's appropriation of a particular narrative or story link into their life circumstances?

Key further reading

Crossley, M.L (1997a). The divided self: the destructive potential of a HIV positive diagnosis, *Journal of Existential Analysis*, 8(2): 72–94.

Crossley, M.L. (1997b) 'Survivors' and 'victims': long-term HIV positive individuals and the ethos of self-empowerment, *Social Science and Medicine*, 45(12): 1863–73.

Crossley, M.L. (1998a) Women living with a long-term HIV positive diagnosis: problems, concerns and ways of ascribing meaning, *Women's Studies International Forum*, 21(5): 521–33.

Crossley, M.L. (1998b) A man dying with AIDS: psychoanalysis or existentialism?, *Journal of Existential Analysis*, 9(2): 35–57.

Crossley, M.L. (1999) Making sense of HIV infection: discourse and adaptation to life with a HIV positive diagnosis, *Health*, 3(1): 95–119.

Davies, M.L. (1997) Shattered assumptions: time and the experience of long-term HIV positivity, *Social Science and Medicine*, 44(5): 561–71.

Frank, A. (1993) The rhetoric of self-change: illness experience as narrative, *The Sociological Quarterly*, 34(1): 39–52.

Notes on further reading

All of the above references explore in detail how people living with life-threatening illnesses use various narratives, with differing degrees of adaptive success, to help them make sense of their diagnosis. Any of these readings could be used as the basis of a seminar session to explore further the ideas disussed in the chapter.

8

Contemporary ways of making meaning

Social and cultural critiques of the 'therapeutic' narrative

In this book so far we have looked at how different contemporary narratives or stories have been used to make sense of personal and traumatizing experiences. We have suggested, sometimes more explicitly than others, that certain stories are more 'adequate' or plausible than others. For example, in Chapter 6, through our analysis of Fraser's autobiographical account of the childhood sexual abuse she suffered, we were concerned to highlight the limitations and inadequacy of the 'therapeutic' narrative which is becoming increasingly popular in contemporary culture. As we also saw in Chapter 7, this 'therapeutic' narrative is also used by some HIV-positive individuals (in the form of the 'conversion/growth' narrative) to help them come to terms with their trauma.

To recap, in Chapter 6 we argued that the 'healing' or 'therapeutic' narrative is all about achieving integration, adaptation, peace and closure. In order to accomplish this, Fraser builds up an image of her father as a victim himself, an unfortunate recipient, just like she was, of a family history constituting a 'tragedy in progress'. By conceiving of her father in this way, Fraser is able to understand, forgive and love and thus move on the 'healing process'. In doing so, she is able to appreciate the full 'mystery' of the world and all the wonders it has to offer. Although this message of 'personal redemption' may be seen as advantageous from the point of view of the individual, however, we argued that the effect of this kind of narrative is to reduce incest from a 'crime' to a 'disease' – a psychological illness involving the entire family. In this way, the therapeutic narrative operates to depoliticize the crime of incest and serves to erase feminist questions about the implications of sexual violence for relations between men and women. It thereby encourages a passive adaptation and adjustment to exploitative social norms and values (Davies 1995a: 139).

Ehrenhaus (1996) puts forward a very similar argument against the therapeutic story in relation to his exploration of the narratives surrounding Vietnam in the USA. He argues that discussions about Vietnam are dominated by a 'therapeutic motif' which 'contains and co-opts the Vietnam veteran as a voice of political opposition' (Ehrenhaus 1996: 78). According to Ehrenhaus, the therapeutic motif casts all issues and questions in matters related to Vietnam, whether they are personal, cultural or political, in terms of healing and recovery (Ehrenhaus 1996: 81). In an 'apologetically integrative' narrative, the 'nation implicitly asks its veterans for forgiveness. And the veterans' implicit acceptance constitutes relational healing, a repair of the social fabric' (p. 87). Ehrenhaus argues that the therapeutic motif has a 'tyrannizing power' insofar as in its 'celebration of unity (personal, relational, national)', it cannot 'abide discourse that engenders division' (p. 83). Thus, it centres all matters on issues of relationship, removing the actions of war from the 'historical, cultural and political context of the Vietnam war' (p. 90). Rendering veterans harmless by casting them in terms of metaphors of psychological dysfunction, emotional fragility, healing and personal redemption, in effect, the therapeutic motif serves to '. . . silence the voice of the veteran as a source of legitimate knowledge about the nature of contemporary warfare, thus subverting a potentially effective challenge to discourses advocating the use of "legitimate", state sanctioned violence as a tool of national policy' (Ehrenhaus 1996: 78).

These arguments, concerned with the inadequacy of the therapeutic narrative in depicting experiences of childhood sexual abuse and veterans' experiences of Vietnam, are typical of some of the social and cultural critiques of therapy which began to emerge during the 1970s. Basically, these critiques saw the increasing interest in therapy and self-development as a turning away from the engagement of the previous decade with the public world and radical politics. Marxists especially saw in the new therapies an obsession with the self and the 'apotheosis of the celebration of the individual in capitalist ideology' (see Rose 1989: 215).

One of the most influential theorists in this area was Christopher Lasch (1980; 1984) who argued that the ways in which people are able to make sense of themselves in late modernity can basically be characterized as 'morally deprived'. Lasch coined this state of affairs a 'culture of narcissism', or, in his more recent work, a 'culture of survivalism'. Basically, this notion of 'survivalism' refers to the idea that modern life becomes increasingly patterned after the 'survival' strategies of individuals who are forced to confront situations of great adversity with 'minimal' selves. These 'minimal' selves are typical of the kinds of selves most of us live with in contemporary society. They are called 'minimal' because they are related to features of modern society such as the decline in traditional institutions like the church and family life. The decline in such institutions tends to lead to the individual's loss of a sense of history, continuity, feelings of belonging, morality and responsibility. This leads to a society made up of individuals who tend to feel that their responsibility is only to themselves and the sphere of their own perceived self interest. This kind of self is analogous to the 'empty' self characterized by Cushman (1990) in Chapter 1.

'Minimal' or 'empty' selves are related to the increasing popularity of therapy and rise of a 'therapeutic culture', because people tend to become dependent on various forms of therapy to survive the vicissitudes of the lonely, modern world. Lasch thereby suggests that therapy is just a means of adjusting dissatisfied individuals to a flawed social environment; a narrow substitute for the deeper range of involvements that used to be available in pre-modern settings. Therapy therefore becomes a form of indulgence promoting narcissistic withdrawal, dependence and passivity, and a reluctance to address the inescapable moral and existential dimensions of life problems. As Giddens (1991) admits, there tends to be an inherently 'privatizing' dimension in therapy in which the individual is encouraged to see the project of the self in terms of self-determination alone, accentuating the separation of life events from moral considerations.

In addition, it has been argued that far from representing an enlightened approach to the individual, the therapeutic or 'psy' culture (incorporating a whole range of 'psychological'-type professions) constitutes an extension of power, 'discipline and professional control over life itself' (see Rose 1989: 240). In compelling and inciting subjects to 'disclose' themselves, finer and more intimate regions of personal and interpersonal life come under surveillance. 'In the name of the recognition of the subjectivity of the client or patient, a more profound subjection is produced' (Rose 1989: 241). This more 'profound subjection' is related to the way in which individuals in therapeutic-type cultures begin to 'internalize' the process of self-surveillance, constantly reflecting back and monitoring the meanings, reasons and motivations underlying their thoughts and actions. Indeed, it could be argued that the increasing interest in individual 'stories' and 'voices', and, relatedly, the narrative psychology project we have pursued throughout this book, exploring the narrative processes by which we and others constitute ourselves in order that we might effect liberating transformations, is simply one more manifestation of the 'profound subjection' inherent in a culture where psychology and psychologically related professions are increasingly coming to 'colonize' our experiences and understanding of ourselves.

Both Lasch (1985) and Melucci (1996a,b) fear that the 'narcissistic withdrawal' associated with the 'minimal self' paves the way to a society replete with irrationality, violence and hostility. Some illustrations of how this might be the case can be seen from my work with HIV-positive individuals. For instance, one of the main ways in which the propensity for 'narcissistic withdrawal' became apparent was in terms of the 'problem' of self-determination, especially in relation to discussions about sex and sexuality. With regard to these issues, a substantial proportion of HIV-positive individuals tended to be concerned almost exclusively with 'me' and 'my' needs, often to the detriment and potential harm of others. In the discussions we had, there seemed to be a widespread assumption that HIV-positive individuals had the 'right' to sexual freedom, especially insofar as this freedom was instrumental in enabling them to regain a sense of psychological control over their lives. This is clear in the following comment by David, a 48-year-old gay man:

> I remember one day I was at Open Door, I said, 'I must take back my sexuality' and I borrowed someone's leather jacket and I went up to the Heath and I stood by a tree and I would not leave that tree until I had got fucked rotten, to put it bluntly. I had to take it back, take the power back for me, *not let the doctors or anybody else, there are plenty of people who say, you mustn't, you drop it all now* (. . . there was a lot of guilt associated and fear, 'you don't do this and you don't do that'). . . . Well, you tell Jo Bloggins at the age of 30 that he can have no more sex, he can have no more company, he can have nothing, see if he can deal with it. They can't and I have had to deal with it by taking the power back for me. . . . And through that I have become much stronger, it is not a negative thing, it is very positive, this is me, who I am. . . .

Similarly, another gay man claimed that he had never lost his sex drive and that it had, in fact, got stronger as he 'denied' himself because of his fear of contaminating other people. But more recently, having been in therapy, he had '. . . started feeling that I have got *a right* to have a sexual relationship with other people, with willing partners because I am number one at the moment. . . .'

This notion of having a 'right' to sexual freedom was expressed in a number of ways and when pushed regarding the issue of responsibility towards other people and the possibility of transmitting infection, the most common response was one in which individuals claimed that their main responsibility consisted of a responsibility to themselves rather than to other people. For instance, the following comments were typical: 'It is my obligation to protect myself, it is not my obligation to protect him'; 'If I look after me I am automatically taking care of the other person and I can't take responsibility for another person'. This commitment to take care of oneself and not to bear greater responsibility in the context of sexual encounters resulted in one gay man's decision not to make explicit the fact of his HIV positivity to potential sexual partners because it was 'just assumed' that everyone on the gay scene was HIV-positive anyway. Another gay man's rationalization of his failure to inform a man whom he had sexual relations with is shown in the following quote:

> . . . it turned out he didn't realize I was positive and got really panicked when he realized. . . . I got really angry about that . . . he was so fucking ignorant . . . heavily into scatia [sexual relations involving faeces]

but he never had Hep B vaccinations . . . that's the best way of getting
Hep B . . . he went very quiet and then said, 'the things we have done,
I mean, I couldn't have caught anything could I?'

The important point to note about these examples is their ability to highlight
the dangers of a culture in which the individual is encouraged to see his/her
life in terms of self-determination alone and a reluctance to address the
inescapable moral and existential dimensions of living with others in a social
world.

A more positive view of
'therapeutic' narratives?

But are things really as bad as all this? Other authors have suggested a less
pessimistic view with regard to the relationship between dominant ways of
understanding ourselves (such as the therapeutic narrative) and the possibility of achieving both self-actualization and a moral society (see Baumeister 1991; Gergen 1991; Giddens 1991; Sugarman and Martin 1995; Melucci
1996a,b; McLeod 1997). Giddens, for instance, throws some doubt on the
idea of the 'minimal self', arguing that Lasch's depiction of the negative con-
tours of the contemporary self are based on an inadequately passive conception of the human agent. This conception fails to take account of the fact
that all human agents stand in a position of *appropriation* in relation to the
social world, which is to say that they respond *reflexively* and *creatively* to
the changes going on around them. Hence, although it is true that modern
social life may, in some ways, impoverish individual action, it is also true
that it creates greater opportunities and new possibilities to individuals that
were not even conceivable in previous eras (this is similar to Gergen's concept of the 'saturated' self discussed in Chapter 2). Giddens extends this critique to what he sees as Lasch's overly negative interpretation of the rise of
'therapeutic culture'. The idea that therapy is just an 'apolitical' means of
adjusting dissatisfied individuals to a flawed social environment fails to
appreciate the potentially empowering nature of therapy which, ideally,
enables individuals to respond creatively and reflexively to ongoing changes
in their social environments (see also Gergen 1991).

Central to Giddens' argument is his critique of Lasch's concept of the
'minimal' self. According to Lasch, this 'minimal' self is characteristic of
contemporary culture and is often constructed in therapy or through thera-
peutically informed narratives such as pop-psychology self-help books and
tapes. Lasch argues that in our state of minimal selfhood, our concerns are
focused more or less exclusively on narrowly defined 'survival' strategies
which 'work for us'. This implies a retreat into a narcissistic, 'personal' or
'private' realm in which we are concerned only about our own thoughts and
feelings and not about the effects of our actions on the wider 'public' or
'political' sphere. A good example is the attitudes of some HIV-positive

individuals towards sex, just discussed. Another classic example would be voting behaviour. In recent years there has been a great deal of concern over the fact that such a large proportion of young people fail to vote in either local or general elections. When asked in national polls why this is so, many young people have responded by commenting to the effect that they 'can't see what's in it for them' or 'it makes no difference to me so why bother?' This could be characterized as an example *par excellence* of Lasch's 'minimal' survivalist self, concerned only with his/her own needs to the detriment of the community in which s/he lives.

Giddens, however, argues that Lasch's characterization of the 'minimal' self as a 'private' self existing in defensive separation from the 'public' or 'political' sphere, fails to appreciate the political implications of the 'refashioning of self' which is taking place in contemporary culture. These changes are crucially important to the task of reconstructing political endeavours and dealing with problems which have become important in our current phase of postmodernity (such as ecological problems, adapting to chronic illnesses, 'surviving' various traumas and so on). Crucial to Giddens' argument is the distinction he draws between what he calls 'emancipatory politics' on the one hand, and 'life politics' on the other.

Emancipatory politics, related to the relatively early phases of modern development and institutions, promotes the principle of emancipation. Giddens defines emancipatory politics as a general outlook which is concerned, above all, with liberating individuals and groups from constraints which adversely affect their life chances. It works with a hierarchial notion of power: power is understood as the capability of an individual or group to assert its will over others. It is concerned to reduce or eliminate exploitation, inequality and oppression. The aim to liberate people from situations of oppression implies the adoption of moral values – making primary the imperatives of justice, equality and participation.

By contrast, the concept of 'life politics' is premised on a certain level of emancipation from the fixities of tradition and conditions of hierarchical domination. It is only when we have achieved a certain level of emancipation that we enter the arena of 'life politics'. This kind of politics does not primarily concern the *conditions* which liberate us in order to make choices (the task of emancipatory politics). Rather, life politics is a politics *of* choice – a politics of lifestyle; it is the politics of postmodernity and constitutes what Giddens calls the 'reflexively mobilized order'. What he means by this is a social order which, although subject to massive changes of a global order, can still be oriented too 'reflexively' (that is, thoughtfully and creatively), on an individual level. Hence, life politics is a politics of life decisions. These decisions are peculiar to contemporary society because they come about only when we have a wide range of choices available to us. A good example of the kind of 'life politics' questions that many of us continually ask ourselves today is related to the project of self-identity, a project framed by the many options and choices available to us: 'Who do I want to be?'; 'What do I want to become?' It may be useful at this point to draw an analogy with C. Taylor's (1989) work on the contemporary self discussed in Chapter 1. Recall that he, too, believed that the questions troubling us today about our selves and the direction of our lives are very different from the kinds of predicaments experienced in previous civilizations. This is because in earlier times people lived with 'unchallengeable frameworks' of meaning which made 'imperious demands' on them. In today's society, by contrast, our 'frameworks of meaning' have themselves become problematic and we now have a sense that no one framework is shared by everyone and that 'the' framework of meaning no longer exists.

One illustration of the shift from emancipatory politics to life politics can be seen in the women's movement. Melucci (1996a: 137) has described how the political path of women in Western societies highlights the eclipse of protest and the decline of women's mobilization. This has been brought about by the redistribution of political and social benefits won during the 1970s. The institutionalization of women's political action has been accompanied by an increased capacity for social and political bargaining and by the development of 'cultural' forms of politics constructed and expressed in the everyday lives of women. These 'cultural' forms of politics involve the search for another kind of freedom: no longer a freedom from want but the freedom *to* want; no longer a struggle for equality but a struggle for difference; no longer a freedom to act but the freedom to be (Melucci 1996a: 135).

Giddens recognizes that such 'life politics' or 'identity' questions can be seen, in Lasch's terms, as a turn towards 'private', narcissistic closure. But his main point is that these kinds of questions tend to develop when a certain level of emancipation has been reached and, rather than resulting in 'narcissistic' and moral closure, actually serve to open us up more and more to engaging with moral and existential dilemmas. It is the reflexive concern with life, self and the body (evident, for instance, in widespread interest in issues of abortion, euthanasia, alternative medicine, ecological issues and so on) characteristic of contemporary culture, that, according to Giddens, is resulting in a widespread resurgence of interest in moral, political and ethical issues. Life political issues call for a remoralizing of social life and demand a renewed sensitivity to questions that were undermined by the processes of modernization.

Rose (1989: 241) similarly argues (but in a more critical vein) that the therapeutic narratives, and therapeutic culture more generally, constitute a different way in which human beings have been urged to 'become ethical beings', 'beings who define and regulate themselves according to a moral code, establish precepts for conducting and judging their lives, and reject or accept certain moral goals for themselves'. In this way, therapeutic narratives are linked 'at a profound level' to the 'socio-political obligations of the modern self' (Rose 1989: 253). Such a self should be able to 'steer its individual path through life by means of the act of personal decision and the assumption of personal responsibility'; 'it is the self freed from all moral obligations but the obligation to construct a life of its own choosing, a life in which it realises itself' (p. 254). Thus, life, according to Rose, should be measured by the 'standards of personal fulfilment rather than community welfare or moral fidelity, given purpose through the accumulation of choices and experiences . . .' (p. 254). Therapeutic narratives therefore offer the means whereby the regulation of both ourselves and others can be 'made consonant with contemporary political principles and moral ideals' (p. 257) by promoting 'the obligation to be free' (p. 258). In this way, we are 'obliged to fulfil our political role as active citizens . . . as if we were seeking to realise our own desires' (p. 257).

It is again useful at this point to recall C. Taylor's (1989) historical research on the contemporary self discussed in Chapter 1. Taylor described how the 'interiorization' of the concept of self was immensely important during the Romantic period in terms of how people defined morality and 'the good life'. Prior to this era, whether or not an event or behaviour was seen as 'good', or in line with morality, depended on its 'objective' or 'external' consequences. During the Romantic period, by contrast, whether or not a person's action or behaviour was moral, began, for the first time, to be determined in terms of how they felt 'internally' about the episode. In this way, according to Taylor, the turn towards the 'inner' reached its full height. By endorsing this 'individualistic' stance as ultimately important to therapeutic narratives, Rose displays an essential continuity between concepts of morality emerging during the Romantic period and the reflexive self-exploratory stance characteristic of contemporary therapeutic culture.

Stories of trauma and the 'moral imperative'

How does all this fit into the questions we have been addressing about stories of ourselves, illness and traumas? So far in this book, we have argued that 'healing' or 'therapeutic' narratives, which are increasingly coming to dominate stories spoken or written by 'survivors' of various traumas, are problematic. For instance, we argued in relation to Fraser's account that use of the 'healing' narrative meant that emphasis was shifted away from the social, moral and political context of patriarchal power and exploitation, on to a concern with the psychological dynamics of individual family history. This could be seen as a classic example of Lasch's 'culture of survivalism' in which Fraser retreats into a 'personal' or 'private' realm and neglects the wider implications for the 'public' or 'political' sphere.

But is this true? In light of our discussion of Giddens' work, it could be argued that this conclusion relies on an old-fashioned distinction between 'emancipatory politics' and 'life politics'. In putting forward this argument, are we displaying a very limited understanding of politics, showing a willingness to grant political recognition only to the domain of 'emancipatory politics'? Fraser claims that the traumatic experiences she has been through have enabled her to 'see the world with new eyes' and in place of her 'narrow world of cause and effect', she is now able to recognize the importance and necessity of love, hope, forgiveness and empathy. Is it adequate simply to view such comments as representative of Lasch's 'survivalist' self, a pale imitation of the more explicit, angry, morally charged feminism of the 1960s? Or is Fraser doing here what Giddens says 'life politics' has the potential to do? That is, is she opening us up more fully to moral and existential problems concerning the meaning and values of life, relationships and how to live more deeply and meaningfully? The same question could be asked of those, like Stephen, the HIV-positive man discussed in the last chapter, who make sense of their illness through use of the 'conversion/growth' narrative. As we have previously seen, Stephen uses a relatively sophisticated version of this narrative, which could be said to result, as Giddens optimistically predicts, in a remoralizing of his psychological and social life because it enables him to experience a renewed sensitivity to important 'life' questions that he had formerly 'put on hold'. In the cases of both Fraser and Stephen, we might ask if they are not more likely to become moral and responsible citizens than if they were consumed by anger (as the emancipatory politics perspective would encourage them to be)?

As we have already briefly discussed in Chapter 7, researchers such as Frank (1995), who has also explored how people come to terms with illness experiences, characterize these kinds of stories as 'quest' narratives. The essential features of such narratives is that illness is portrayed as a journey in which the individual experiences crisis and change which ultimately enables him/her to open him/herself to the contingency and mystery of life. Framed by the threat of death and human finiteness, these narratives tend to highlight and exacerbate the importance of moral and existential concerns. They have the ability to painfully bring forth questions of meaning and concern; questions about our relationships with others; questions about how we have lived our lives; questions about values and priorities; questions, in short, about the meaning of life (see also Davies 1997).

Frank (in press) argues that these kinds of testimonies to trauma are very popular in contemporary postmodern culture because they are located in a 'horizon of moral significance', a powerful 'moral ideal' which puts back into its proper place the 'real' value of life. This value is allegedly opposed to the predominantly rationalist world-view (with its emphasis on work, planning for the future, money, pensions, materialist values and so on), and serves to reinstil a sense of awe and respect for a more 'holistic' world-view in which the emphasis is on human relationships and achieving interconnections between self, other and world. This alternative conception of morality is very similar to that put forward by feminist critics such as Gilligan (1982) who challenge the predominance of 'masculine' models of instrumental rationality and pave the way for newer models of intersubjectivity and connexity (see also Melucci 1996a, 1996b; Mulgan 1997).

The main point about such 'quest' narratives is that they serve as a powerful reminder that our everyday lives are lived on the surface and that there may be a deeper and more meaningful way of living. Such stories 'prevent us from always being the same' (Frank in press) and force us to rethink our lives, priorities and values. Frank (1995) develops an argument which encourages us to envisage such 'quest' narratives of illness as examples of Giddens' conception of 'life politics'. The degree of 'reflexivity' incorporated in the quest narrative is related to contemporary postmodern culture insofar as, in the past, when people have become ill, their only responsibility was to try to get well again. In contemporary culture, however, often because many illnesses are chronic and long term, the ill person has also to take responsibility for 'what illness means in his or her life' (Frank 1995: 13). Hence, the telling of an illness story constitutes what Frank calls a 'moral imperative' and 'involves a profound assumption of personal responsibility' (p. 13). More precisely, this 'moral imperative' incorporates a commitment to 'perpetual self-reflection on the sort of person that one's story is shaping one into, entailing the requirement to re-shape that self-story if the wrong self is being shaped' (p. 158). It requires continuous 'reflexive monitoring' in the form of a 'perpetual readjustment of past and present to create and sustain a coherent self-story' and thus to re-create memory and assume responsibility (p. 65). What is clear here is that this 'narrative ethic' incorporates a conception of morality which requires a 'commitment to shaping oneself as a human being' (p. 158).

It is useful at this point to highlight the similarities between Frank's idea of the 'moral imperative' behind illness stories and Rose's (1989) argument that therapeutic culture constitutes a different way in which human beings have been urged to 'become ethical beings'. Such a being, according to Rose, should be able to 'steer its individual path through life by means of the act of personal decision and the assumption of personal responsibility. . . . It is the self freed from all moral obligations but the obligation to construct a life of its own choosing, a life in which it realises itself' (Rose 1989: 254). This also links into our discussion of the narrative configuration of identity in Chapter 3. As we saw there, some philosophers and literary theorists such as Kierkegaard and Ricoeur have argued that it is only through the process of telling of our life stories, selecting and editing the past in order to direct our future, that we become ethical beings responsible for our own lives. Recall that Ricoeur makes such responsibility central to his concept of 'narrative identity' and argues that the self comes into being only in the process of telling a life story (Ricoeur 1986: 132).

The moral imperative of telling an illness story, according to Frank, however, is not just related to the commitment to changing oneself. For instance, when Stephen tells his story of living with an HIV-positive diagnosis, he does not do so just to work through his own changing identity but also 'to guide others who will follow' him (Frank 1995: 17). This is because the storytelling of ill or traumatized individuals is 'informed by a sense of responsibility and represents a way of living *for* the other' (Frank 1995: 17, original emphasis). According to Frank, this idea of telling one's story as a reponsibility reflects the 'core morality of the postmodern' in which storytelling is *for* another as much as it is for oneself. 'In the reciprocity that is storytelling, the teller offers herself as a guide to the other's self-formation' (p. 18). Here, Frank draws on the work of Bauman (1992) who characterizes the ideal 'postmodern self' in terms of the moral philosopher Emmanuel Levinas' ideas. This ideal is one in which I exist and bear responsibility *for* the other (Bauman 1992: 42). The fundamental point to grasp in relation to this concept of morality is that people live *for* others because their own lives as humans require them to live in that way. The self is understood as coming to be human only in relation to others and the self can continue to be human only by living for the other (Frank 1995: 15).

It is important to note that Frank regards the 'quest' narrative as the way of telling an illness story that comes closest to achieving this 'ideal' moral self associated with Levinas' philosophy. This is because those who tell or write about their illnesses or traumas in this way are engaging in an 'ethical practice of self' in which they open themselves up to others. Their desire is to 'touch others and perhaps makes a difference in the unfolding of their stories' (Frank 1995: 127). In this way, the 'self-story' of the quest narrative 'is never just a *self* story but becomes a self/*other* story' (p. 131, original emphasis). Hence, although the decision to testify to illness or trauma may consist of an individual moral choice, at the same time it implies a 'social ethic' (Frank 1995: 145). It should be clear by this point that if we accept the arguments put forward by Frank and Giddens, then our previous understanding of the 'depoliticizing' and 'demoralizing' tendency of therapeutic narratives as manifest in personal accounts such as Fraser's, may be seriously limited and flawed.

What about 'restitution' narratives?

Another point to consider in addressing the adequacy of my earlier position regarding Fraser's account is Frank's argument about 'restitution' narratives of trauma and illness. As we briefly discussed in the last chapter, 'restitution' narratives are characteristic of modernity and constitute the 'culturally preferred narrative' in contemporary culture. To recap, these narratives incorporate the modernist expectation that for every suffering there is a remedy. This 'remedy' could be in the form of some sort of medical intervention which 'cures' the disease or some form of political activism which 'solves' the problem by implementing a particular policy or vision. The important feature of such restitution narratives is that they incorporate the assumption that by *acting* on the world in some way, a 'solution' will be forthcoming. In the last chapter, for instance, we encountered John who, representing the 'normalizing' story's characteristic refusal to accept the limitations imposed by illness, believes that if he just keeps on 'working' and 'doing what he is doing', things will work out all right at the end of the day. This is one example of a restitution narrative. A slightly different 'take' on the 'normalizing' story is evident in the following quote from Danny, a 40-year-old gay man, who, although similarly refusing to accept the limitations of his HIV infection, is more committed to traditional forms of 'active' politics. This is also an example of a 'restitution' narrative:

> We have covered a lot of ground today . . . but I think I would like to say . . . I have always considered myself a strong person, but it is like, *I had to be strong because I had to survive*, and we had to set up support groups . . . we had to fight for literature and medication and information. . . . Whereas *now* everything is handed to people on a plate because all the services and the provision are already set in place . . . it's a hell of a lot easier than it was 10 years ago. And I think if I was diagnosed now, I don't think I would be as strong as I am now . . . do you know what I'm saying? . . . People have said to me 'oh well, I don't see it as a death sentence because I know people like you are living with it'. . . . But it is like, yes, I have lived long, but I have also worked hard and I look after myself in my own ways . . . I have got friends who I have met through HIV, and by being friends with those people, and by helping them to fight, and them helping me to fight, *that's what's kept me alive* . . . [we have got] strength in unity . . . bonds that have developed over time. . . .

Another example of a 'restitution' narrative is the 'old-style' feminist narrative incorporated in certain parts of Fraser's *My Father's House* (discussed in Chapter 6). Incorporated within this narrative is a belief, like Danny's, that if women (in Danny's case, HIV-positive individuals) come together as a collective group committed to the diminution of patriachal power, a 'solution' to male exploitation will eventually be found and implemented. There will be, in Danny's words, 'strength in unity'.

It is clear from these examples that the 'restitution' narrative encourages a belief in striving forward into the future; a belief in progress. In Chapter 6, arguing against the adequacy of the 'therapeutic' or 'healing' narrative in relation to Fraser's account, I argued that the 'old-style' feminist narrative, the 'restitution' narrative in Frank's terms, had more potential to offer a moral and politically informed version of the abusive events Fraser suffered as a child. But is this the case? Is the person who engages in explicitly political activities necessarily 'on the ball' with regard to the moral and existential dimensions of life problems? On the contrary, Frank (1995: 63) would have us believe that our 'normalizing' way of living in the world, naïvely believing in the potential for solutions and the possibility of progress, 'borders on denial'. Living in this state of 'denial' we come close to the condition of 'moral deprivation' described by Lasch in his characterization of our 'survivalist' culture. We are unable to engage in any depth with the 'real' questions life poses for us (see also Steinem 1992; bell hooks 1993).

A particular example of such denial is the treatment of death and issues of mortality in contemporary society. For instance, Bauman (1992) characterizes modern life as one in which we 'deconstruct mortality'. Basically, this means that we exorcise our fear of death by breaking down threats, among which illness is paradigmatic, into smaller and smaller units. Contemporary medical practice, which can be considered exemplary of the 'restitution narrative', is designed to effect this deconstruction, with its division into specialities and sub-specialities. As long as small puzzles can be solved, fixing this or medicating that, the threat of death is deconstructed into small, manageable portions. This ultimately means that the threat of death is denied, the 'big issue' of mortality evaded and thus the whole 'mystery' of life sublimated. In this way, contemporary medical practice, as representative of the 'restitution narrative', seeks to turn 'mysteries into puzzles'. Whereas a mystery can only be faced up to, a puzzle admits solution. The absence of solution makes mysteries a scandal to contemporary medicine (Frank 1995: 81).

An interesting study in relation to this tendency of medicine to deconstruct the fear of death and evade issues of mortality is provided in del Vecchio Good *et al.*'s (1994) study of oncologists (physicians dealing with cancer patients) in the USA. This study described how oncologists work with the fear that 'endings' (death) are undesirable, and thus how both physicians and patients resist the explicit formulation of death during the course of medical treatment and encounters. Physicians attempt to formulate experiences for their patients which instil hope, the continued desire to live, and willingness to invest in arduous and toxic treatments. This involves a certain structuring of clinical time. For instance, one of the important images used in structuring patient experience is that of 'mountain climbing'. This image gives 'a metaphorical equivalent' for medical time which is marked not by degeneration but by progress' (del Vecchio Good *et al.* 1994: 857). It is a metaphor 'of protest, an image which suggests that the oncologist will pull the patient to safer, higher ground' (p. 857). It is also a metaphor which 'taps into American concepts that through mobilising personal will, the patient has resources to engage in the struggle for higher ground, for cure or remission' (p. 857). The cumulative effect of this structuring of experience is that: 'As cancer patients come to live in the immediacy of treatment decisions and therapeutic activities set within the social context of the clinic, they enter into a narrative form in which endings are rarely made explicit and progression is measured in calibrated bits . . .' (p. 858).

Of course, the power of the 'restitution' narrative, as represented in such medical encounters, derives from real progress gained from technological and economic advancement (for example, improvements in medical technology). However, the 'single-minded telos of cure' manifest in contemporary medical culture is also its 'ultimate limitation'. This is because, as Frank argues, 'the confrontation with mortality cannot be part of the story' (Frank 1995: 95). Again, this is apparent in del Vecchio Good *et al.*'s study, which highlights the 'critical dilemma' that frequently arises for oncologists when it becomes clear that it is no longer possible to 'do' any more (in terms of active, medical intervention) with a patient because they are obviously close to death.

At such times, the structuring of experience formulated by the oncologist for the patient may fragment (del Vecchio Good *et al.* 1994: 859). What then

happens is that the oncologist's 'professional' agenda, which is far more pre-
dictive and explicit about time and horizons, may suddenly become quite
central to medical decisions and conversations with patients. It becomes
clear then that treatment is at an end, especially when patients are typically
transferred from hospital-based care to a hospice or home-based hospice
care. At this point, it becomes uncomfortably apparent to all concerned that
'immediacy, or "for the moment", becomes death' (del Vecchio Good *et al.*
1994: 859).

As del Vecchio Good *et al.* point out, such restitution narratives have
consequences not only for patients' experience of treatment, but also for a
society's choice of investment in cancer research and the production of anti-
cancer treatments. As they argue, 'The creation of hope and desire for
particular modes of anti-cancer therapies through metaphors central to
emplotted clinical time can lead to the commodification of "hope" and to
expectations of material salvation through biomedical technologies' (1994:
859).

It is also important to point out that the kind of philosophy associated
with the restitution narrative, exemplified in contemporary medical culture,
is not confined to medicine. It has also infiltrated into the 'patient' or 'survivor' groups which often constitute an intrinsic feature of being 'ill' in postmodern culture. The word 'ill' here is bracketed because the very use of the
term 'survivor' (as in 'surviving' an HIV-positive diagnosis, 'surviving'
mental illness or 'surviving' childhood sexual abuse) implies a commitment
to challenging the sense of passivity associated with illness and patient
status. This became apparent in my interviews with HIV-positive individuals
who were members of the 'National Long-Term Survivors Group'. For
instance, many of these people firmly believed that they had survived so long
with HIV infection because of the actions and behaviours they had under-
taken. One example is Alicia, a 39-year-old woman who said that 'the
reason I am still well and alive is because that is what I have chosen to do'.
The same belief is also evident in the following comment by Danny:

> Whereas I had to fight for whatever I wanted . . . I see people now in
> Body Positive [a self-help organization] groups and they just go
> because it's a social event. They are not interested in the medical side
> or they are not interested in getting involved in newsletters or running
> the group, they just want to go and take . . . and I just think to myself,
> 'God, what would you have been like 10 years ago! [when none of the
> services were in place].

Here, by contrasting himself to other, less politically active, HIV-positive
individuals, Danny expresses his belief that his own actions are intrinsic
to his survival. The necessity of fighting and 'actively' surviving was
also apparent in the many stories told by these people about 'other'
'weak-minded' or 'negative' HIV-positive individuals who, when diagnosed,
become obsessed with the fact that they are going to die, sit there, day-in,
day-out, thinking or talking about it and, in the manner of a self-fulfilling

prophecy, proceed to die. More or less every 'survivor' I spoke to had a story to tell about a friend they had known, or a friend of a friend, who had simply succumbed to the disease in this way. One such story is the following told by Alicia: '. . . some people I have known who have died, especially one woman . . . she had only been infected 6 years when she died and she *chose* to die, the first serious illness that came along, she gave into it and died . . .' (see Crossley 1997b).

This emphasis on fighting, optimism and not giving up is typical of the 'survivalist' philosophy characteristic of the 'restitution' narrative. It is a philosophy which is especially strong in the gay community's response to the AIDS crisis. This also became apparent in some more recent research I have been conducting for an NHS Trust in which the possibility of providing palliative care (care of the terminally ill for whom 'active' interventions or treatments are no longer appropriate) for gay men in a local hospice was explored. Some of the problems highlighted with regard to such provision were that few gay men with AIDS would actually choose to enter a hospice because, as one nurse who had been talking to potential service users reported, 'they live for the day when there will be a cure or something that will arrest the disease'. The relatively young age of many AIDS patients means there is a non-readiness to accept that they have an incurable disease. In addition, as I have previously suggested, in the gay community the main focus is on fighting, optimism and not giving up, a philosophy that sits some-what uneasily with the hospice philosophy of accepting death peacefully and gracefully. It is not surprising, therefore, to find that hospices are primarily viewed by the gay community as inappropriate because they represent an admission of failure (Tehran 1991; Crossley and Small 1998).

This brings us back to the 'ultimate limitation' of the 'single-minded' focus and belief in cure and survival so characteristic of the 'restitution' narrative. As Frank (1995) reminds us: 'The confrontation with mortality cannot be part of the story'. A clear example of this is evident in the follow-ing quote from Tim, a 41-year-old HIV-positive man who expressed reser-vations about what he called 'the whole survival thing':

> It's not a criticism of the Survivors Group but it is like the whole fight-ing thing. You know, that you have to fight and you must fight until the end, and it is that fighting that keeps you alive. But in some way I think it is actually just recognizing that there is a point where there is actually no point any more in just fighting. Because in fact I would rather just relax and that for me is the big, there is *a big question in my life at the moment, which is, where am I now?, sort of thing.* You know, because my partner and my parents and everyone are saying, come on, take more drugs, eat more, relax more and all that and you will be fine, you will pick up your weight, you will. But my body, in a way, is telling me otherwise, you know, my body is actually just getting tired now. It's saying 'just enough already'.

Tim went on to say that he was very aware, being a white South African, of the need for political activism. He had seen what 'positive action' could do with the political activism of the African National Congress, for instance. Also, being Jewish, he had always asked his parents why the 'Jews just walked like sheep to their deaths' and could not understand why they did not rebel more. But now, Tim felt that he had a greater understanding of their actions. This was because he felt that there is also a time when you just have to 'give up fighting', characterized in his use of the terms 'I'm all right already', 'just enough already', in other parts of the interview.

Tim talks about the 'big question' in his life at the moment, the question that he feels a great need to feel free to address, 'where am I now sort of thing?'. What he makes lucidly clear here is the fact that we all eventually have to face the 'reality and responsibility of mortality, and its mystery' (Frank 1995: 84). But he also points to the problems of a culture geared up to the denial of death and the ultimate inability of 'survivor-speak' to enable him to address his 'big question'. This is also the main criticism of Frank (1995) with regard to restitution narratives. Frank argues that different types of narrative accord different sorts of agency and responsibility. In the restitution narrative responsibility is limited to specific acts such as taking one's medicine, attending a meeting, wellness or activity being defined in contrast to illness or passivity. In Tim's terms, his partner and parents are pressurizing him to 'take more drugs, eat more, relax more and all that and you will be fine, you will pick up your weight' and so on. But what Tim realizes in this situation is that this is not where his direction or responsibility lies. It could be argued that he is more in need of a 'quest' narrative which would enable him to experience a renewed sensitivity to important 'life' questions, to open himself to the contingency and mystery of life and to 'make return to the same life that was lived before impossible as a moral choice' (Frank 1995: 91). In opening himself to such a story, Tim would 'refuse denial and thus stand against social pressures' (Frank 1995: 63). But as any of us who have sat uncomfortably around the hospital bed of a dying or seriously ill person will know, those social pressures are very strong. For, as Bauman writes:

> Perhaps it is not just the delicacy of manner that deprives us of speech [when we encounter the dying] but also the simple fact that, indeed, we have nothing to say to a person who has no further use for the language of survival; a person who is about to leave the world of busy pretence that language conjures up and sustains.
>
> (Bauman 1992: 129)

In defence of 'restitution' narratives: narrative responsibility and life circumstances

Restitution narratives are criticized in Frank's (1995) work for 'bordering on denial' and being unable to liberate the individual to his/her 'narrative responsibility'. Such a responsibility, exemplified in the 'quest' narrative of illness (such as Fraser's and Stephen's), would encourage the development of a more ethical, reflexive being who is able to share his/her traumatizing experiences with others and thus remain open to the mysteries and contingencies of life and death. From this perspective, the question faced by traumatized individuals should not be 'What am I going *to do* about this?' but 'How do I rise to the occasion?' According to Frank, this is achieved by telling a 'good' story. This good story would be 'the measure of his/her success' (Frank 1995: 62). And as we have previously seen, such a story would 'refuse denial and stand against social pressures' (p. 63).

We should, however, pause for a moment and reflect a little more on what this notion of a good story means. I am especially concerned about how, if a good story is all about opening up to contingency and mystery, as Frank's prioritization of the 'quest' narrative seems to suggest, this relates to the question of 'historical truth'. We first touched on this question in Chapter 3 when we explored the relationship between 'narrative truth', 'historical truth' and psychotherapy. In the attempt to create a 'good' story from a client's 'broken' world, Spence suggested that 'narrative truth is what we have in mind' (Spence 1982: 32). Such a story should be both plausible and coherent. But simultaneously, the narrative truth of the good story has to remain truthful to life as it is lived, in other words to the 'historical truth'. Factual truths that do not fit in with or that disturb the elegance, coherence and persuasiveness of the narrative should still be included in order that a realistic assessment of the past and future can be made. A personal story that neglects or denies the events of one's life in order to make it more pleasing or coherent is 'counter to the therapeutic commitment to truth' (Polkinghorne 1988: 181). This commitment to a true historical narrative of oneself is a 'value' commitment made in the interests of both psychological growth and in recognition of the imbalanced power relations intrinsic to many human relationships.

But how can this commitment to 'historical truth' be reconciled with the commitment to a 'good' story which stands against social pressures and opens one to mystery and contingency? An example will be useful at this point. Take the case of John, the 25-year-old HIV-positive haemophiliac discussed in the last chapter as representative of the 'normalizing' story. John, stoically unconcerned as he is about moral, political and existential dilemmas, 'merely' concerned with getting by from day to day, could be seen as an archetypal example of Lasch's 'minimal' self, 'bordering on denial' and existing in a 'culture of survivalism'. But the question is: Is this necessarily a 'bad' story? When John's particular circumstances are taken into account it becomes clear that his 'minimalist' self is probably entirely necessary for the life he finds himself in. As Shelly Taylor's study of cancer patients demonstrated, sometimes such 'denial' or 'illusions' are psychologically and socially functional insofar as they enable people to adapt to a radically unpredictable world in a way which enables them to impose a modicum of order and control on it (S. Taylor 1989).

So we are left with the question of whether it is necessarily a bad thing that John sets his sights less on the 'open' moral horizon of the universe, less on the kind of pondering on self and world typical of the 'quest' narrative, given that he has his mortgage to pay and his wife to support? And, conversely, given that Stephen (who was discussed in Chapter 7 as representative of the 'quest' narrative) is financially well off with no dependants, and given that he is struggling to come to terms with the death of his long-term partner, perhaps it is a 'good' thing that he can 'open' himself to questions of personal and psychological growth, to pursue, in Giddens' terms, his 'life politics' project? My point here is that questions of narrative truth and responsibility are subject to certain historical and material conditions and not all such conditions are equally amenable to the mysterious 'pondering' so favoured by the 'quest' narrative. Isn't it sometimes entirely necessary, functional and, indeed, psychologically and socially beneficial, to live and tell stories which 'border on denial'?

The ultimate implication of this argument is that the question of what constitutes a 'good' story cannot be answered in isolation from a consideration of the individual's interpersonal, social, economic and political context. In some ways, although this conclusion serves to individualize and relativize the question of narrative responsibility, at the same time it serves to create a moral vision which appreciates more fully the integration between individuals, stories and the cultures in which they live. This argument brings us back full circle to Chapter 1 where we discussed Charles Taylor's (1989) and MacIntyre's (1988) contention that concepts of self, morality and narrative are inextricably intertwined. Hence, questions of 'the good' can be defined only in relation to the 'interchange of speakers' in a 'defining community', of which one forms a constituent part.

Chapter summary

By the end of this chapter you should appreciate the following concepts and issues:

- The link between 'therapeutic' and 'quest' narratives.
- Debates around the adequacy of 'therapeutic' or 'quest' narratives: Do they demoralize or remoralize personal and social life? How these issues relate to 'postmodern' culture.
- The link between 'restitution' narratives, medical and 'survivor' culture, and modernism.
- Debates around the inadequacy of restitution narratives, for example the denial of death and 'big' issues.
- The inextricable connection between a 'good' narrative and life/historical circumstances.

Discussion points

- Lee is a 32-year-old HIV-positive heterosexual haemophiliac who lives with his wife and three young children. He is unemployed and the family are struggling to live on disability benefits. Discuss some of the advantages and disadvantages of him appropriating a 'quest'-style narrative on the one hand, or a 'restitution'-style narrative on the other.
- Do you think therapeutic-style narratives result in a demoralizing of personal and social life?
- In what ways has your narrative psychology project engaged you in 'life politics' issues? Do you think this has resulted in increased moral and political engagement with your own personal and social world?
- What do you think of people who appear on talk shows? Is it 'all talk'/'all show'? Or are they engaging in 'life politics'? How does this phenomenon highlight some of the problems and potentials of 'life politics' in contemporary society? (see Priest 1996).
- Discuss critically some of the ways in which contemporary medicine operates in accordance with a 'restitution'-style narrative.

Key further reading

Crossley, M.L. (1999b) Stories of illness and trauma survival: liberation or repression?, *Social Science and Medicine*, 48: 1685–95.

*del Vecchio Good, M., Munakata, T., Kobayashi, Y., Mattingly, C. and Good, B. (1994) Oncology and narrative time, *Social Science and Medicine*, 38: 855–62.

Frank, A. (1995) *The Wounded Storyteller: Body, Illness and Ethics* (Chapters 1, 3 and 7). Chicago: University of Chicago Press.

Frank, A. (in press) Stories of illness as care of the self: a Foucauldian dialogue, *Health*.

Giddens, A. (1991) *Modernity and Self Identity: Self and Society in the Late Modern Age* (Chapters 5–7). Cambridge: Polity Press.

*Priest, P. (1996) 'Gilt by association': talk show participants televisually enhanced status and self-esteem', in D. Grodin and T. Lindlof. (eds) *Constructing the Self in a Mediated World*, pp. 69–83. London: Sage.

Notes on further reading

The Giddens and Priest readings provide further exploration of the relationship between 'therapeutic' and 'confessional'-type narratives and self/

identity in contemporary society. This relationship, and its specific application to illness, is addressed further in the Frank readings, and the Crossley reference, which attempts to expand on Frank's (1999) paper.

The *del Vecchio Good *et al.* reference constitutes a fascinating exploration of how oncologists attempt to structure time for their patients, in a manner which attempts to miminize and contain anxiety about death. This reading raises important moral and ethical considerations which can be used as a way of expanding on the ideas covered in this chapter.

Concluding synopsis

In *Introducing Narrative Psychology,* I have attempted to provide a broad flavour of the kinds of theoretical, methodological and practical issues narrative psychology is concerned with. In the early chapters of the book we saw how narrative psychology conceptualizes the distinctively human order of meaning as one intrinsically involved with language, temporality, other people and morality. We saw how images of self are connected to particular cultural contexts such as the contemporary 'inward' Western self and the moral implications of such conceptualizations. Such issues and questions have been followed through over the course of this book both with application to our own autobiographical narratives and also in relation to case-studies of various traumatizing events such as childhood sexual abuse and the study of illness narratives.

It is through such applications that we also come to realize the importance of theoretical debates first encountered in Chapter 2. There, we argued that a narrative psychological approach attempts to retain a sense of the culturally discursive structuring of experience while trying not to lose sight of the very personal nature of that experience. Analysis of our own autobiographies and trauma narratives illustrated why the process of deconstruction is so important. We need to understand how dominant cultural narratives are inscribed in experiential accounts, invisibly working to produce certain versions and visions of reality which subdue others and frequently serve to perpetuate existing social relations of power. But we have also found that this is not necessarily a 'bad' thing. On a personal level, the appropriation of such dominant cultural narratives *may* constitute the best way in which we can adjust to the social world and live a fulfilling and meaningful life. The important point here is that our process of deconstructing cultural narratives should leave us in a position where we can empathically appreciate the role those narratives play in making sense of our own lives and the lives of others, building up a sense of meaning, identity and morality. Our analysis of traumatizing events, which involve the breakdown of temporal coherence and narrative structure, have alerted us to just how central such processes are to our lives.

We have also come to realize that there are no easy answers to what constitutes a 'good' or an 'adequate' personal narrative. Such questions, and answers, relate to wider moral and cultural debates in particular societies. As such, engagement with such issues serves to reframe the whole psychological enterprise. Psychology, from a theoretical point of view informed by narrative thinking, can (and should) no longer be viewed as an 'objective', 'value'-free, 'neutral' or 'amoral' science. Instead, by engaging with issues of personal meaning and subjectivity, it goes right back to the heart of what matters to people: joys, tragedies, sadness, happiness, meanings, moralities, identities. We are no longer satisfied with sitting behind our computers feeding dummy data into SPSS (or more 'sophisticated' statistical packages). We need, and want, to find out more. As narrative psychologists our aim, in a thoroughly postmodern way, is to boldly open ourselves to questions and issues that have been artificially closed off by a discipline that has trained us to think and act in severely limited and circumscribed ways. It is my hope that this book has taken the first tentative steps to showing you how to do this. And further, it is my hope that, along with many other critical approaches developing in this discipline at present, psychology will at last have the capacity to become human again.

Bibliography

Abraham, C. and Hampson, S. (1996) A social cognition approach to health psychology: philosophical and methodological issues, *Psychology and Health*, 11: 233–41.

Adler Cohen M. (1990) Biopsychosocial approach to the human immunodeficiency virus epidemic: a clinician's primer, *General Hospital Psychiatry*, 12: 98–123.

Allen, H. (1986) Psychiatry and the feminine, in P. Miller and N. Rose (eds) *The Power of Psychiatry*. Oxford: Polity Press.

Allen, V. (1980) *Daddy's Girl*. New York: Harper and Row.

Anderson, R. and Bury, M. (eds) (1988) *Living with Chronic Illness*. London: Unwin Hyman.

Angelou, M. (1969) *I Know why the Caged Bird Sings*. New York: Virago.

Armstrong, L. (1987) *Kiss Daddy Goodnight: Ten Years Later*. New York: Pocket Books.

Armstrong, L. (1996) *Rocking the Cradle of Sexual Politics: What Happened When Women Said Incest*. London: Women's Press.

Aronson, E., Wilson, T. and Akert, R. (1994) *Social Psychology: The Heart and The Mind*. New York: Harper Collins.

Augustinous, M. and Walker, I. (1995) *Social Cognition: An Integrated Introduction*. London: Sage.

Bakhtin, M. (1984) *Problems of Dostoevsky's Poetics*. Minneapolis: University of Minnesota Press.

Bass, E. (1983) Introduction: in the truth itself, there is healing, in E. Bass and L. Thornton (eds) *I Never told Anyone: Writings by Women Survivors of Childhood Sexual Abuse*, pp. 1–22. New York: Harper and Row.

Bass, E. and Thornton, L. (eds) (1983) *I Never told Anyone: Writings by Women Survivors of Childhood Sexual Abuse*. New York: Harper and Row.

Bauman, Z. (1992) *Mortality, Immortality and other Life Strategies*. Cambridge: Polity Press.

Baumeister, R. (1991) *Meanings of Life*. New York: Guilford Press.

Beckham, D. (1988) Group work with people who have AIDS, *Journal of Psychosocial Oncology*, 6: 213–18.

bell hooks (1993) *Sisters of the Yam: Black Women and Self-Recovery*. Boston: South-end.

Bell, M. (1990) How primordial is narrative?, in C. Nash (ed.) *Narrative in Culture: the Uses of Storytelling in the Sciences, Philosophy and Literature*, pp. 172–99. London: Routledge.

Bellah, R., Madsen, R., Sullivan, W., Swindler, A. and Tipton, S. (1985) *Habits of the Heart: Individualism and Commitment in American Life*. New York: Perennial Library.

Bem, D. (1972) Self perception theory, in L. Berkowitz (ed.) *Advances in Experimental Social Psychology*, Volume 6, pp. 1–62. New York: Academic Press.

Benson, S. (1997) The body, health and eating disorders, in K. Woodward (ed.) *Identity and Difference*, pp. 121–83. London: Sage.

Berger, P. and Luckman, T. (1967) *The Social Construction of Reality: A Treatise on the Sociology of Knowledge*. New York: Anchor Books.

Bertenthal, B. and Fisher, I. (1978) Development of self-recognition in the infant, *Developmental Psychology*, 14: 44–50.

Best, S. and Kellner, D. (1991) *Postmodern Theory: Critical Interrogations*. Basingstoke: Macmillan.

Bettelheim, B. (1976) *The Uses of Enchantment: The Meaning and Importance of Fairy tales*. New York: Knopf.

Billig, M. (1987) *Arguing and Thinking: A Rhetorical Approach to Social Psychology*. Cambridge: Cambridge University Press.

Billig, M. (1991) *Ideology and Opinions*. London: Sage.

Birren, J. and Birren, B. (1996) Autobiography: exploring the self and encouraging self development, in. J. Birren, G. Kenyon, J. Ruth, J. Schroots and T. Svensson (eds) *Aging and Biography: Explorations in Adult Development*, pp. 52–77. New York: Springer.

Bourdieu, P. (1990) Time perspectives of the Kabyle, in J. Hassard (ed.) *The Sociology of Time*, pp. 17–45. London: Macmillan.

Brady, K. (1979) *Father's Days: A True Story of Incest*. New York: Dell.

Brody, H. (1987) *Stories of Sickness*. Yale UP: New York.

Brown, M. (1996) Desperately seeking strategies: reading in the postmodern, in D. Grodin and T. Lindlof (eds) *Constructing the Self in a Mediated World*. London: Sage.

Broyard, A. (1992) *Intoxicated By My Illness, and Other Writings on Life and Death*. New York: Clarkson, Patter.

Bruner, J. (1990) *Acts of Meaning*. Harvard, MA: Harvard University Press.

Bruner, J. (1991) The narrative construction of reality, *Critical Inquiry*, 18: 1–21.

Carr, D. (1986) *Time, Narrative and History*. Bloomington: Indiana University Press.

Case, R. (1991) Stages in the young child's first sense of self, *Developmental Review*, 11: 210–30.

Cherry, K. and Smith, D.H. (1993) Sometimes I cry: the experience of loneliness for men with AIDS, *Health Communication*, 5(3): 181–208.

Cocks, J. (1984) Wordless emotions: some critical reflections on radical feminism, *Politics and Society*, 13(1): 27–57.

Conrad, P. (1987) The experience of illness: recent and new directions, *Research in the Sociology of Health Care*, 6: 1–31.

Cooley, C. (1902) *Human Nature and the Social Order*. New York: Scribner.

Cooper, D. (1990) *Existentialism*. Cambridge: Blackwell.

Coulter, J. (1979) *The Social Construction of Mind*. London: Macmillan.

Coulter, J. (1983) *Rethinking Cognitive Theory*. London: Macmillan.

Cousins, S. (1989) Culture and self-perception in Japan and the United States, *Journal of Personality and Social Psychology*, 56: 124–31.

Cox, M. and Theilgaard, A. (1987) *Mutative Metaphors in Psychotherapy: The Aeolian Mode*. London: Tavistock.

Crites, S. (1986) Storytime: recollecting the past and projecting the future, in T.

Sarbin (ed.) *Narrative Psychology: The Storied Nature of Human Conduct*, pp. 153–73. New York: Praeger.

Crossley, M.L. (1997a) The divided self: the destructive potential of an HIV positive diagnosis, *Journal of Existential Analysis*, 8(2): 72–94.

Crossley, M.L. (1997b) 'Survivors' and 'victims': long-term HIV positive individuals and the ethos of self-empowerment, *Social Science and Medicine*, 45(12): 1863–73.

Crossley, M.L. (1998a) Women living with a long-term HIV positive diagnosis: problems, concerns and ways of ascribing meaning, *Women's Studies International Forum*, 21(5): 521–33.

Crossley, M.L. (1998b) Sick role or empowerment: the ambiguities of life with an HIV positive diagnosis, *Sociology of Health and Illness*, 20(4): 507–31.

Crossley, M.L. (1998c) A man dying with AIDS: psychoanalysis or existentialism?, *Journal of Existential Analysis*, 9(2): 35–57.

Crossley, M.L. (1999a) Making sense of HIV infection: discourse and adaptation to life with an HIV positive diagnosis, *Health*, 3(1): 95–119.

Crossley, M.L. (1999b) Stories of illness and trauma survival: liberation or repression?, *Social Science and Medicine*, 48: 1685–95.

Crossley, M.L. (in press) Sense of place and its import for life transitions, in R. Josellson, A. Lieblich and D. McAdams (eds) *The Narrative Study of Lives*. London: Sage.

Crossley, M.L. (forthcoming) *Rethinking Health Psychology*. Buckingham: Open University Press.

Crossley, M.L. and Small, N. (1998) *Evaluation of HIV/AIDS Education Training Services provided by London Lighthouse at St Ann's Hospice*, Stockport: Stockport Health Authority.

Crossley, N. (1995a) Body techniques, agency and intercorporeality: on Goffman's *Relations in Public*, *Sociology*, 29(1): 133–49.

Crossley, N. (1995b) Merleau-Ponty, the elusive body and carnal sociology, *Body & Society*, 1(1): 43–63.

Crossley, N. (1996a) *Intersubjectivity: The Fabric of Social Becoming*. London: Sage.

Crossley, N. (1996b) Body-subject/body power, *Body & Society*, 2(1): 99–116.

Crossley, N. (forthcoming) *Embodied Sociology: Habit, Identity and Desire*. Sage: London.

Crossley, N. and Crossley, M.L. (1998) HIV, empowerment and the sick role: an investigation of a contemporary moral maze, *Health*, 2(2): 157–74.

Csikszentmihalyi, M. and Figurski, T. (1982) Self awareness and aversive experiences in everyday life, *Journal Of Personality*, 50: 15–28.

Cushman, P. (1990) Why the self is empty: toward a historically situated psychology, *American Psychologist*, 45: 599–611.

Cushman, P. (1995) *Constructing the Self, Constructing America: A Cultural History of Psychotherapy*. Massachusetts: Addison-Wesley.

Daly, M. (1979) *Gyn/Ecology: The Metaethics of Radical Feminism*. Boston: Beacon Press.

Davies, M.L. (1993) Healing Sylvia: accounting for the textual 'discovery' of unconscious knowledge, *Sociology*, 27(1): 110–20.

Davies, M.L. (1995a) *Healing Sylvia: Childhood Sexual Abuse and the Construction of Identity*. London: Taylor and Francis.

Davies, M.L. (1995b) Final report to the Health Directorate DGIV of the European Community: *An Exploration of the Emotional, Psychological and Service*

Delivery needs of people who have been living with an HIV positive diagnosis for five years or more. Brussels: European Community.

Davies, M.L. (1997) Shattered assumptions: time and the experience of long-term HIV positivity, *Social Science and Medicine*, 44(5): 561–71.

Davis, K. (1994) What's in a voice? Methods and metaphors, *Feminism and Psychology*, 4(3): 353–61.

de Wit, J., Tennis, N., Godfried, N., van Griensven, J. and Sandfort, T. (1994) Behavioural risk reduction and strategies to prevent HIV infection amongst homosexual men: a grounded theory approach, *Aids Education and Prevention*, 6(6): 493–505.

del Vecchio Good, M., Munakata, T., Kobayashi, Y., Mattingly, C. and Good, B. (1994) Oncology and narrative time, *Social Science and Medicine*, 38: 855–62.

duBois, P. (1991) *Torture and Truth*. New York: Routledge.

Dunne, J. (1995) Beyond sovereignty and deconstruction: the storied self, *Philosophy and Social Criticism*, 21: 137–57.

Dwivedi, K. (1997) (ed.) *The Therapeutic Use of Stories*. London: Routledge.

Dwivedi, K. and Gardner, D. (1997) Theoretical perspectives and clinical approaches, in K. Dwivedi (ed.) *The Therapeutic Use of Stories*, pp. 19–42. London: Routledge.

Early, E. (1982) The logic of well being: therapeutic narratives in Cairo, Egypt, *Social Science and Medicine*, 16: 1491–7.

Edwards, D. and Potter, J. (1992) *Discursive Psychology*. London: Sage.

Egendorf, A. (1986) *Healing from the War*. Boston: Shambala.

Ehrenhaus, P. (1996) Cultural narratives and the therapeutic motif: the political containment of Vietnam veterans, in D. Mumby (ed.) *Narrative and Social Control: Critical Perspectives*. London: Sage Annual Review of Communication, Volume 21.

Elias, N. (1992) *Time: An Essay*. Oxford: Blackwell.

Farmer, P. (1994) AIDS talk and the constitution of cultural models, *Social Science and Medicine*, 38(6): 801–9.

Featherstone, M. (1988) In pursuit of the postmodern, *Theory, Culture & Society*, 5(3): 195–216.

Fein, G. (1991) The self building potential of pretend play or 'I got a fish all by myself', in M. Woodhead, R. Carr and P. Light (eds) *Becoming a Person*, pp. 25–42. London: Routledge.

Finney, L. (1990) *Reach for the Rainbow: Advanced Healing for Survivors of Sexual Abuse*. Malibu: Changes Publishing.

Flowers, P., Smith, J., Sheeran, P. and Beail, N. (1997) Health and romance: understanding unprotected sex in relationships between gay men, *British Journal of Health Psychology*, 2: 73–86.

Forman, F. and Sowton, C. (eds) (1989) *Taking our Time: Feminist Perspectives on Temporality*. Oxford: Pergamon.

Foucault, M. (1979) *Discipline and Punish: The Birth of Prison*. New York: Vintage.

Frank, A. (1993) The rhetoric of self-change: illness experience as narrative, *The Sociological Quarterly*, 34(1): 39–52.

Frank, A. (1995) *The Wounded Storyteller: Body, Illness and Ethics*. Chicago: University of Chicago Press.

Frank, A. (in press) Stories of illness as care of the self: a Foucauldian dialogue, *Health*.

Frankl, V. (1984) *Man's Search for Meaning*. Washington: Pocket Books.

Fraser, S. (1989) *My Father's House: A Memoir of Incest and Healing*. London: Virago.

Freeman, M. (1993) *Rewriting the Self: Memory, History, Narrative*. London: Routledge.

French, M. (1987) *Her Mother's Daughter*. New York: Summit.

Freud, S. (1956) Remembering, repeating and working through, in *The Standard Edition of the Complete Psychological Works of Sigmund Freud*, vol. 12. London: Hogarth Press.

Frosh, S. (1997) Screaming under the bridge: masculinity, rationality and psychotherapy, in J. Usser (ed.) *Body Talk: The Material and Discursive Regulation of Sexuality, Madness and Reproduction*, pp. 70–85. London: Routledge.

Fumento, M. (1990) *The Myth of Heterosexual AIDS: How a Tragedy has been Distorted by the Media and Partisan Politics*. Washington: Regnery Gateway.

Fussell, P. (1975) *The Great War and Modern Memory*. London: Oxford University Press.

Fussell, P. (1989) *Wartime*. New York: Oxford University Press.

Gallup, C. (1977) Self recognition in primates: a comparative approach to bidirectional properties of consciousness, *American Psychologist*, 32: 329–38.

Garfinkel, H. (1984) *Studies in Ethnomethodology*. Cambridge: Polity Press.

Garro, L. (1994) Narrative representations of chronic illness experience: cultural models of illness, mind and body in stories concerning the temporomandibular joint (TMJ), *Social Science and Medicine*, 38(6): 775–88.

Geertz, C. (1973) *The Interpretation of Cultures*. New York: Basic Books.

Geertz, C. (1979) From the native's point of view: on the nature of anthropological understanding, in P. Rabinow and W. Sullivan (eds) *Interpretive Social Science: A Reader*. California: University of California Press.

Gergen, K. (1973) Social psychology as history, *Journal of Personality and Social Psychology*, 26: 309–20.

Gergen, K. (1991) *The Saturated Self: Dilemmas of Identity in Contemporary Life*. New York: Basic Books.

Gergen, K. (1996a) Beyond life narratives in the therapeutic encounter, in J. Birren, Kenyon, J. Ruth, J. Schroots and T. Svensson (eds) *Aging and Biography: Explorations in Adult Development*. New York: Springer.

Gergen, K. (1996b) Technology and the self: from the essential to the sublime, in D. Grodin and T. Lindlof (eds) *Constructing The Self in a Mediated World*, pp. 127–41. London: Sage.

Gergen, K. and Gergen, M. (1983) Narratives of the self, in T.R. Sarbin and K. Scheibe (eds) *Studies in Social Identity*, pp. 54–74. New York: Praeger.

Gergen, K. and Gergen, M. (1993) Autobiographies and the shaping of gendered lives, in N. Coupland and J. Hussbaum (eds) *Discourse and Lifespan Identity*, pp. 154–69. London: Sage.

Giddens, A. (1991) *Modernity and Self Identity: Self and Society in the Late Modern Age*. Cambridge: Polity Press.

Gilligan, C. (1982) *In a Different Voice: Psychological Theory and Women's Development*. Harvard: Harvard University Press.

Glucksmann, M. (1998) 'What a difference a day makes': a theoretical and historical exploration of temporality and gender, *Sociology*, 32(2): 239–58.

Good, B. and del-Vecchio Good, M. (1994) In the subjunctive mode: epilepsy narratives in Turkey, *Social Science and Medicine*, 38(6): 835–42.

Gouldner, A. (1971) *The Coming Crisis of Western Sociology*. London: Heinemann.

Griffin, S. (1980) Thoughts on writing a diary, in J. Sternberg (ed.) *The Writer on Her Work*, pp. 33–55. New York: W. Norton.

Gusdorf, G. (1980) Conditions and limits of autobiography, in J. Olney (ed.) *Autobiography: Essays Theoretical and Critical*, pp. 22–54. Ewing, NJ: Princeton University Press.

Habermas, J. (1971) *Toward a Rational Society*. London: Heinemann.

Habermas, J. (1987) *The Theory of Communicative Action*. Boston, MA: Beacon Press.

Hammond, M., Howarth, J. and Keat, R. (1991) *Understanding Phenomenology*. Cambridge: Blackwell.

Harré, R. and Gillet, G. (1994) *The Discursive Mind*. London: Sage.

Heidegger, M. (1962) *Being and Time*. Oxford: Blackwell.

Henriques, J., Hollway, W., Urwin, C., Venn, C. and Walkerdine, V. (1998) *Changing the Subject: Psychology, Social Regulation and Subjectivity*. London: Routledge.

Heritage, J. (1984) *Garfinkel and Ethnomethodology*. Cambridge: Polity Press.

Hildebrand P.H. (1992) A patient dying with AIDS, *International Review of Psychoanalysis*, 19: 457–69.

Hodgkinson, N. (1996) *AIDS: The Failure of Contemporary Science: How a Virus that Never was Deceived the World*. London: Fourth Estate.

Hoffman, L. (1993) *Exchanging Voices: A Collaborative Approach to Family Therapy*. London: Karnac.

Holifield, E. (1983) *A History of Pastoral Care in America: From Salvation to Self-Realisation*. Nashville: Abingdon Press.

Hollway, W. (1984) Gender differences and the production of subjectivity, in J. Henriques, W. Hollway, C. Urwin, C. Venn and V. Walkerdine (eds) *Changing the Subject*, pp. 227–64. London: Methuen.

Howard, G.S. (1991) Culture tales: a narrative approach to thinking, cross-cultural psychology and psychotherapy, *American Psychologist*, 46(3): 187–97.

Hutchby, I. and Wooffitt, R. (1988) *Conversation Analysis*. Cambridge: Polity Press.

Ingham, R. and Kirkland, D. (1997) Discourses and sexual health: providing for young people, in L. Yardley (ed.) *Material Discourses of Health and Illness*, pp. 150–76. Routledge: London.

Irigiray, L. (1985) *This Sex Which is Not One*. New York: Cornell University Press.

Janoff-Bulman, R. (1992) *Shattered Assumptions: Towards a New Psychology of Trauma*. New York: Free Press.

Johnson, T. (1972) *Professions and Power*. London: Macmillan.

Joffe, H. (1997) Intimacy and love in late modern conditions: implications for unsafe sexual practices, in J. Ussher (ed.) *Body Talk: The Material and Discursive Regulation of Sexuality, Madness and Reproduction*, pp. 159–76. London: Routledge.

Josselson, R. (1995) Narrative and psychological understanding, *Psychiatry*, 58: 330–43.

Kahneman, D. and Tversky, A. (1973) Subjective probability: a judgement of representativeness, *Cognitive Psychology*, 3: 430–54.

Kaplan, E. (1987) *Rocking around the Clock*. New York: Methuen.

Katz, A. and Shotter, J. (1996) Hearing the patient's voice: toward a social poetics in diagnostic interviews, *Social Science and Medicine*, 43(6): 919–31.

Kelly, G. (1955) *The Theory of Personal Constructs*. New York: Norton.

Kierkegaard, S. (1987) *Either/Or, Part 2*. Ewing, NJ: Princeton University Press.

Kitzinger, J. (1992) Sexual violence and compulsory heterosexuality, *Feminism and Psychology*, 2(3): 399–418.

Kleinman, A. (1988) *The Illness Narratives: Suffering, Healing and the Human Condition*. New York: Basic Books.

Kohler Riessman, C. (1990) Strategic uses of narrative in the presentation of self and illness: a research note, *Social Science and Medicine*, 30(11): 1195–200.

Kondo, D. (1990) *Crafting Selves: Power, Gender and Discourses of Identity in a Japanese Workplace*. Chicago: Chicago University Press.

Kristeva, J. (1981) Women's time, *Signs*, 1: 16–35.

Kunzmann, K. (1990) *The Healing Way: Adult Recovery from Childhood Sexual Abuse*. Hazledon: Centre City.

Kvale, S. (ed.) *Psychology and Postmodernism*. London: Sage.

Lacan, J. (1987) *The Four Fundamental Concepts of Psychoanalysis*. Harmondsworth: Peregrine.

Laclau, E. (1991) *New Reflections on the Revolution of our Time*. London: Verso.

Laclau, E. and Mouffe, C. (1985) *Hegemony and Socialist Strategy: Towards a Radical Democratic Politics*. London: Verso.

Landrine, H. (1992) Clinical implications of cultural differences: the referential versus the indexical self, *Clinical Psychology Review*, 12: 401–15.

Langellier, K. and Peterson, E. (1996) Family storytelling as a strategy of social control, in D. Mumby (ed.) *Narrative and Social Control: Critical Perspectives*, pp. 49–75. London: Sage Annual Review of Communication, Volume 21.

Lasch, C. (1980) *The Culture of Narcissism*. London: Abacus.

Lasch, C. (1985) *The Minimal Self*. London: Picador.

Lewis, C.S. (1952) *Mere Christianity*. New York: Macmillan.

Lienhardt, G. (1985) Self: public and private: some African representations, in M. Carrithers, S. Collins and S. Lukes (eds) *The Category of the Person*, pp. 74–102. Cambridge: Cambridge University Press.

Lifton, R. (1968) *Death in Life: Survivors of Hiroshima*. New York: Random House.

Lifton, R. (1969) *Boundaries*. New York: Random House.

Lifton, R. (1973) *Home from the War: Vietnam Veterans: neither Victims nor Executioners*. New York: Simon and Schuster.

Lovlie, L. (1992) Postmodernism and subjectivity', in S. Kvale (ed.) *Psychology and Postmodernism*, pp. 118–34. London: Sage.

Lowy, E. and Ross, M. (1994) 'It'll never happen to me'. Gay men's beliefs, perceptions and folk constructions of sexual risk, *AIDS Education and Prevention*, 6(6): 467–82.

Lucas, J. (1997) Making sense of interviews: the narrative dimension, *Social Sciences in Health*, 3(2): 113–26.

McAdams, D. (1993) *The Stories we live by: Personal Myths and the Making of the Self*. New York: Morrow.

McHale, B. (1987) *Postmodern Fiction*. New York: Methuen.

MacIntyre, A. (1981) *After Virtue*. Notre Dame, NY: Notre Dame University Press.

MacIntyre, A. (1988) *Whose Justice? Which Rationality?* Notre Dame, NY: Notre Dame University Press.

McLean, S. (1994) Mapping the human genome – friend or foe, *Social Science and Medicine*, 39(9): 1221–7.

McLeod, J. (1997) *Narrative and Psychotherapy*. London: Sage.

McNamee, S. (1996) Therapy and identity construction in the postmodern world, in

D. Grodin and T. Lindlof (eds) *Constructing the Self in a Mediated World*, pp. 141–63. London: Sage.

Mair, M. (1989) *Between Psychology and Psychotherapy*. London: Routledge.

Markus, H. and Kitayama, S. (1991) Culture and the self: implications for cognition, emotion and motivation, *Psychological Review*, 98: 224–54.

Martin, B. (1988) Lesbian Identity and autobiographical difference(s), in B. Brodzki and C. Schenck (eds) *Life/Lines: Theorising Women's Autobiography*, pp. 77–107. Cornell: Cornell University Press.

Maslow, A. (1970) *Motivation and Personality*, 2nd edition. New York: Harper and Row.

Maslow, A. (1972) *The Farther Reaches of Human Nature*. New York: Viking.

Matthews, C.A. (1990) *Breaking Through: No Longer a Victim of Child Abuse*. Albatross Books.

Mead, G.H. (1967) *Mind, Self and Society*. Chicago: University of Chicago Press.

Melucci, A. (1996a) *Challenging Codes: Collective Action in the Information Age*. Cambridge: Cambridge University Press.

Melucci, A. (1996b) *The Playing Self: Person and Meaning in the Planetary Society*. Cambridge: Cambridge University Press.

Messer, S., Sass, L. and Woolfolk, R. (eds) (1988) *Hermeneutics and Psychological Theory*. New Brunswick, NJ: Rutgers University Press.

Montemayor, R. and Eisen, M. (1977) The development of self-conceptions from childhood to adolescence, *Developmental Psychology*, 13: 314–19.

Mulgan, G. (1997) *Connexity: How to Live in a Connected World*. London: Chatto and Windus.

Nash, C. (ed.) (1990) *Narrative in Culture: The Uses of Storytelling in the Sciences, Philosophy and Literature*. London: Routledge.

Nelkin, D. and Tancredi, L. (1990) *Dangerous Diagnostics: The Social Power of Biological Information*. New York: Basic Books.

Olsen, T. (1983) *Silences*. New York: Dell Lorel.

Omer, H. (1993) Short-term therapy and the rise of the life-sketch, *Psychotherapy*, 30: 59–66.

Ortega y Gasset, J. (1953) In search of Goethe from within. Trans. Willard R. Trask, in W. Phillips and P. Rahv (eds) *The New Partisan Reader*, pp. 151–74. New York: Harcourt Brace.

Pancer, M. (1997) Social psychology: the crisis continues, in D. Fox and I. Prilleltensky (eds) *Critical Psychology: An Introduction*, pp. 150–66. London: Sage.

Parker, I. (1990) Discourse: definitions and contradictions, *Philosophical Psychology*, 3: 189–204.

Parker, I. (1991) *Discourse Dynamics: Critical Analysis for Social and Individual Psychology*. London: Sage.

Parry, A. (1991) A universe of stories, *Family Process*, 30: 37–54.

Pascal B. (1889) *The Thoughts of Pascal*. Trans. from the text of M. Molinier. London: Kegan Paul.

Penn, P. and Frankfurt, M. (1994) Creating a participant text: writing, multiple voices, narrative multiplicity, *Family Process*, 33: 217–32.

Pilgrim, D. and Rogers, A. (1997) Mental health, critical realism and lay knowledge, in J. Ussher (ed.) *Body Talk: The Material and Discursive Regulation of Sexuality, Madness and Reproduction*, pp. 33–50. London: Routledge.

Polkinghorne, D.P. (1988) *Narrative Knowing and the Human Sciences*. Albany, NY: SUNY Press.

Pollner, M. (1987) *Mundane Reason*. Cambridge: Cambridge University Press.

Poston, C. and Lisbon, K. (1989) *Reclaiming Our Lives: Adult Survivors of Incest*. Boston, MA: Little, Brown.

Potter, J. and Wetherell, M. (1987) *Discourse and Social Psychology: Beyond Attitudes and Behaviour*. London: Sage.

Potter, J., Wetherell, M., Gill, R. and Edwards, D. (1990) Discourse: noun, verb or social practice? *Philosophical Psychology*, 3: 205–17.

Povinelli, D. (1993) Reconstructing the evolution of mind, *American Psychologist*, 48: 493–509.

Priest, P. (1996) 'Gilt by association': talk show participants' televisually enhanced status and self-esteem, in D. Grodin and T. Lindlof (eds) *Constructing the Self in a Mediated World*, pp. 68–84. London: Sage.

Pucci, E. (1992) Review of Paul Ricoeur's *Oneself as Author*, *Philosophy & Social Criticism*, 18: 185–209.

Radley, A. (1994) *Making Sense of Illness: The Social Psychology of Health and Disease*. London: Sage.

Radley, A. (1997) What role does the body have in illness? in L. Yardley (ed.) *Material Discourses of Health and Illness*, pp. 50–68. London: Routledge.

Radley, A. and Green, R. (1987) Illness as adjustment: a methodology and conceptual framework, *Sociology of Health and Illness*, 9: 179–207.

Rappoport, J. and Simkins, R. (1991) Healing and empowerment through community narrative, *Prevention in Human Services*, 10: 29–50.

Rennie, D. (1994) Storytelling in psychotherapy: the client's subjective experience, *Psychotherapy*, 31: 324–43.

Ricoeur, P. (1984) *Time and Narrative*, Volume 1. Chicago: University of Chicago Press.

Ricoeur, P. (1985) *Time and Narrative*, Volume 2. Chicago: University of Chicago Press.

Ricoeur, P. (1986) Life: a story in search of a narrator, in M. Doeser and J. Kray (eds) *Facts and Values*, pp. 34–68. Dordrecht: Martinus Nijhoff.

Ricoeur, P. (1988) *Time and Narrative*, Volume 3. Chicago: University of Chicago Press.

Ricoeur, P. (1991) Life in quest of narrative, in D. Wood (ed.) *Paul Ricoeur: Narrative and Interpretation*, pp. 20–33. London: Routledge.

Roberts, J. (1994) *Tales and Transformations*. London: Norton.

Robinson, I. (1990) Personal narratives, social careers and medical courses: analysing life trajectories in autobiographies of people with multiple sclerosis, *Social Science and Medicine*, 30(11): 1173–86.

Rogers, C. (1961) *On becoming a Person: A Therapist's View of Psychotherapy*. London: Constable.

Rose, N. (1989) *Governing the Soul: The Shaping of the Private Self*. London: Routledge.

Rosenberg, S. (1977) New approaches to the analysis of personal constructs, in W. Landfield (ed.) *1976 Nebraska Symposium on Motivation*. Lincoln, NE: University of Nebraska Press.

Roth, P. (1963) *Timetables: Structuring the Passage of Time in Hospital Treatment and other Careers*. Indianapolis: Bobs Merrill.

Russell, D. (1995) *Women, Madness & Medicine*. Cambridge: Polity Press.

Russell, R. and Luciarello, T. (1992) Narrative Yes; Narrative Ad Infinitum, No! *American Psychologist*, 47: 671–2.

Ryle, G. (1973) *The Concept of Mind*. Harmondsworth: Penguin.

Sandstrom, K. (1990) Confronting deadly disease: the drama of identity construction among gay men with AIDS, *Journal of Contemporary Ethnography*, 19(3): 271–94.

Sarbin, T.R. (eds) (1986) *Narrative Psychology: The Storied Nature of Human Conduct*. New York: Praeger.

Sartre, J.P. (1947) *Existentialism*. New York: Philosophical Library.

Schafer, R. (1992) *Retelling a Life: Narration and Dialogue in Psychoanalysis*. New York: Basic Books.

Scheper-Hughes, N. (1994) AIDS and the social body, *Social Science and Medicine*, 39(7): 991–1003.

Schutz A. (1962) *Collected Papers I*. The Hague: Martinus Nijhoff.

Schwartzberg, S. (1993) Struggling for meaning: how HIV positive gay men make sense of AIDS, *Professional Psychology: Research and Practice*, 24(4): 483–90.

Schwartzberg, S. and Janoff-Bulman, R. (1991) Grief and the search for meaning. Exploring the assumptive worlds of bereaved college students, *Journal of Social and Clinical Psychology*, 10(3): 270–88.

Segall, L. (1997) Sexualities, in K. Woodward (ed.) *Identity and Difference*, pp. 183–229. London: Sage.

Shapiro, R. (1991) *The Human Blueprint: The Race to Unlock the Secrets of our Genetic Script*. London: Cassell.

Shilling, C. (1997) The body and difference, in K. Woodward (ed.) *Identity and Difference*, pp. 63–121. London: Sage.

Shotter, J. (1993) *Cultural Politics of Everyday Life: Social Constructionism, Rhetoric and Knowing of the Third Kind*. Buckingham: Open University Press.

Shotter, J. (1997) The social construction of our inner selves, *Journal of Constructivist Psychology*, 10: 7–24.

Shotter, J. and Gergen, K. (eds) (1992) *Texts of Identity*. London: Sage.

Showalter, E. (1997) *Hystories: Hysterical Epidemics and Modern Culture*. Basingstoke: Picador.

Silverman, D. (1993) *Interpreting Qualitative Data*. London: Sage.

Simonds, W. (1996) All consuming selves: self-help literature and women's identities, in D. Grodin and T. Lindlof (eds) *Constructing the Self in a Mediated World*, pp. 15–29. London: Sage.

Simpson, T. (1996) Constructions of self and other in the experience of rap music, in D. Grodin and T. Lindlof (eds) *Constructing the Self in a Mediated World*, pp. 163–83. London: Sage.

Smith, J. (1995) Semi-structured interviewing and qualitative analysis, in J. Smith, R. Hare and L. Van Lagenhove (eds) *Rethinking Methods in Psychology*, pp. 9–27. London: Sage.

Smith, J. (1996) Beyond the divide between cognition and discourse: using interpretative phenomenological analysis in health psychology, *Psychology and Health*, 11: 261–71.

Smith, J., Flowers, P. and Osborn, M. (1997) Interpretative phenomenological analysis and the psychology of health and illness, in L. Yardley (ed.) *Material Discourses of Health and Illness*, pp. 68–92. London: Routledge.

Smith, M. (1994) Selfhood at risk: postmodern perils and the perils of postmodernism, *American Psychologist*, 49(5): 405–11.

Social Science and Medicine (1990) *Qualitative Research on Chronic Illness*, 30(11): special issue.

Sontag, S. (1978) *Illness as Metaphor*. New York: Vintage.

Soper, K. (ed.) (1990) Feminism, humanism, postmodernism, in K. Soper (ed.) *Troubled Pleasures: Writings on Gender, Politics and Hedonism*, pp. 50–74. London: Verso.

Spence, D. (1982) *Narrative Truth and Historical Truth*. New York: Norton.

Spring, J. (1987) *Cry Hard and Swim: The Story of an Incest Survivor*. London: Virago.

States, B. (1988) *The Rhetoric of Dreams*. Ithaca, NY: Cornell University Press.

Steinem, G. (1992) *Revolution from within: a book of self-esteem*. Boston, MA: Little, Brown.

Stevens, R. and Wetherell, M. (1996) The self in the modern world: drawing together the threads, in R. Stevens (ed.) *Understanding the Self*, pp. 339–70. London: Sage.

Strack, F., Martin, I. and Stepper, S. (1988) Inhibiting and facilitating conditions of the human smile: a nonobtrusive test of the facial feedback hypothesis, *Journal of Personality and Social Psychology*, 54: 768–77.

Sugarman, J. and Martin, J. (1995) The moral dimension: a conceptualisation and empirical demonstration of the moral nature of psychotherapeutic conversations, *The Counseling Psychologist*, 23: 324–47.

Tal, K. (1996) *Worlds of Hurt: Reading the Literature of Trauma*. Cambridge: Cambridge University Press.

Taylor, C. (1989) *Sources of the Self: The Making of Modern Identity*. Cambridge: Cambridge University Press.

Taylor, S. (1983) Adjustment to threatening events: a theory of cognitive adaptation, *American Psychologist*, 38: 1161–73.

Taylor, S. (1989) *Positive Illusions: Creative Self Deception and the Healthy Mind*. New York: Basic Books.

Tehran, C. (1991) The cost of caring for patients with HIV in hospice, in A. O'Rawe and C. Tehran (eds) *AIDS and the Hospice Community*, pp. 156–77. New York, London: Howarth Press.

Triandis, H., Betancourt, H., Iwav, S. *et al.* (1993) An eticemic analysis of individualism and collectivism, *Journal of Cross-Cultural Psychology*, 24: 366–83.

Turkle, S. (1996) Parallel lives: working on identity in virtual space, in D. Grodin and T. Lindlof (eds) *Constructing the Self in a Mediated World*, pp. 156–77. London: Sage.

Ussher, J. (1991) *Women's Madness; Misogyny or Mental Illness?*, London: Harvester Wheatsheaf.

Van den Berg, J. (1972) *The Psychology of the Sickbed*. New York: Humanities Press.

Viney L. (1991) The psycho-social impact of multiple deaths from AIDS, *Omega*, 24(2): 151–63.

Viney, L. and Bousfield, L. (1991) Narrative analysis: a method of psychosocial research for AIDS affected people, *Social Science and Medicine*, 32(7): 757–65.

Vygotsky, L. (1978) *Mind in Society: The Development of Higher Psychological Processes*. Cambridge: Harvard University Press.

Vygotsky, L. (1986) *Thought and Language*. Cambridge, MA: Massachusetts Institute of Technology Press.

Walters, S. (1996) Terms of enmeshment: the cultural construction of the mother–daughter relationship, in D. Grodin and T. Lindlof (eds) *Constructing the Self in a Mediated World*, pp. 31–52. London: Sage.

Ward, E. (1984) *Father–Daughter–Rape*. London: Women's Press.

Warner, S. (1997) Review article of Davies' *Healing Sylvia*, Orrs' *No Right Way* and Reder *et al.*'s *Beyond Blame*, *Feminism and Psychology*, 3: 377–83.

Watzlawick, P., Weakland, J. and Fisch, R. (1974) *Change: Principles of Problem Formation and Problem Resolution*. New York: W. Norton.

Waugh, P. (1992) Modernism, postmodernism, gender, in P. Waugh (ed.) *Practising Postmodernism/Reading Modernism*, pp. 20–44. London: Edward Arnold.

Wax, M. (1995) How secure are Grunbaum's foundations?, *International Journal of Psychoanalysis*, 76: 547–56.

Weitz, R. (1989) Uncertainty and the lives of persons with AIDS, *Journal of Health and Social Behaviour*, 30: 270–81.

Wertsch, J. (1991) *Voices of the Mind: A Sociocultural Approach to Mediated Action*. London: Harvester Wheatsheaf.

Wertz, D. (1992) Ethical and legal implications for the new genetics: issues for discussion, *Social Science and Medicine*, 35(4): 495–505.

White, H. (1973) *Metahistory*. Baltimore: Johns Hopkins University Press.

White, M. and Epston, D. (1990) *Narrative Means to Therapeutic Ends*. New York: Norton.

Widdershoven, G. (1993) The story of life: hermeneutic perspective on the relationship between narrative and history, in R. Josselson and A. Lieblich (eds) *The Narrative Study of Lives*, Volume 1, pp. 1–20. London: Sage.

Wiener, W. and Rosenwald, G. (1993) A moment's monument: the psychology of keeping a diary, in R. Josselson and A. Lieblich (eds) *The Narrative Study of Lives*, pp. 30–58. London: Sage.

Wilkinson, S. (1997) Feminist psychology, in D. Fox and I. Prilleltensky (eds) *Critical Psychology: An Introduction*, pp. 247–65. London: Sage.

Williams, G. (1984) The genesis of chronic illness: narrative reconstruction, *Sociology of Health and Illness*, 11(2): 135–59.

Williams, S. (1996) The vicissitudes of embodiment across the chronic illness trajectory, *Body & Society*, 2(2): 23–47.

Wittgenstein, L. (1953) *Philosophical Investigations*. Oxford: Blackwell.

Wittgenstein, L. (1980) *Remarks on the Philosophy of Psychology*. Oxford: Blackwell.

Wood, D. (1991) *Paul Ricoeur: Narrative and Interpretation*. London: Routledge.

Woodward, K. (1997) Motherhood, identities, meanings and myths, in K. Woodward (ed.) *Identity and Difference*, pp. 7–63. London: Sage.

Yardley, L. (1997) (ed.) *Material Discourses of Health and Illness*. London: Routledge.

Zerubavel, E. (1979) *Patterns in Hospital Life*. Chicago: Chicago University Press.

Zerubavel, E. (1981) *Hidden Rhythms: Schedules and Calendars in Social Life*. Chicago: Chicago University Press.

Index

20275491R00116

Printed in Great Britain
by Amazon